CHARACTER ANIMATION
WITH POSER® PRO

LARRY MITCHELL

Charles River Media

A part of Course Technology, Cengage Learning

COURSE TECHNOLOGY
CENGAGE Learning

Australia, Brazil, Japan, Korea, Mexico, Singapore, Spain, United Kingdom, United States

Character Animation with Poser® Pro

Larry Mitchell

**Publisher and General Manager,
Course Technology PTR:**
Stacy L. Hiquet

Associate Director of Marketing:
Sarah Panella

Manager of Editorial Services:
Heather Talbot

Marketing Manager: Jordan Casey

Acquisitions Editor: Megan Belanger

Project Editor: Dan Foster, Scribe Tribe

Contributing Editors:
Kathie Berry and Phil Cooke

CRM Editorial Services Coordinator:
Jennifer Blaney

Copy Editor: Julie McNamee

Interior Layout: Jill Flores

Cover Designer: Mike Tanamachi

DVD-ROM Producer: Brandon Penticuff

Indexer: Jerilyn Sproston

Proofreader: Sue Boshers

Poser® Pro is a registered trademark of Smith Micro Software, Inc. All other trademarks are the property of their respective owners.

Library of Congress Control Number: 2007935956

ISBN-13: 978-1-58450-517-4

ISBN-10: 1-58450-517-6

Course Technology
25 Thomson Place
Boston, MA 02210
USA

Cengage Learning is a leading provider of customized learning solutions with office locations around the globe, including Singapore, the United Kingdom, Australia, Mexico, Brazil, and Japan. Locate your local office at: **international. cengage.com/region**

Cengage Learning products are represented in Canada by Nelson Education, Ltd.

For your lifelong learning solutions, visit **courseptr.com**

Visit our corporate website at **cengage.com**

Printed in the United States of America
1 2 3 4 5 6 7 11 10 09

Acknowledgments

Writing a book is no small task, by any measure of the mind. In support of getting the book completed, I'd like to acknowledge the following:

My publisher, who survived my many delays

My dear wife Teri, who at times had only the thought of me to hold on to

My parents, who stepped in to lend assistance when needed

Ami, Kathy, and Phil, who helped me not look "oh so dim"

Scott, who encouraged me to complete this work

To the aspiring authors who read this, all I have to say to you is, "See one, do one."

Larry

About the Author

Larry Mitchell has been working as a digital media artist and producer for more than 20 years and has created graphics and software for TV shows, arenas, video games, and commercials. He has taught and lectured on computer animation at international conferences and at various institutes and universities in the U.S., Japan, and the UK. He has taught 3D design and animation to teams from a major theme park, the Department of Defense, and broadcast facilities. Larry is the author of several 3D animation training titles at Lynda.com and is the CEO of Liquid Digital (*http://ld-e.com/ent*), a digital media production company in Central Florida.

Contents

Introduction

Have you ever been thoroughly impressed by some character animation wizardry at the movies and then rushed home to jump into Poser and animate your block-buster, only to once again get stumped, not knowing where to begin? Well, this is the Poser character animation book for you. For many, it can be very frustrating to have a powerful 3D character application such as Poser and yet be unable to really bring characters to life.

If you can pose characters, animating them shouldn't be so tough, right? Well, it's not really a matter of being tough. It's really a matter of understanding the techniques and principles that govern 3D character animation.

When you watch excellent character animation, it's important to remember that the animators have had years of experience using key techniques and principles and aren't just winging it.

SPINNING LOGOS

So what is a frustrated animator to do who can animate 3D characters? Spinning logos, of course, or at least that's what they did back in the day. Most 3D anima-tors don't animate characters—not that they don't want to—they just don't know how to start.

This book can't answer every 3D character animation question, but it gives a clear sense of various methods and workflows used to achieve the believable illusion of character animation.

POSER 7 AND POSER PRO

Please note that with the exception of the PoserFusion exercises in Chapter 8, everything in this book applies to both Poser 7 and Poser Pro.

WHY I WROTE THIS BOOK

The idea behind writing this book is to present the fundamental principles of character animation applied to Poser, along with very creative workflows and solutions to assist the widest audience of animators, ranging from the guy at home to the student of animation to the small 3D production company.

So, now, get ready to bring your Poser characters to life, and let's roll!

1 Principles of Animation

In This Chapter

- Introduction
- Timing
- Squash & Stretch
- Anticipation
- Overlapping Motion: Primary, Secondary, Tertiary
- Pose-To-Pose

INTRODUCTION

Before you can bring Poser® Pro figures to life so they become characters in a story, you must understand some underlying principles upon which character animation is based. Application of these principles can turn bad animation into good animation. Mastery of these principles can turn good animation into great animation.

In truth, you can ignore these principles and still create animation, but you can't make animation that is emotion based without these principles. Your animation, without these, will be more mechanical (which can still have use for technical animation when you need to show how an engine works). But still, even in technical mechanical animation, you're probably going to use the principle of timing to make a convincing presentation.

This chapter deals with making your animation more appealing to an audience so that the audience can relate to the characters in the animation, and you can tell your story effectively. This is necessary because people looking at animation often recognize elements of the animation based upon prior real-life experience—they see a person walk and automatically recall how people walk. So they automatically judge the animated walk, even if they do it subconsciously. And by judge, I mean they look at the walk and they decide, "Is this how a person walks?" If it's supposed to be comical and the character walks comically, that's acceptable. But if you're trying to make the characters walk realistically and they look totally bizarre, the viewer will assume that you can't tell your story very well, so you lose your theme and won't communicate your idea effectively.

Now let's look at how these principles of animation apply to Poser Pro.

When it comes to principles of animation, there are quite a few, depending on whom you speak to. If you ask how many principles of animation there are, you may be told 12 or even as many as 28. It all depends upon the school of animation training in which the principles are taught.

We will look at a *subset* of principles of animation that apply to Poser Pro because Poser Pro actually does quite a few things for you automatically under the hood, so that you don't have to think about and manage them.

TIMING

Timing is a foundational element of storytelling and is the most elemental characteristic of motion. Timing is a characteristic of every form of animation from cartoon and mechanical animation to sophisticated 3D character animation, and even 3D motion graphics.

In this chapter, we will look at two different case scenarios of timing in Poser Pro. First, we will deconstruct the elements necessary to create a bouncing ball animation, and then we will explore how timing affects character animation.

You will first create a very basic animation. We're trying to create the illusion that this ball is bouncing on the floor (see Figure 1.1).

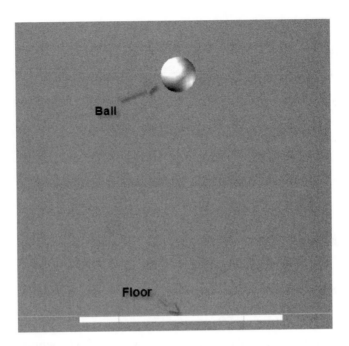

FIGURE 1.1
Image of the ball and the floor on which it must bounce.

In the DVD-ROM, Project Files/Chapter 01 folder, play the video 01-Ball_Bounce_Bad.mov to see a very poor animation of a bouncing ball. Although there is motion, you can't say this ball is really bouncing. It almost looks like it is on a yo-yo string. From the same folder, open 01_Ball_Bounce_Bad.pz3 in Poser to see how this animation is constructed. You don't have the timing that would illustrate bounce. The timing is a function of a few things. It's not just basic things like having keyframes because as you can see by looking at the Keyframes Editor, you really do have keyframes in here at the start, middle, and end of the 60-frame animation (see Figure 1.2).

FIGURE 1.2
Three keyframes of the 60-frame animation.

Select the ball, and then click the Next Key Frame button (see Figure 1.3) to advance the animation to the ball's next keyframe at frame 30. You see here that the ball is now down on the floor on frame 30 and up in the air on frame 60. So these elements of the bounce are in place, but they're not the only elements to be factored in.

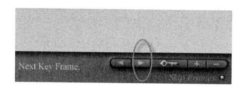

FIGURE 1.3
The Next Key Frame button.

In the Keyframes Editor, with Ball 1 selected, expand its hierarchy to see that the keyframes are all made on the y-translate. This makes sense because in Poser Pro, the y-axis is used to position objects up and down.

Not all 3D applications follow this convention. In some 3D applications, the z-axis goes up and down.

NOTE

So you see that you have keyframes that identify when the ball is in different positions (at a different height). You can further look at this by getting into the Graph Editor (see Figure 1.4), and with Ball 1 still selected, choosing yTran.

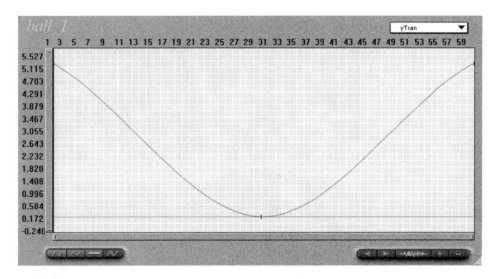

FIGURE 1.4
Graph Editor of the ball's Y translation. Notice the very smooth shape of the curve directly reflecting its helium-like motion.

In Figure 1.4, you see that the ball is transitioning smoothly between the keyframes, which is precisely why the animation doesn't look like a bounce.

By simply looking at a Graph Editor curve, you can easily know what type of animation will occur.

NOTE

ON THE DVD   In the DVD-ROM, Project Files/Chapter 01 folder, play the video 01-Ball_Bounce_Good.mov to see a better animation of a bouncing ball. From the same folder, open 01_Ball_Bounce_Good.pz3 in Poser to see how this animation is constructed.

Why is the timing now behaving properly? In the Keyframes Editor, scroll through the keyframes to see that you have a few more keyframes here. New keyframes have been added to help affect the ball's movement in the y-axis. But it's not just a matter of how many keyframes you have and where you place them in time, but also how they affect the y-translation curve.

Open the Graph Editor curve, and look at the ball's yTran again. You see a difference now as shown in Figure 1.5.)

Keyframe Editor

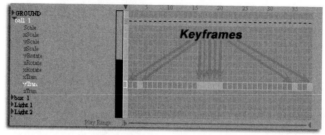

Graph Editor

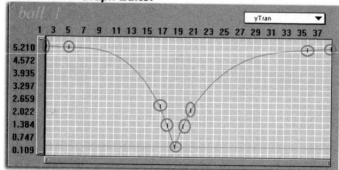

FIGURE 1.5

Additional keyframes are added and adjusted to make the ball's motion in the y-axis into a bounce.

Rather than having that very smooth balloon helium-type curve, you have something that accelerates. It's clear to see that additional keyframes were added and adjusted to change the shape of the curve to achieve a sharply spiked point in the center. It's crucial to achieve acceleration (a sharply spiked point) for the bounce to be realistic. You may want to adjust this kind of a curve to be a bit wider if it's going to be, for example, a soft bouncing rubber ball. Or, make the distance between these two keyframes very close if it's maybe a bouncing golf ball (something that has very high tension and high rebound energy).

So adjusting the timing for a bouncing ball is limited to editing the keyframes and graph curve of movement in the y-axis. It is a matter of creating keyframes in the right location, and you may even need to move your keyframes, which you can achieve by simply dragging them to adjust the timing. That is another way to adjust timing. It is also a matter of adjusting your curve and setting the curve on the correct keyframe. By simply selecting a keyframe, you can move it up or down, which would have great impact on the sharpness of the bounce. It gets more interesting as you do more challenging animations containing multiple objects whose timing must be considered.

Next, we will look at another example of how Poser Pro can adjust the timing; however, this time it's in the context of character animation.

You start by working with project 01_Timing_Punch_Slow-1.pz3, which is found in the Chapter 01 exercise files. In this project, a character is set up to punch a box object (see Figure 1.6).

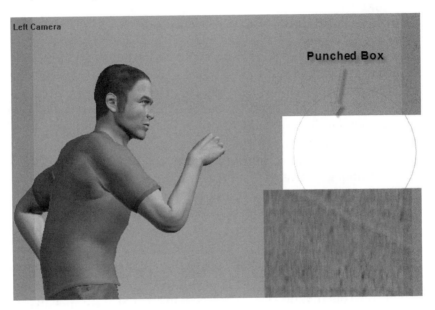

FIGURE 1.6
Simon has punched the block.

Set the Tracking to Fast, and click Play It to see slow animation timing. We are assuming that the surface between these two objects is not very high in friction and that the box isn't terribly heavy, so that the amount of slide occurring on this top block makes sense.

Let's look at our keyframes in the Keyframes Editor to see what's really happening (see Figure 1.7). You have keyframes on the Waist, Abdomen, and Chest as they twist for the punch, and the Right Collar, Right Shoulder, Right Forearm, and Right Hand as they are engaged in throwing the punch. On Simon, you have a start position, an impact position when he hits the block, and an end position where he retracts his hand. Looking at the Keyframes Editor, as you scrub through the timeline, you see that even though the block is moving at frame 18, the hand reaches its full extent at frame 30, and not when it visually appears to hit the block. Simon's hand visually appearing to hit the block is the cue to start animating the block so it appears to respond to the punch.

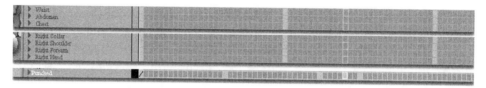

FIGURE 1.7
Keyframes for the slow version of the block punch.

In the Keyframes Editor, scroll down to the punched object. Twirl this open to look at the zTran channel. Now you see that you are simply keyframing where this object is in the z-axis. In this animation, the z-axis defines movement horizontally. It may appear to be left to right on the screen, but you are looking at this from the side, so it is really front to back. You also have keyframes for the travel motion and the slowing down, ending with the keyframe where the motion comes to a halt. Notice, however, that the timing of the arm still continues. This kind of overlap between timing is realistic. Just because you punch a box in the real world, and the box hits the wall and stops, that does not mean that your arm actually stops. Your arm has its own independent physics and its own constraints and dependencies to deal with. So in animation, you need to factor these into the timing. You want to make sure that it looks like what people expect because if not, and you have bad timing in your animation, it will distract your audience from what you are trying to communicate. Rather than see your story, they will see your errors. They will likely be turned off, tune out, and simply wish they could forget what they've seen. To get around this, you need good timing within each element and good timing between the elements.

So you have good timing of the hand coming in punching, good timing of the block moving in response to the punch, and good timing in their relationship to each other. Now let's look at what happens when you try to speed up this animation. You can't simply make all the frames closer and have the whole thing speed up because that would actually not be great timing. If you think about it, if you hit a block very slowly, the block moves a certain distance. If you hit it very quickly, it should move a further distance, so simply moving your keyframes closer would not solve the problem.

ON THE DVD Open the project 01_Timing_Punch_Fast-1.pz3 in the Chapter 01 exercise files. In the Keyframes Editor, you can see that the keyframes are very short (see Figure 1.8). A bit more activity fine-tunes this animation, and keyframes appear over a shorter period of time.

FIGURE 1.8
Keyframes for the fast version of the block punch.

Play the animation in Fast Tracking. You can see that the punch is happening much faster and the result is that the block is moving both faster and further.

 ON THE DVD Using the Quicktime™ videos 01-Timing-Punch-Slow.mov and 01-Timing-Punch-Fast.mov in the Chapter 01 exercise files, you can see the comparison. Figure 1.9 compares the final result at the end of each animation. In the slow punch, you can see that the distance traveled by this block is fairly short, which is reasonable for the animation as it is set. As you punch faster, you have it traveling a farther distance.

NOTE *Depending on the project you are working on, you may need to get technically accurate. This may involve using motion references and working with material property specifications. It all depends upon the focus of the animation. If the focus of the animation is to show that a vitamin you're taking gives you more strength, then it's not going to be so crucial to get the accuracy of the distance that this block will travel. However, if you are trying to show something for a forensic case for a courtroom debate, you need very accurate information. In that case, you need to understand the co-efficiencies of friction involved between the different materials of the block that is moving and the block that is stationary, as well as the applied force of the punch. It may get very deep. Generally, however, that is a rare case, and you can often get away with what looks good. Again, you must pay attention to the actual specifications of your project to determine how accurate it must be.*

FIGURE 1.9
Comparison showing the different results of the slow punch and fast punch animations.

SQUASH & STRETCH

The *squash & stretch principle* of animation refers to the expectation that as an object collides with another object, there will be some change in shape while maintaining the same volume. This change is based upon the following properties of both colliding objects:

- Momentum
- Inertia
- Mass
- Flexibility
- Angle of impact
- Speed of impact

Although these principles can be evaluated mathematically, we're not going into the math geek–level of explaining this here. You simply want to visualize it to tell a story. Squash & stretch applies in cases where you either have a sudden change in momentum or direction of an object. It's also used in instances where there is no collision whatsoever and no physics but is used instead as a gag or storytelling method, which you may see in some animations or films where you have eyes stretching out of their sockets or the head changing into a different form. Let's look at how you apply this principle in different cases in Poser Pro.

ON THE DVD In the first tutorial, we'll apply squash & stretch to a bouncing ball. Open up project 02_Ball-S&S-Bad.pz3 in the Chapter 01 exercise files. When playing this animation, you see a ball that's bouncing okay but there is no kind of squash & stretch (see Figure 1.10). There's no change in shape when the ball touches the ground. If you were animating a bouncing golf ball, then this animation behavior would be a good start.

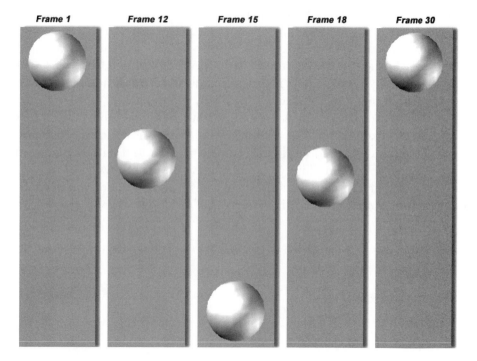

FIGURE 1.10
The ball bounces well but doesn't squash & stretch in this animation.

To learn about the animation principle of squash & stretch, we'll look at three methods for how you squash & stretch animated objects in Poser Pro. In this first method, you'll be scaling the object to change its shape without changing its volume by scaling in either two or three axes.

Squash & Stretch: Method 1 (Scaling)

For the first method, take the ball and simply adjust its scale down in the y-axis to squash it and out in the x-axis to stretch it.

Being careful to stretch only as much as you squash is the key to maintaining the animated object's volume. When making these adjustments in Poser, it's helpful to use opposing percentages. So if you squash the y-axis to 66%, then stretching the x-axis to 133% allows you to maintain the animated object's volume.

To see this in action, open up project 02-Ball-Squash&Stretch-M1.pz3 in the Chapter 01 exercise files. When playing this method back, you will see that the ball is flattening and widening upon impact (see Figure 1.11). This method is useful when you don't want to employ any physics assist and the squash & stretch doesn't need to be physically accurate—it just needs to look good. Although there are quite a few physics assist areas in Poser Pro, the disadvantage at times can be that it takes more time to set up, and it is definitely more involved. Even when it works, the squash & stretch can be so accurate that it can become more difficult to produce expressive animation. The advantage of physics-assisted squash & stretch is that the end result is more realistic and can yield predictable results for more technically accurate animation. However, your animation will not always call for that kind of realism but rather just a little touch of realism. In those cases, you would then use this kind (scaling in the x-axis and y-axis) of technique where you adjust your scale.

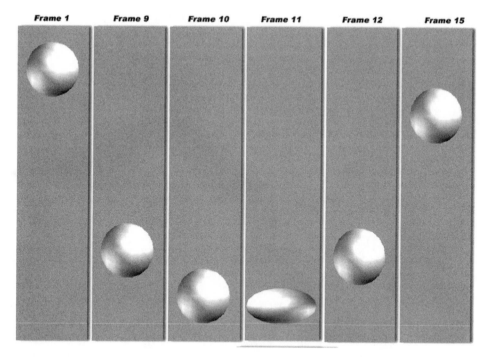

FIGURE 1.11
Bouncing ball using the squash & stretch principle of animation (nonphysics method).

When manually animating squash & stretch, find the keyframe where your ball touches the floor, and add a keyframe for the xScale and yScale to establish the start of the squash & stretch.

Open Object Properties, (make sure it's the properties window for ball_1), where you can adjust the parameters.

Advance one frame on the timeline, and set the yScale to 66 and the xScale to 133. This sets the squash & stretch action. In the prior frame, both xScale and yScale are at 100. You will also need to adjust the yTran value to keep the ball on the floor.

Advance one more frame, and set the xScale and yScale back to 100 to restore to the animated object's original shape.

If the scale squashes too early, you can adjust it by opening the Keyframes Editor, select Ball_1 xScale and yScale, and drag them right or left to adjust timing. By doing that, you have edited the ball so it only changes form when there is impact. One of the problems you will quickly see is that the animation will overshoot its keyframes both before and after where you might expect to see the animated object changing shape due to the interpolation method of the keyframes. A look at the Graph Editor display of the xScale (see Figure 1.12) shows the problem clearly.

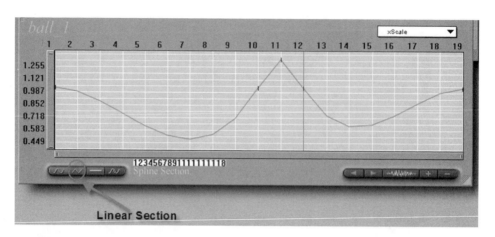

FIGURE 1.12

The xScale curve shows a change in value before and after the keyframes. This leads to constant changing in shape.

To correct this, select each keyframe, and set the interpolation method to Linear Section. Do this to both the xScale and yScale. The Graph Editor display of your xScale and yScale should be as shown in Figures 1.13 and 1.14.

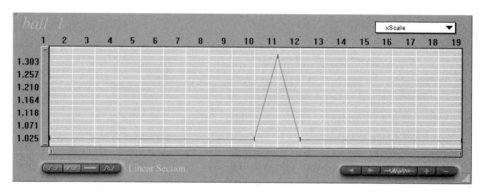

FIGURE 1.13

Figure 1.13 Linear interpolation of the ball's xScale keyframes.

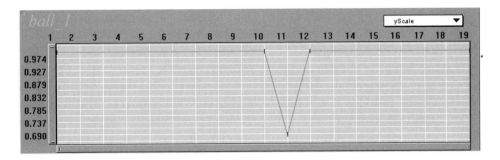

FIGURE 1.14
Linear interpolation of the ball's yScale keyframes.

There aren't many frames here (see Figure 1.15). So you don't have a lot to play with. Fortunately, when a ball bounces, there are generally going to be few frames. So the fact that you can't see a nice smooth transition is both acceptable and normal. The ball's yTran curve is shown in Figure 1.16.

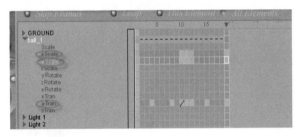

FIGURE 1.15
In the Keyframes Editor, the ball's xScale, yScale, and yTran keyframes are displayed.

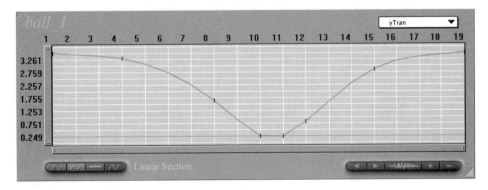

FIGURE 1.16
The ball's yTran curve.

Next, you will take a look at how to apply the animation principle of squash & stretch to character animation in Poser Pro. From the DVD-ROM, open the project 02-Penguin-Squash&Stretch-Bad.pz3 in the Chapter 01 folder. Play the animation to see the penguin jump with no squash & stretch added. The original jump animation without squash & stretch may be suitable for some projects, depending on the customer needs and the objective. This is a great feature, but if you need to use squash & stretch, you will need to adjust it. You can play the 02-Penguin_S&S-Bad.mov video file from the Chapter 01 folder to see the rendered result.

Open the project 02-Penguin-Squash&Stretch-Good.pz3, and play it to see the animation with squash & stretch applied. The penguin actually appears to have some mass because you have applied squash & stretch. The squash & stretch method of adjusting an object's scale while maintaining its volume was applied to the jumping penguin as shown in Figure 1.17.

FIGURE 1.17
A good example of the penguin's squash & stretch.

Squash & stretch is not a button in Poser Pro; it is a method and principle of animation. You can use the Edit tools to adjust scale, for example. Alternatively, you can select an object, go to its properties, and adjust its independent axis scale, meaning its y-axis scale, not just scale in general. You get the object to change shape based on an event, such as colliding, expressing, or changing direction or velocity.

Now select Object Properties>Parameters, and select Body as the actor on the Preview tab. When moving through the keyframes, observe that you are changing the x-scale and the y-scale interactively. At frame 1, the xScale is 100% and the yScale is 100%, which means this is the default, natural state. When you go to the next keyframe, the penguin is preparing to jump, so he is a little bit wider and shorter. This is the squash. In keyframe 12, he is at his full size and, even though you are not focusing on it, other animation parameters cause his wings to flap. (Our focus in this tutorial is only squash & stretch.) In frame 24, he's back down at 100%, followed by squashing and again returning to normal. You can play the 02-Penguin_S&S-Good.mov video file from the Chapter 01 folder to see the rendered result.

ON THE DVD

So, to recap, to manually squash & stretch an animated object using scaling, at the point of impact (or incident), set keyframes to establish the start of the squash & stretch, scale the object's axes while maintaining its volume, set keyframes to establish the end of the squash & stretch, and use linear interpolation on keyframes to contain the squash & stretch within its intended location in time.

SQUASH & STRETCH: METHOD 2 (CLOTH)

In this second method of creating squash & stretch animation, we'll use Poser Pro's physics-based tools to simulate the change in the object's shape to create more physically accurate deformation.

ON THE DVD

For this next project, open 02-Ball-Squash&Stretch-M2_start.pz3 in the Chapter 01 exercise files. We've applied a texture to the ball in this project because friction causes the ball to rotate due to the simulation nature of this method. Without the texture, you wouldn't be able to see this rotation. In this method, you are not animating by creating keyframes, and there is no adjustment of the scale in the x-axis and y-axis. Instead, you are using the Poser Cloth room. You turn this ball into a cloth object, letting gravity pull it down and allowing the cloth dynamics to cause the soft body deformation, which means the squash & stretch is really due to the cloth ball falling and colliding with the hard floor. This is the most realistic squash & stretch you'll get in Poser Pro, and it is very similar to what you get in other applications, such as Maya™ and CINEMA 4D™.

1. With the ball selected, enter the Cloth room, and click New Simulation to begin the process of making the ball able to react and change shape when it hits the floor.
2. For the purpose of creating a squash & stretch animation of this ball hitting the floor, set the End frame value to 120 so that there will be enough time for the action to occur.

3. Select which object is to become the cloth by clicking Clothify. Use the drop down menu provided to select the ball, and click Clothify to complete this step.

4. Select Collide Against, and then click Add/Remove to choose box_1 (the floor object) to tell the simulation what the ball will collide with.

NOTE

The Dynamics Controls is where you set the parameters, such as the Fold Resistance (the resistance to permanently changing shape), the Stretch Resistance (the resistance to changing shape), and Friction (which causes it to interact in a realistic way with the floor that it is hitting). After these parameters are set, you simply click Calculate Simulation, which then builds the keyframes to create the simulation dynamics animation that causes the squash & stretch.

5. Set the Dynamics Controls parameters as shown in Figure 1.18.

FIGURE 1.18
Dynamics Controls parameters
settings for a good ball bounce.

ON THE DVD Back in the Pose room, you can play back and render the result. If you want to compare your results with the finished project file on the accompanying DVD-ROM, open project 02-Ball-Squash&Stretch-M2.pz3 in the Chapter 01 exercise files, and play the animation to see the ball bounce, squash & stretch, and roll on the floor.

Now, if you drag through the keyframes slowly, you can see the point of squashing. The stretching is minimal in this case, which is a function of the parameters for your dynamics. So the more flexible you make this material, the more it will both squash & stretch. Again, it is based on what your story or project needs. The advantage of this method over the previous method is that it is more realistic and, depending on the complexity of your project, could actually end up taking less time. See Figure 1.19 for an example.

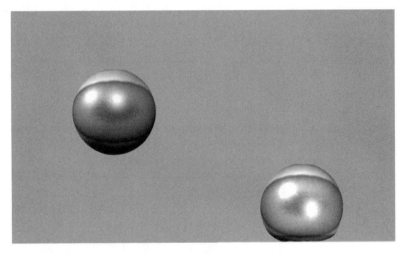

FIGURE 1.19
Cloth ball showing the squash & stretch.

If your project calls for several objects to squash & stretch and if they must collide with and bounce off of each other, then dynamics solutions are effective tools for the job.

NOTE

The initial setup time to set the parameters is longer than making a few keyframes, as in the previous method. This method saves you time, however, when the ball has to bounce down many steps, go into a hallway, hit a can and be hit by a bottle, and so on. In cases like that, this method makes your life easier by doing all the calculations for all those collisions for you, as well as all the squashing and stretching.

Now that you know both methods, you should be able to select which method is most appropriate to tell your story effectively.

SQUASH & STRETCH: METHOD 3 (DEFORMATION)

ON THE DVD Another method for creating squash & stretch animation in Poser Pro is to start with, for example, Figures>Additional Figures>Head Man, which loads the figure of a male head. Then, go to Props>Poser 1-5>Magnets. Here you have a variety of prepositioned magnets that you can apply to this figure. If you add a Chin Magnet, for example, you can pull out his chin for animation.

You can create your own magnets by going to Object>Create Magnet, and then you can position them as you wish.

TIP

Switch to Right Camera view. Select Props>Chin Mag in the Actor list, and then use the Move tool to stretch the chin outward. If you stretch too far, you will see that the chin starts breaking due to some of the principles of magnets. For example, the zone is limited here. (You could expand the zone to animate the chin even more.) Nevertheless, the point is you can squash & stretch independent areas of an object.

ON THE DVD Based upon this, open the project 02-Head-Squash&Stretch.pz3 from the Chapter 01 folder. Several magnets have been applied to the head so that it resembles a "fish-man" at this point (see Figure 1.20).

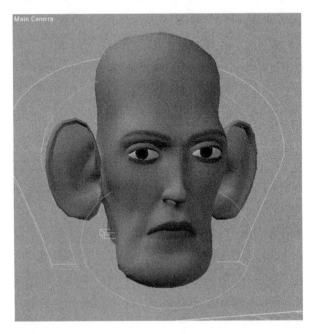

FIGURE 1.20
Head squashed and stretched with magnets.

ON THE DVD Play back the rendered video 02-Head-Squash&Stretch.mov in the Chapter 01 folder to see the finished animation. You can see how multiple squashes and stretches can happen on independent timing. This is achieved by moving different magnets positioned in various elements of the head.

With the Chin Mag selected as the Actor, as you drag (and release) through the timeline frames, you can see the xTran, yTran, and zTran parameters change, indicating where the magnet is moved to deform the head. You can see this even better if you look at the keyframes for the Chin Magnets (see Figure 1.21), and even more if you look at the Graph (see Figure 1.22).

FIGURE 1.21
Figure 1.21 The Chin Mag keyframes.

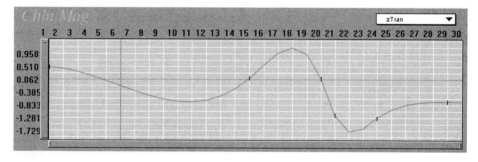

FIGURE 1.22
The Chin Mag keyframes graph display (zTran).

Again, this is not some advanced animation concept; these are very basic principles of adjusting the position or scale of each magnet over time. Bear in mind that magnet principles are going to give you limits at times. The large horseshoe outline around the head is the *magnet,* and the circle below is the *zone,* which is the area of the magnet's influence. If you want the magnet to stretch the face out and deform it more, you need to be sure that the zone will be large enough. As the zone gets larger, it affects more of the character, which can be good or bad.

In this third method of creating squash & stretch animation, it's very important to note that maintaining volume can be a difficult task requiring a lot of visual inspection.

ANTICIPATION

The next principle of animation is Anticipation. *Anticipation* is basically what it sounds like. Just like in the real world, when you are about to do something, you perform some action that is in preparation for the real motion. For example, before the pitcher throws the ball, in anticipation, he'll first do a wind up and then perform the main action of throwing the ball. In animation, the principle of anticipation causes the viewer to not only identify with the action but also to invest emotionally because anticipation aids in the process of creating a believable illusion that supports storytelling.

To see how anticipation is applied to character animation in Poser Pro, first look at a sample of animation that lacks anticipation by loading 03-Anticipation-punch-bad.pz3 from the Chapter 01 folder to see Simon about to throw a punch. In the "bad" (no anticipation applied) version of this animation, Simon throws the punch without preparing for it.

Again, it's worth pointing out that for some projects, this may be acceptable. However, if you need more realism to engage the audience, especially if you support it with dialog, sound effects, and a soundtrack that creates a sense of thrill, suspense, or some impending action, you'll want to support your storytelling with the animation principle of anticipation.

Anticipation is the visual element of the principles of animation where the audience members start to hold their breath because something is coming. Here you have the punch being thrown without anticipation, so the viewing audience members never hold their breath and are never really engaged. From a physiological perspective, by animating without anticipation, you jump ahead of the viewer rather than staying emotionally in sync. So let's look at how you would correct this.

Open the 03-Anticipation-punch-good.pz3 project in your Chapter 01 folder, and play it back. You see that before Simon punches, his torso twists, his head rotates, and his arms are also getting into it.

Play back 03-Anticipation_Punch_Bad.mov in your Chapter 01 folder, which is the rendered video clip, and compare it to 03-Anticipation_Punch_Good.mov to really note the difference in how this subtle change adds real value to the overall believability of the animation. In the good clip, he winds up, which makes sense because he is building up energy in his body to deliver the punch. Again, there is no magic anticipation button in Poser Pro. Creating anticipation is a matter of using the basic editing tools to twist his torso and make the adjustments in his neck, head, and arms to tell the story. Paying attention to a reference video will guide you in making these decisions. When you know you have an animation coming up with a guy throwing a punch, get some videos and look at how the body really works.

What is the biomechanical action happening during that punch? During this punch, there are elements simply being rotated. Nothing fancy is happening, but when it's done well, it looks more sophisticated than it really is (see Figure 1.23).

FIGURE 1.23
The audience anticipates Simon's punch as he draws back.

The element of anticipation is extremely important for making your story believable and engaging the interest of your audience. These subtle cues, such as squash & stretch, anticipation, and timing, tell people that they are watching something they can relate to from the real world.

OVERLAPPING MOTION: PRIMARY, SECONDARY, TERTIARY

The animation principle of *overlapping motion* addresses the relationship in character animation among the primary motion that is the core focus of the animation, the secondary motion that naturally supports the primary motion, and the tertiary motion that may be present and is a response to the primary and secondary motion.

When people walk, the main thing that causes them to move from one spot to another is that their legs are taking steps. Keeping their arms firmly planted at their sides will not inhibit their ability to move from one spot to another but will lessen the normalcy of their motion. So the legs moving is the primary motion and the arms swinging in support is the secondary motion. Add a super hero cape to this walking person, and you have tertiary motion of the cape moving and deforming in response to the primary and secondary motion of the legs and arms.

In the case of a character walking in Poser Pro, to achieve the primary motion (the legs walking), you can either keyframe this in Poser Pro by manually positioning the body and the legs to make the figure walk, or you can use the Walk Designer to define the walking style and make the figure walk along a walk path. The Walk Designer also provides the secondary motion of the arms automatically. As in the real world, the arms oppose the direction of the legs, so that when the right leg is forward, the right arm is back and vice-versa.

ON THE DVD

1. In the Chapter 01 folder, view 04-Overlapping_Pri.mov to see Simon walking with only the primary motion of the legs walking.
2. View 04-Overlapping_Pri_Sec.mov to see the motion of the swinging arms added to support the primary motion of the legs.
3. View 04-Overlapping_Pri_Sec_Ter.mov to see the addition of tertiary motion of the hat as it responds to the body movement caused by Simon walking (see Figure 1.24).

FIGURE 1.24
Primary, secondary, and tertiary animation of Simon walking while wearing a hat.

The secondary and tertiary videos are examples of the principle of overlapping animation applied to character animation.

To create the tertiary animation in Poser Pro, there are two ways of handling this. One way is to keyframe the hat so that its scale and rotation change in response to the figure's walk; however, you'll have to put in a lot of time to make it look good.

The second way is usually preferred, which is to make your hat object into a cloth object and let the character's head become what the cloth collides against. You would have to play with your Collision Parameters (dynamics parameters as shown earlier in the ball squash & stretch method using the Cloth room) to get the kind of bounce and the material structure that you want, but it is a more dependable way of creating the tertiary animation.

Tertiary animation also refers to things like clothing in general. The clothing worn by the character in these video clips is conforming clothing—not dynamic— and therefore it automatically bends to whatever deformation is caused by the body. Dynamic clothing would actually collide against the body, just like your clothes act when you wear them. You may not think about it, but your clothing is actually hitting against your body, is held in place by your body, and dynamically reacts to all of your motions. In Poser Pro, you can make tertiary animation by making the clothing dynamic as well, just like you made the hat dynamic by making it into cloth. The more things you have to be concerned about, the more involved it gets, such as having the body and clothing intersecting and peeking through, which can cause clothing accidents. It can also take a great deal of time to calculate. However, the results can be amazing when done well. If you have super heroes in your project, their capes are good examples of tertiary animation, as is hair, which is dynamic.

Again, the primary is the origin of the character's motion (in this case, the legs that are moving the figure). Secondary motion is the arms, working in concert with (and in support of) the legs, even if they are out of phase. Tertiary is additional animation, resulting from the primary and secondary motion affecting things such as clothing, accessories, and even body fat.

When you create a figure—let's say an alien—bear in mind that primary and secondary motion, at a bare minimum, are a whole lot more interesting to watch than just primary motion. The more there is going on, such as arms or appendages corresponding to the primary motion, the more alive it will appear to be and easier for the human mind to engage with.

POSE-TO-POSE

In the principles of animation, pose-to-pose animation allows you to define the interpolation (changes) that occurs between a character's extreme poses. Extreme poses are those poses that define a character's action. For example, in the creation of the animation of a baseball pitcher throwing a ball, the following poses are the extremes:

1. Initial state before throwing.
2. Hands come up and elbows move back.
3. The pitcher winds up.
4. The pitcher throws the ball.
5. His body follows through.
6. He finally recovers.

For this to create meaningful animation, these extreme poses must be placed at appropriate keyframes in the timeline.

In Poser Pro, you create pose-to-pose animation by posing the character at key points on the timeline that correlate with the story.

In the next exercise, you'll see how to use the pose-to-pose principles with a woman who gets up from a seated position in a chair.

ON THE DVD

1. Begin with the 05-Pose-To-Pose_start.pz3 project in the Chapter 01 folder. Here you have Sydney standing in front of a sofa (see Figure 1.25). You will animate this using poses from the Library. First, make sure you have SydneyG2 selected in the Figure list on your Preview pane.

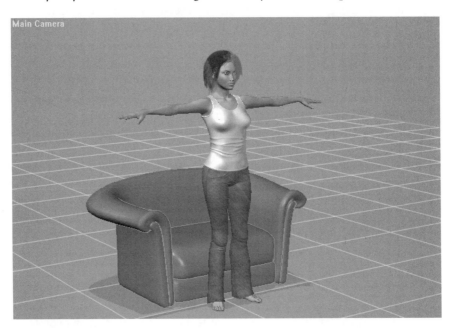

FIGURE 1.25
Sydney standing in front of the sofa.

Failure to ensure you have the correct figure selected can result in the wrong character or object being animated, or nothing at all may be animated.

2. Open the Library>Pose>Universal Poses>Sitting>On Chair. Select On Chair 10. Click Apply Universal Pose (see Figure 1.26).

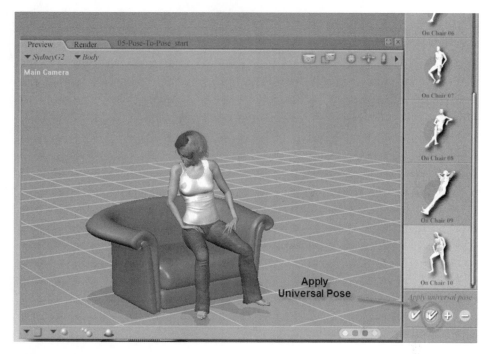

FIGURE 1.26
Sydney sitting on the sofa.

3. Though Poser provides some excellent figure poses, you'll usually have to tweak the applied poses by using the editing tools to adjust the figure's actors so that body parts make appropriate contact with props and the character's emotional state is presented. Open 05-Pose-To-Pose_step-01.pz3 to see what these adjustments should look like for this animation. In Figure 1.27, the figure has been adjusted to fit better on the chair. The chair has been scaled up a bit, plus other minor details have been added to make it look nicer.

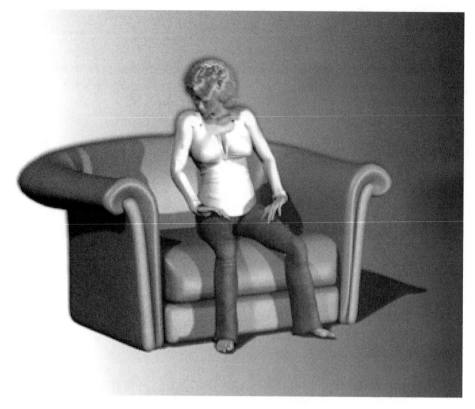

FIGURE 1.27
Sydney is better adjusted to the sofa.

4. Because this is currently a 1-second animation (only 30 frames), increase the number of frames to 90. At the end of the animation, apply a pose of her standing. First, select SydneyG2 as your Figure, then select Library>Pose>Universal Poses>Standing>Stand04, and click Apply Universal Pose.

NOTE

Be sure that the figure's Body is selected and not just some body part.

5. Because the standing pose will move her out of position in relation to the sofa, you'll need to move her into position. Switch to Top Camera, and using the Translate>Pull tool, drag her into position (see Figure 1.28).

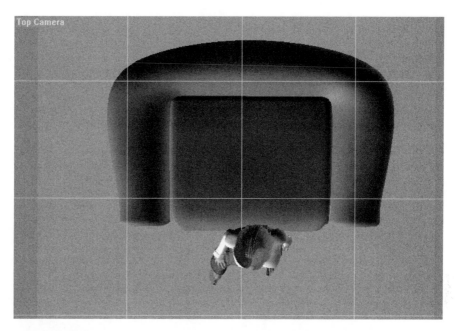

FIGURE 1.28
Sydney moved into position in front of the sofa shown from the top view.

6. Switch back to Main Camera, and play the animation (select Fast motion tracking for faster playback) to see Sydney go from sitting to standing very smoothly but not very realistically.

7. At this point in the pose-to-pose animation, the problem is that Sydney's motion is so unrealistic that it could distract a sophisticated audience from the story you are trying to tell. You need to add more animation detail between the two extremes of sitting and standing.

8. To see how this is resolved, open the 05-Pose-To-Pose_step-03.pz3. In step three, keyframes are set on frame 30 to pose Sydney to stabilize herself by placing her left hand on the left armrest of the sofa.

9. This is where you begin setting specific detail to make this animation occur. Because this is a very well rigged Poser figure, you can use the Advanced Body Controls in Properties (see Figure 1.29) to maneuver the body into the position shown in Figure 1.30.

ON THE DVD

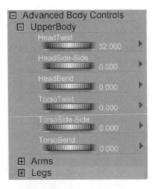

FIGURE 1.29
The Advanced Body
Controls allow you to
control the Properties.

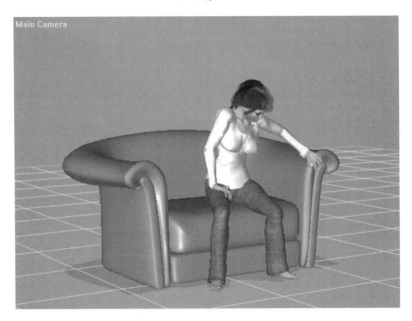

FIGURE 1.30
Sydney braces herself on the sofa's left armrest in preparation for standing.

Here you can twist the head (with a numeric control specifically designed for that), bend the torso, and so on. It is more predictable to use these tools than to use the traditional editing tools and will speed up your workflow. There are also specific controls for working with the arms, so you can shrug the shoulders, for example. Although these controls are high level and easy

to use, they are also a bit limited in that you cannot get very granular—
down to adjusting the fingers, for example. However, you can get some
general positioning here that can speed up the manual posing process. On
frame 30 in this project, you have the left arm placed on the armrest (this
is more animation detail than provided in the initial pose-to-pose animation where the character managed the feat of getting up without any kind
of support). Here you have the arm placed on the sofa armrest for support.

*This is done to create the illusion that Sydney has to compensate for the fact that
her center mass is heavier than the rest. So, realistically, the arm is acting as a support mechanism. In such animation, it's helpful to perform the task yourself by, for
example, sitting on a real sofa and then slowly going through the motion of standing up, taking close note of each action you take, why you take those actions, and
even what's happening to your skeleton and muscles.*

You also have her weight dragged across because it is natural to scoot over
a bit, readying herself to use her left arm for support. Therefore, her weight
has been shifted, which is done by selecting her hip and dragging her over.
Her head has been turned to look at her left hand because that is also a natural thing to do—making sure the hand has something sturdy to hold on
to that will hold her weight.

10. Now, go back to frame 15, and position the head to look at where the hand
    is going to go, as a person really would do. This way, rather than assuming
    her hand will land in the correct place, she looks ahead and makes sure this
    is where she wants to secure herself to lift her body to stand up.

*You didn't do this first because by going to frame 30 and establishing where she is
supposed to be looking and then going back to frame 15, you get a smoother rotation curve for the head. If, for example, you set her head to look over here on frame
15, then when you at frame 30, after adjusting her body, weight, and hand, you
may find her head is no longer facing to the right place. In that case, you would
have to make additional adjustments, which often create an unnatural movement.
This method can help to compensate for that.*

ON THE DVD   Open the next project 05-Pose-To-Pose_step-04.pz3. Go to frame 60—the
midpoint of getting her to stand up (see Figure 1.31). Here Sydney is right between
where she was sitting and standing straight up. Now her head is twisting away
from the armrest to looking forward. There could be another person to interact
with, or she's getting her path set to whatever it is she'll be doing next. Her head is

tilting upward, now dealing with eye-level activity, and her hip is raised. Raising the hip is literally a matter of selecting her hip and raising her using the Move tool to get her to stand up.

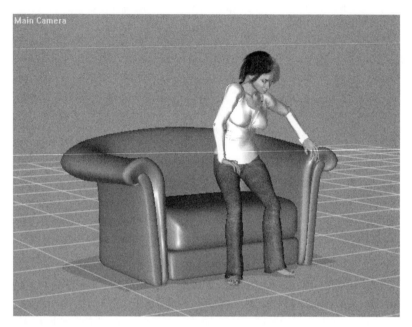

FIGURE 1.31
Sydney in the raised pose between sitting and finally standing up.

When you are doing this kind of work, such as raising the hips and especially the hand placements, you will want to work with multiple cameras, such as the Auxiliary Camera, to orbit around and see if you have any instances of the hand penetrating the sofa. You also need to work with the Hand Cameras to get a close look at the hands.

In the project example, the Main Camera is designated as the nonanimated camera, so that this pose is always guaranteed. This helps in the posing process. So when you're in the Main Camera mode, you never use the track ball. If you want to look around, go to the Auxiliary Camera. This way, as you work through all these different steps, you can be certain that you're looking at the Main Camera view from the same angle each time. If you're making a movie or music video, you may put some cinematic camera movement on this main view, but this current exercise is about creating the animation itself.

ON THE DVD
Now, open project 05-Pose-To-Pose_step-05.pz3. In this step, you're looking at frame 90. At this point, Sydney is standing (see Figure 1.32). The head is oriented for a casual, natural look forward; the arms are slightly placed out from the sides of her body; and the torso is straightened but favoring weight on her left leg. It is not symmetrical intentionally, so it looks more like the way a real person would stand. Her hands have been relaxed, which means going in and manually adjusting her fingers. Additionally, in the previous step, her right foot was farther over to the right. Here the foot has been dragged over, closer to her left foot, for a more natural stance. The torso is not only straightened, but you have a bit of work going on in there because you had her weight shifted in the previous step. In other words, the abdomen, chest, hips, and waist were all adjusted. So now they are all being twisted and adjusted to give the impression of a person who actually has mass and weight.

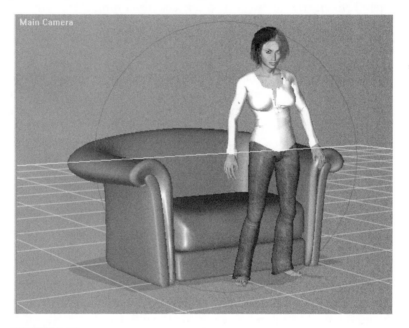

FIGURE 1.32
Sydney standing in a relaxed pose.

TIP

When animating, it's important to make sure you portray that the character has mass. When you stand up, your skeleton and your muscles are holding you up. It's an actual act—it takes effort and energy, and there's weight displacement. It is important to reflect these kinds of factors when you animate in 3D, so that it comes across as believable. Now, if you are making a loopy, quick and dirty animation that is about a humorous, nonrealistic thing, it may be good not to pay attention to the realistic details. But it's beneficial to learn how to do it at the higher levels of realism so that you can handle any kind of animation that is thrown at you.

ON THE DVD   Open the next step, 05-Pose-To-Pose_step-06.pz3. Here it's all about fine-tuning. It is not about making any significant adjustments but rather small, fine-tuning adjustments. As you make keyframes for an animation, especially when there is interaction between two objects, it's common for something, such as the hands, to go through the chair at some point. Therefore, after the major keyframes are set (as in the previous steps), it's important to go back and make all of those adjustments because the prior frames affect what happens in between. You don't want to spend all your time making those adjustments as you go forward because you will end up creating erratic-looking animation where a hand or arm is jumping or twisting as if there's a spasm. To prevent that, first do your major animation, and then go back and do all the tweaking.

ON THE DVD   Look at the rendered animations in the Chapter 01 folder to see the results of all this. First, look at the 05_Pose-To-Pose_start.mov, and then look at 05_Pose-To-Pose_end.mov. You see that there is definitely a significant increase in realism. Although it is not 100% realistic, that would simply be a matter of using those same techniques and putting more time and effort into it, to make incredibly realistic animation. This is especially true if you use some kind of reference video that can give you more hints about those little things you do that make the motion so natural and so believably human.

So, to recap pose-to-pose, you pose the character at the extreme poses and then edit poses to add detail in between. An essential key to great pose-to-pose animation is to place the extreme poses at the point in the timeline that believably tells your story.

SUMMARY

Familiarizing yourself with these principles before developing animation will not only save you time and result in more effective and fulfilling animation, it will also protect you from developing ineffective bad habits.

Remember that proper use of (1) timing to communicate the temporal relation between elements of an animation can help an animation be more realistic or more comical when done right, (2) squash & stretch can help support the animation principles of anticipation and weight, (3) anticipation can set up the upcoming action—engaging the viewer for a visual payoff, (4) overlapping motion can add hierarchical layers of visibly interesting complexity and (5) pose-to-pose is an excellent way to develop the overall key points in the animation before adding levels of motion detail.

So, not only have you learned what some of the basic principles of animation are, but you now know how to apply them within Poser.

2 Advanced Poser Figure Posing

In This Chapter

- Introduction
- Reference Photo Photography Issues
- Preparing Photos in Adobe® Camera Raw for Use as Pose References
- Masking in Adobe Photoshop® Using Fluid Mask
- Aligning Reference Photos and Poser Figures
- Posing to the Reference Photos

INTRODUCTION

When animating characters in Poser or any 3D application, you must first be able to pose the characters before you can animate them. In this chapter, you'll learn how to take reference photos for use in Poser, how to mask those photos, and how to pose figures in Poser Pro based on those photo references.

If you already have some experience using the editing tools and the pose library to pose your figures, note that this chapter goes beyond basic posing concepts and uses actual photographs as the posing reference using the parameter controls rather than the editing tools to provide a clear and predictable workflow for controlled figure posing. You will learn critical aspects of taking and processing photos for use as Poser Pro pose references.

There are some unique things to plan for and ways to handle the photos to make sure they make effective references in Poser Pro. You'll also learn how to use a turnstile (lazy susan) when photographing your models, and you'll learn about some basic lighting issues you'll need to know when capturing such photo references. If you don't take these basic lighting issues into account, you may end up with photos that are either unusable or that waste much of your time in preparation. You'll learn how to prepare the photo background (the backdrop for your subject) and get some helpful information on choosing the camera's digital color and pixel resolution settings that are most optimal for this workflow.

You'll work in Adobe Camera Raw and consider the advantages of using this photo processing application in the workflow for prepping the photos to ensure you have the cleanest and fastest workflow. The photos will be prepared for masking with Fluid Mask (by Vertus™) in Adobe Photoshop. Although you can mask in many ways, the Fluid Mask is the fastest way to get the results you'll need. As a digital media production professional, when you start shooting many photos for the sake of bringing them into Poser Pro as photo references, time becomes a serious issue. You will save the photos from Photoshop for use in Poser, set up those reference shots in Poser, and finally pose figures from the reference photos.

REFERENCE PHOTO PHOTOGRAPHY ISSUES

When producing photos for use as references in Poser Pro, *turnstiles* are useful because they let you take photos that are 90 degrees apart. You place a person, an actor or model, in position on a turnstile; take a photo; rotate the turnstile 90 degrees; and take another photo so that you have a front and a side reference to work with.

As you can see in Figure 2.1, the construction of the turnstile used to produce the reference photos for this book is simple. A single turnstile (lazy susan) element is attached with 4 screws to a piece of plywood, 4' × 4' wide. This is a very inexpensive turnstile, which you should be able to put together for well under $40 (USD)—and maybe even as low as $20 (USD) if you're a frugal shopper.

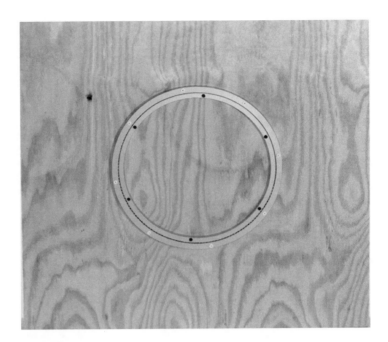

FIGURE 2.1
Turnstile used to create the reference photos for this chapter.

A turnstile allows you to photograph a perfectly still person from different angles by rotating the subject (person on the turnstile) while keeping the camera planted. This way, the model doesn't need to move out of the pose for you to capture front and side shots. The turnstile is an essential element in producing reference photos in which you will use more than a single view of your subject.

Figure 2.2 shows the turnstile in operation. In some cases, you may want to use a mat or some other solid color (other than the unfinished wood surface) to simplify the masking process. This provides a solid color that can aid in the process of cutting or masking out your subject. This simple, additional step can help in the end. If the model is wearing black and the mat is black (as shown in Figure 2.2), you could face some difficulty during the masking process. This can be resolved in Photoshop using Levels by raising the Midtone slider (or in Adobe Camera Raw by raising the Exposure) to create an apparent difference between the black clothing and the black mat (see Figure 2.3). This should be done to a duplicate of the original photo layer so that you preserve the original color and lighting of the photo.

It would in practice be more helpful to simply not have the model wearing black against a black background and thereby have an easier workflow.

NOTE

Front   **Right**   **Back**

FIGURE 2.2
A stationary model on a turnstile is photographed and rotated 90 degrees twice to capture a total of three reference photos.

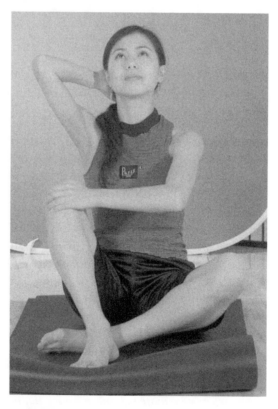

FIGURE 2.3
Midtones are raised to differentiate between black clothing and the black mat.

To gain the greatest control when trying to create a visual difference between different black objects, work with wide dynamic range (16-bit–32-bit) raw photos.

When photographing a subject for use as reference photos in Poser Pro, one of the most elementary issues in photography to be factored in is the lighting. You must make sure your subject is well lit so that features and details appear without unwanted shadows. Additionally, to aid the masking process, you should use a solid colored background and light it with its own light. This is not a general concern for regular photography, but when using reference photos, you want to light the solid background (shown in Figure 2.4) to have clear distinct edges on your subject (the model) and to eliminate shadows cast by the subject.

FIGURE 2.4
A light is positioned to specifically illuminate background and eliminate shadows cast by the subject.

In Figure 2.4, you can see one light dedicated to lighting the green backdrop. Two additional lights are out of this shot and are lighting the subject to assure good tone and detail.

The required intensity of the lights is not defined so much by the wattage, as by making sure you have a clear picture with a high amount of detail in your subject and the elimination of unwanted shadows. In this reference photo, there are three incandescent lamps, each with a 500-watt bulb. However, depending upon the type of lights you use, the bulbs do not necessarily need to be 500 watts. It all depends on the exact light technology employed in your lights, the size of the area you must light, the color of the walls, and the level of subject detail you must capture.

The background needs to have reduced noise and reduced motion. For example, you shouldn't shoot a reference photo against a background of a rose garden, dots, or clouds—unless you absolutely have to—because this only adds to the complexity in masking out your subject. Additionally, you should photograph your subject against a perfectly still background. A worst-case scenario is photographing against a moving crowd, for example. This becomes even more of an issue as we look at the use of video as reference later in this chapter. In setting up the lighting, you should have at least three lights distributed between lighting your background and the subject.

When you want to mask out a subject, a moving background is not advisable because it will simply multiply the amount of work you have to do.

NOTE

The reference photos used in this chapter were captured using a Fuji™ S3 Pro camera. You can, of course, use any other digital camera to capture the reference photos for your project. You are definitely not limited to the use of any specific type of camera. One of the benefits of using a camera like the S3 Pro is that it has a very high resolution in both color and pixels.

The pixel resolution for these shots is 12 megapixels. The color resolution, set at wide dynamic range, is 16 bit. The pixel resolution of 12 megapixels gives a lot of detail for creating crisp edges when you mask the photo. The benefit of 16- or 32-bit wide color resolution is that when you are working in Camera Raw to process the incoming photos, you have a greater amount of control to do color correction, which can increase the amount of detail and make your workflow in the masking process much easier. This measurement, 16 or 32 bit, refers to the number of bits of color per channel. A standard photograph has 8 bits of color per channel. This means that the red, green, and blue have 8 bits or 258 shades of color. As you go to 16 and 32 bit, the number of shades increases exponentially and can provide significantly higher fidelity to the original photo, as it was in the real world.

In addition to having the appropriate camera settings—set at the highest color and pixel resolution you can—you also should mount your camera onto a tripod to not only ensure good focus but to also maintain equal distance between the camera and the subject. Meaning, when the subject on the turnstile is turned 90 degrees, the camera's distance from the subject does not change. This way, the photo sizes are all appropriate and equal, so when you go to Poser, you don't have the camera closer when they are facing you and farther away when they are rotated 90 degrees because you happened to move your position. So, using a tripod in this process is absolutely essential in this case because you are working with more than one photo to be used as referencing for the same person.

PREPARING PHOTOS IN ADOBE CAMERA RAW FOR USE AS POSE REFERENCES

We will begin by working in the Adobe Camera Raw application. Because Photoshop cannot process raw images directly, opening raw camera files automatically launches Adobe Camera Raw. If you haven't worked with raw files, all you need to know about them for this workflow is that they are the unprocessed files from your digital camera. *Raw files* are what is really captured by the camera's imaging sensor before the camera makes all kinds of internal generalized color correction decisions and stores the image as a JPEG, TIFF, BMP, or some other format. Raw is the untouched format professional photographers use to gain maximum control over the processing of a digital photograph. The issues we will look at that are relevant to preparing reference photos for pose reference use in Poser Pro are limited in scope. Although we will cover what you need to know about Adobe Camera Raw to prep your files for masking, we won't cover all that Raw has to offer because that would fill another book.

ON THE DVD

1. From the accompanying DVD-ROM, in Exercise files/chapter 02/Reference Photos, open Ami-Front.raw and Ami-Side.raw in Adobe Camera Raw. After the reference photos are open in Raw, starting with the front view and using the Crop tool, start by cropping the photos to make sure you work with the areas that are of interest (clearly showing the model). When you crop, it's important to leave some space around the subject to allow for easier masking (see Figure 2.5). Cropping to the precise boundaries of the subject will only increase the steps required to mask the subject. Do the same thing to the side view photo (see Figure 2.6). From this point on, you will actually be working with both photos at the same time. Select both photos, by holding down the Shift key, so that as you make adjustments, these adjustments occur on both images.

FIGURE 2.5
Ami-Front.raw cropped to allow space around the subject.

2. Look at the Exposure level (see Figure 2.6). The exposure level in this case happens to be correct, but if your lighting was not appropriate, you can adjust your exposure setting here to set lighting after the photograph has already been taken.

3. Look at the level of detail (see Figure 2.6) by going into 100% Magnification. You can see a bit of grain in this photo, so you will adjust that in the Detail tab. Increase the Luminance Smoothing as well as the Color Noise Reduction. Although you want to have a crisp edge for your masking, if you take Sharpness all the way up, you will in some cases end up with grain on the edge, which can make the edge detecting for your masking a bit problematic. You'll often keep this close to the low side rather than all the way up.

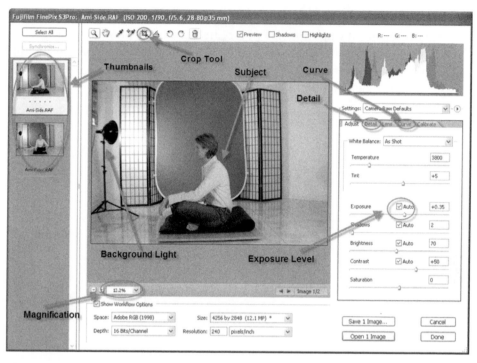

FIGURE 2.6
Adobe Camera Raw interface.

Because this photo was taken with the camera set to Wide Dynamic Range, the depth of this image is set to 16 bits. You have an option of 8 or 16 bits—it all depends on what your camera is capable of producing. This is something you may want to factor in when buying a camera for use in this kind of workflow. Look for wide dynamic range or 16 to 32 bits per channel to gain better exposure control to manipulate the image lighting without exceeding (clipping) the white or black limits. Here, the pixel resolution is set to 6 megapixels. You can see this if you clear the crop; otherwise, it will show the megapixels of the cropped area only.

Often, setting your camera to a lower ISO speed setting can reduce grain in the image but then requires more light to produce the same level of subject detail.

At times, depending on how the illumination of your lighting is distributed in the photo (where some areas can be too dark or too bright), you may need to adjust the Curves in the Curve tab. You can adjust your curve and you can add knots (see Figure 2.7) to your curve by clicking into the curve. Unlike using brightness, contrast, or level adjustments, using curves allows you to adjust the bright areas and/or dark areas of a photo without affecting other areas. This helps you balance the lighting in a photo. In this project photo, you won't need to adjust the curves, but now you know where and why you should make this kind of adjustment for future reference photos. You can also delete knots by clicking on them and deleting them.

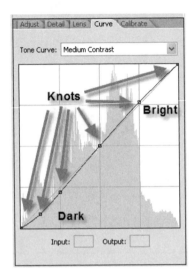

FIGURE 2.7
The Curve tab showing knots in
bright and dark areas.

Your images have now been processed in Raw, and you're ready to move on. Here you have two options. You can save the images, or you can open them. As a matter of good safe workflow, you should save them rather than open them to ensure the work you've done to this point is stored, in case you later need to restart the masking process. When you save them, you can work with them again in the future beyond this one session, but if you open them in Photoshop and process your work, you will be limited to the use of Photoshop's History function and would have to go through the Camera Raw process if a program crashes or if you exit Photoshop. Still in Raw, save these two images. With both image thumbnails selected, they will both be saved. Enter the model's name, and choose the format. Using the TIFF or PSD file formats will ensure that there's no compression applied to the photo, and the photo will not be degraded in any way. If you use JPEG, you will get a nice small file at the expense of having compression applied to it.

MASKING IN ADOBE PHOTOSHOP USING FLUID MASK

ON THE DVD

Now, you're about to mask the reference images in Photoshop using Fluid Mask from Vertus (*http://www.vertustech.com/*). You have front and side view reference photos of the model. Either load the images you previously saved from Raw, or go to the Exercise files/Chapter 02/reference photos folder, and open Ami-Front_source.PSD and Ami-Side_source.PSD in Photoshop. These images are still in 16-bit mode, which means many features in Photoshop will not be available to process these images. Some Photoshop features are only accessible in 8-bit mode. In the Filter menu, the grayed out options are the features you will not be able to use while working with 16-bit and 32-bit images. For this project, this limitation is not a problem. You only need to access two things: Image/Adjustment/Levels and the Filter/Vertus/Fluid Mask.

NOTE

For this part of the process, you need to install either the free downloadable demo of Fluid Mask or the full licensed version. This adds Fluid Mask functionality to Photoshop as a filter plugin. If you've never used the application before, go through their impressive tutorials, which will expose you to the interface. Our exploration of Fluid Mask will be limited to processing these images as references for use in Poser Pro only.

You will now mask out the model in the front view. First we'll go through all of the workflow steps to process the front reference image, and then you'll repeat these steps to process the side view.

1. Right now, only one layer is shown, which is the background layer. Right-click on this layer, choose Duplicate Layer, and then hide the default background layer. You're doing this because you will modify the contrast of this new duplicated layer to be processed in Fluid Mask. You will use the mask that is then generated to copy the original background. This may sound confusing at first, but you'll see shortly why this gives you more flexibility.

2. On this duplicate layer, you need to make one adjustment. As you can see, the model is wearing dark colored jeans on a black mat. This gives you the chance to work with low-contrast conditions. Traditionally, this would be difficult to mask, but you can remove the difficulty. From the main menu, choose Image>Adjustments>Levels. You just want to adjust one thing to see the difference between the jeans and the mat clearly. Drag the Midtone slider to the left to approximately 1.83 (see Figure 2.8), and click OK. This creates a strong contrast between the dark colored jeans and the black mat.

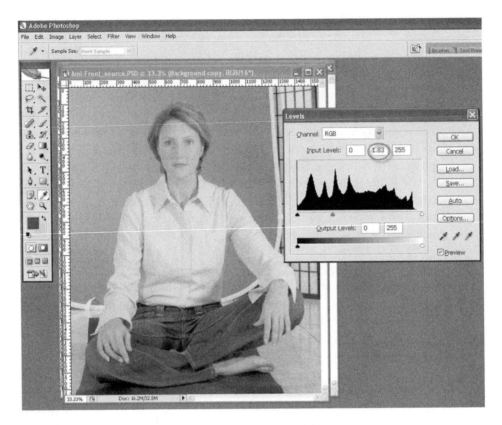

FIGURE 2.8
Midtone level adjusted to create high contrast for masking.

NOTE

The resulting image will appear to be poorly lit. This lighting will not be used in Poser; it will only be used for the masking process in Fluid Mask.

3. Now you're ready to take this image into the Fluid Mask. In Photoshop, launch Fluid Mask by going to the main menu and choosing Filter>Vertus>Fluid Mask. Fluid Mask immediately analyzes the image to try to identify where the edges are. Fluid Mask looks at the image and breaks up the differences in color information into shapes. After the analysis is complete, you will make some adjustments to get lines that are more appropriate for the image.

4. Working in the Fluid Mask Edge Detection Options, increase the Edge Sensitivity from 11 to 15 to increase the number of detected edges, and decrease the In-Focus Edge Width to 3 to create crisper masked edges. Click Apply to analyze again. The length of the time to analyze the image is affected by the

amount of resolution involved. Remember, the original resolution on this photo was quite high, as a 6-megapixel, 16-bit image. If you work with lower-resolution images, the analyzing process will be quicker (see Figure 2.9).

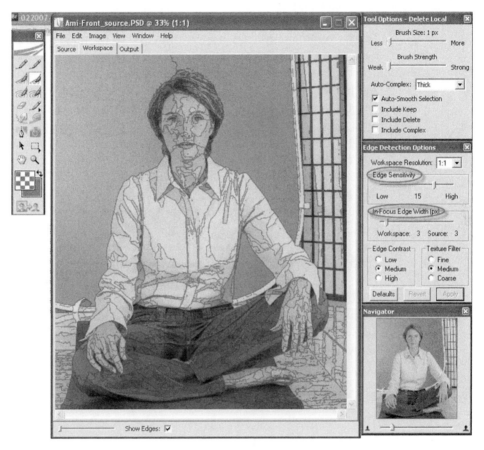

FIGURE 2.9
Vertus Fluid Mask Edge Detection settings adjusted and image re-analyzed.

5. You can now see that more shapes of similar color in the image are defined. As you move the mouse around, you can see the brush, which may be a bit large for working with this kind of image. If needed, in the Tool Options, reduce the Brush Size, and set the Brush Strength to Weak. The Brush Strength determines how far from the area of selection the effect of masking extends. Keeping it at the weakest strength gives you greater control over how the masking effect works. As you get into more detailed areas of a photo, you'll need to reduce the brush size to limit selection to only those areas to be removed.

The higher you take the brush strength, the more memory is required. Even working with this reference photo on a 2 GB RAM system, it is actually possible to run out of memory. So, unless you have a very good reason, you will want to keep the Brush Strength at Weak.

6. To give you the simplest demonstration of how the mask selection process works, simply click once in the green screen area in the background. Fluid Mask has now identified that the green background is all one colored area and has removed it. So rather than having to trace along the subject, you can just click on those areas that should be removed. In some areas, you must go in and do some manual cleanup, however, and Fluid Mask has cool tools for that as well. You are not limited to just clicking on each section to be removed. You can also drag across several areas outside of the subject to process all those areas at once. Just be cautious when you see that the contrast between different areas is low.

7. From the Fluid Mask toolbar on the left, zoom in to do more detailed work. You can also zoom in by dragging the slider at the bottom right of the Fluid Mask interface. In most areas, the contrast is obvious, but the area between a small dark piece of the black mat and the dark jeans (see Figure 2.10) has an open gap. To mask this area, switch from the Delete Local (the default) to Delete Exact (see Figure 2.11). With Delete Exact, you draw manually to define the mask. In many ways, working with Fluid Mask feels like working with magic. If you've ever masked images in Photoshop, you know the amount of time and pain associated with it. Fluid Mask gets rid of most of that.

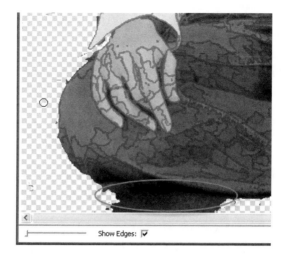

FIGURE 2.10
The low contrast area.

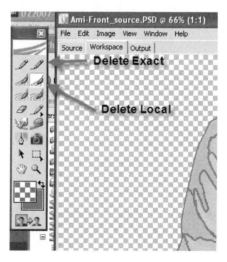

FIGURE 2.11
Delete with the Local and Exact tools.

8. The contrast difference is not very high around the fingers, so if you are not careful, you could easily cut fingers off. Zoom in on the fingers, and turn off the Show Edges (bottom left of the current Fluid Mask workspace) to see the original picture. Use Delete Exact, reduce your brush size, and then trace manually along the edges of the fingers. Don't worry if you accidentally cut a piece of the finger. We'll look at such reconstruction when we get back into Photoshop.

NOTE

Remember, the goal is just a reference to use in Poser, so you do not need to go overboard with the level of detail here. When making these reference photos, remember that you may have quite a few of them to do if you are making an animation, so don't get into the habit of spending hours making each of these masks. You'll want to get it down to masking an image in about five minutes.

NOTE

This is another reason for making a copy of the background because the background image will be the source to fill this back in.

9. Although there is an incredible amount of magic to using Fluid Mask, you still need to do some manual cleanup to make sure the work looks professional. Even though you are not going for a fine-art portrait print quality mask here, you may be working with a team and handing off these masks to other artists. You'll want to make sure they're not ratty, yet still produce them within a reasonable amount of time. Do a general cleanup of the mask by selecting the Clean icon from the Fluid Mask tools on the left, and clicking into the general mask (empty) area.

10. Now you're ready to take this pose reference photo back to Photoshop. Go to the Fluid Mask main menu and choose Image>Create Cutout. Then choose File>Save and Apply to open the masked reference photo in Photoshop.

11. Here you will reconstruct the missing portion of the fingers (if your photo needs it). First, hold the Ctrl key, and select the Background Copy layer thumbnail image (this is the layer just processed in Fluid Mask) to get the mask. Then turn on and select the Background layer, and copy and paste to create a new layer named Layer 1. Layer 1 is the original color of the background layer but with the shape of the mask created in Fluid Mask. Delete the Background Copy layer.

12. Magnify the fingers (or the area that needs reconstruction). Select the background layer. With the Lasso tool selected, trace the finger, and then copy and paste (to create a layer containing just the missing finger information). Turn off the background layer to see the fingers reconstructed (see Figure 2.12).

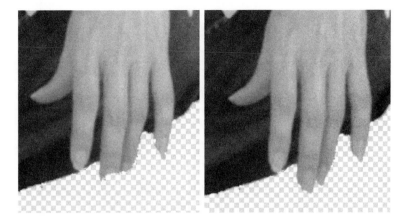

FIGURE 2.12
The fingers are reconstructed.

13. Manually clean up any remaining areas that need it. After the fingers are re-constructed, they must be merged with the masked layer. (You can safely delete the Background Copy layer because you don't need it anymore.) Merge the top three layers for the final masked image. The masking is now complete!

14. Using the same workflow, go ahead and mask the side view image. When you are finished, you will continue processing the image in Photoshop to save it out for Poser Pro.

15. To convert this image from a 16-bit to an 8-bit image, choose Image>Mode>8 Bits from the main menu. You are now ready to save the images for use in Poser Pro.

16. Save the front image as a JPEG file named Ami-Front.jpg, and save the side image as Ami-Side.jpg.

17. Now that you've saved the color images, you'll need to save a black-and-white image for each reference photo. The color image and black-and-white image will be used in the Poser Material room.

18. Fill the bottom empty layer with black. Fill the top layer with white so that you have a silhouette of the subject. Save this as a JPEG image as well, and name it Ami-Front_alpha.jpg. Save a similar image for the side view.

You must save two images for every reference image—the color image and the alpha. They will both be used in the Materials room in Poser Pro when you create the reference for use in the posing process. Also, keep in mind the resolution of the image. You can check your resolution in Image>Image Size. This will come in handy when you want to adjust the size of the object that you are mapping the image onto.

Table 2.1 Importing the Reference Photos into Poser Pro

Reference Images	Pixel Resolution
Ami-Front.jpg	500 x 592
Ami-Front-mask.jpg	500 x 592
Ami-Side.jpg	528 x 592
Ami-Side-mask.jpg	528 x 592

ON THE DVD

19. Now working in Poser Pro, get a female figure set up in a T-pose, or you can load the Exercise files/chapter 02/SyndneyT.pz3 project as a starting point (see Figure 2.13).

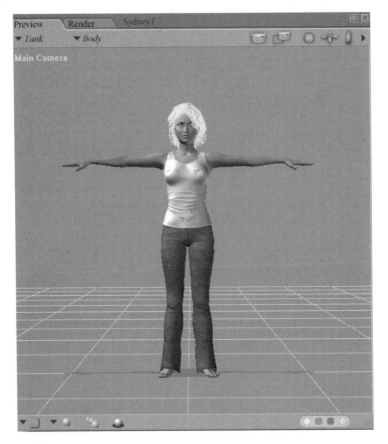

FIGURE 2.13
Sydney in the T-Pose.

20. You now add the objects that you will map the reference photos onto. Add the one-sided square from Library>Props>Primitives. Adjust the size of this one-sided square to match the resolution of the front reference photo. This is where the resolution image information you saw earlier comes in handy. Set the xScale of the square to the horizontal value of the front reference image (500), and set the yScale to 592 accordingly (see Figure 2.14).

The actual position and final scale are not yet set. We just want to get the correct aspect ratio for now.

NOTE

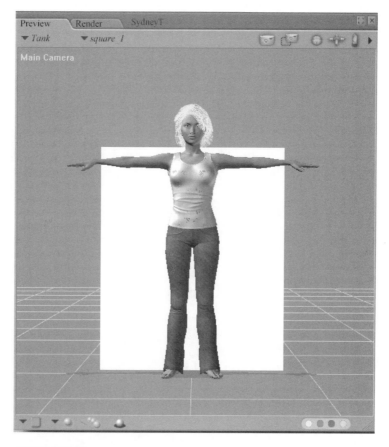

FIGURE 2.14
The one-sided square scaled to 500 x 592.

21. Now you will rename the square because just having something named "square" does not give you the information you need. Just imagine the chaos you would have if you just added these squares for a scene with 10 characters and had to switch between square 13 and square 7. That's the stuff that gets away from you. So get into the habit of naming them from now to have a much better workflow, especially when working with a team. Go to Properties, and rename the square Ami_Front.

22. You will now create the material for this object. Go to the Material room, and make sure the Ami_Front object is still selected. Right-click to create a new node in the Material room (see Figure 2.15).

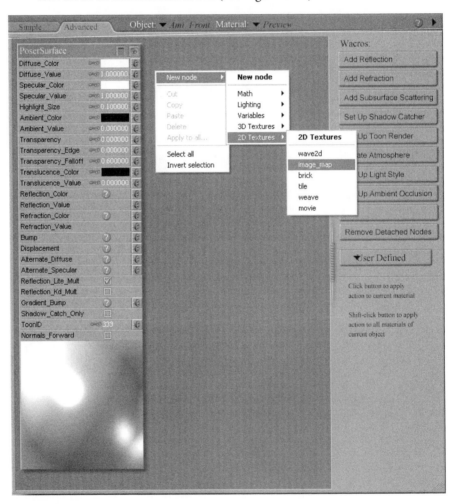

FIGURE 2.15
Creating a new node in the Material room.

ON THE DVD

23. You will now add the 2D Textures/image_map. In this first image map, bring in the masked image. Browse the Image Source to find the image in the exercise files on the accompanying DVD-ROM, located in Exercise files/chapter 02/Photo references/Ami-Front_mask.jpg. In this node, you can hide or show the contents of the node and hide or show the image that is associated with it (see Figure 2.16). This does not affect functionality; it only provides feedback. You will now connect this with the Transparency channel and adjust the Transparency channel to 1. The result is that the cutout of the object is showing behind Sydney (see Figure 2.17).

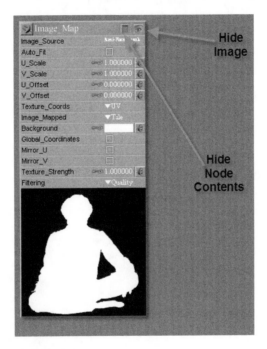

FIGURE 2.16
The 2D Texture node.

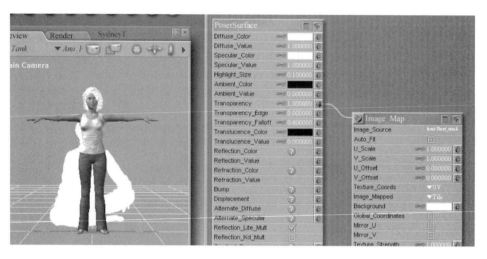

FIGURE 2.17
Mask image connected to the material transparency input with the Transparency value
set to 1 (maximum).

24. Right-click to add a new node. This will be another image map from 2D
    texture. Browse and select Ami-Front.jpg. This is the color image. Connect
    this texture node to the Diffuse/Color channel. Now you have the full color
    image showing behind Sydney (see Figure 2.18).

FIGURE 2.18
Reference material for the front view is
now complete.

25. Return to the Pose tab, and open the Library. Add another one-sided square. Rotate the square 90 degrees in the Parameters yRotate. Looking at this from the front, it will seem to disappear, but it's simply on its side (as you can see if you rotate the camera). Use the resolution information for the reference image, just as you did with the front. Set your xScale to 528, and the yScale to 592. In Properties, rename this square to Ami_Side. With the Ami_Side object selected, go back to the Material room. When Ami_Side is selected, you will see it has no nodes yet.

26. Right-click to add two nodes for Ami_Side. You will use 2D Texture image maps, as before. Browse the Image Source, and select Ami_Side for the first node and Ami-Side_mask for the second node. Connect the color image to the Diffuse_Color channel, and connect the masked image into the Transparency channel. Be sure to set your Transparency to 1. You can either use the slider or enter it numerically. When you go back to the Pose room, you can now see that both the front and side image are mapped and in place when you rotate the camera (see Figure 2.19). Now you need to set the relationship of how those two mask objects are going to intersect each other.

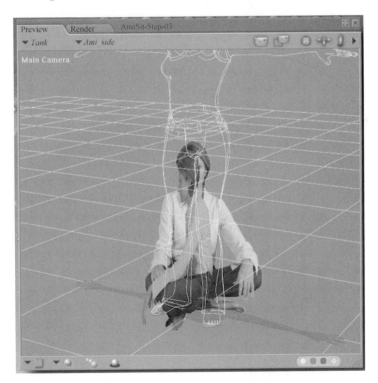

FIGURE 2.19
Both reference photos are now mapped and oriented.

ALIGNING REFERENCE PHOTOS AND POSER FIGURES

Here you will learn the workflow of posing the figure based on the reference images you have just set up in the Materials room. This process helps eliminate much of the guesswork out of creating believable realistic poses for your figures. You'll learn both the benefits and limitations of this method.

1. Go to the Four View viewport mode. You will work with the Parameters, not the Properties. Also, set the entire display to Outline, select Ami_Front and Ami_Side, and set them to Texture Shaded from the main menu using Display>Element Style>Texture Shaded. That way you don't have the 3D figure obscuring your view (see Figure 2.20). You want the figure side and front view reference images to be positioned so you can have a good placement of the 3D Poser figure.

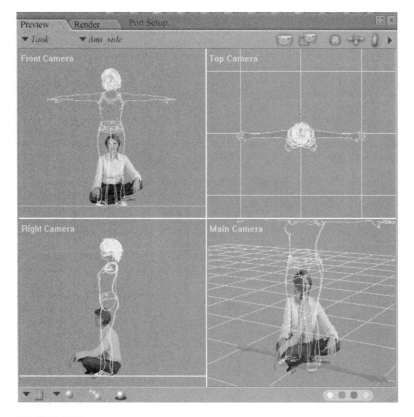

FIGURE 2.20
Four View viewport mode showing Sydney in outline and the reference photos as Texture Shaded.

2. Select the side view, and adjust its zTrans until the necks of the Ami_Front and Ami_Side objects intersect. Then switch back to the single viewport.

The choice of working with single- or four-viewport views is simply a matter of gathering enough information so you know you're moving in the right direction. It's not like a particular rhythm you need to achieve, where you have to go to four viewports first and then one; it's just a matter of making sure you get enough information to understand the spatial relationship between the front and side reference photos.

3. You also need to adjust the position of the front reference to line up the necks. Work with the xTrans for that. When both the front and side line up with the Poser figure, you are good to go.
4. To match the reference photos to the Poser Pro figure, you need to adjust the scale. You adjust the scale of the reference photos, not the scale of the Poser Pro figure.
5. If you think for a moment about why you adjust the size of the reference photos rather than the size of the figure, there are some case scenarios to consider. For example, if the Poser figure is part of an animation, and you adjust the scale of the figure to match the scale of the reference photos, obviously this would be a problem because the figure would go from one size to a whole other size, just to match a pose. Also, if a figure were part of an environment that had already been matched to that figure, then of course you would want to adjust the reference photos, not the figure. In general, because the reference images are introduced to the scene, often the scene will include a figure that is already set to match the scale of the scene. Therefore, as a general rule, you need to match the scale of the reference photos to match the scale of the 3D figure. To do this, make sure you have one of the reference photos selected (in this case, Ami_Front is selected). Remember, this is just a square that has the material mapped onto it. You will adjust the uniform Scale, not the xScale, yScale, or zScale. The Scale is a uniform scale adjustment, which means it will scale equally in X, Y, and Z. Set this to a scale of 66%.

66% is simply the value that matches the size of this object. If you have different reference photos with different resolutions, you'll need to match them up to the Poser figure.

6. Select the second reference, and scale it to 66% as well. Make sure everything still lines up. You don't really need to make an adjustment to that. When you're posing the figure to match the reference photos, you can

make the fine adjustments of the positioning (in the Z, for example) on the figure. It's a pretty easy adjustment. Now you're ready to fit the Poser figure to the reference photos.

POSING TO THE REFERENCE PHOTOS

To fit the Poser figure to the reference photos, follow these steps:

1. Switch back to the four-viewports view because you need to see both reference photos simultaneously with the Poser figure, from both the front view and the right view. The perspectives here help you make sure they are matched up, as far as the end result of the posed figure. You'll start by matching up the general body. Select the Body, but make sure you have the correct figure (SydneyG2) because, by default, you may have the Tank top selected. This is something to keep a very close eye on at all times!
2. Select the Right viewport and use the Move tool. Move the figure downward until it's lined up nicely with the reference photo. (You can zoom in and reposition to get maximum use of the viewport as shown in Figure 2.21.)

FIGURE 2.21
The Poser figure is moved down to
line up with the side reference photo.

NOTE

It may be tempting to use highly interactive editing tools, but there are a couple of things to keep in mind before doing so. When you use these tools and select the area in which to use them, it's very easy to either click the wrong body part or to move uncontrollably in an unintended axis. So at this point, a lot of the work you do to pose the figure will be done with the parameter controls.

3. With SydneyG2/Waist selected, use the Bend parameter to bend her forward a bit (see Figure 2.22). (Depending on your model photo reference, you may also need to adjust the Hip a bit before you continue adjusting the waist and abdomen.)

The Poser Pro figure will never perfectly match the reference photos. The reference photos are a posing guide to get the Poser figure into the general pose.

FIGURE 2.22
Waist bent slightly to match reference photo.

4. Now continue up the hierarchy to the Abdomen. Again, use the Bend parameter to bend the upper torso to match the reference photo (see Figure 2.23).

NOTE

Besides going through the drop-down menu when selecting the body parts, you can also go through the hierarchy of the figure by using the up and down arrows.

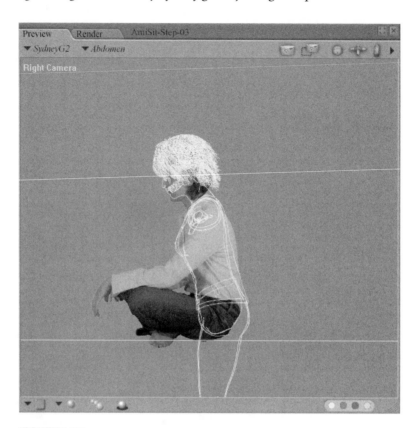

FIGURE 2.23
Abdomen bent slightly to match reference photo.

5. Select the lButtock. To allow direct posing control, turn off the IK (inverse kinematics) for the Left Leg and Right Leg. If you don't turn it off, the IK tries to fight your movement of the joints independently. IK overrides forward kinematics, and we're using traditional forward kinematics (FK) that can adjust its parameters manually. With IK turned off, the leg bends as it should. Bend the lButtock and then the Left Thigh to match the reference photo (see Figure 2.24). Next, adjust the Side-Side parameter to move the leg out toward the left. (You can see the outward bend in the Front and Top Camera views.)

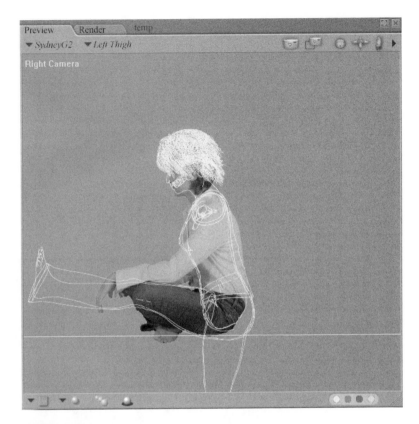

FIGURE 2.24
lButtock and Left Thigh bent to match reference photo.

6. Move on to the Left Shin, and set the Bend parameter to about 163 degrees. Also apply the Twist parameter (approx. -30), to get the foot to taper up a bit.

7. Select the Left Foot, and give it a 50-degree Bend. Keep your eye on the Front Camera this time to make sure it's bending the appropriate way. Then add a little bit of the Twist (-30), to twist the foot upward. Now you're ready to do the other leg.

8. Start from the rButtock, and work with the Bend, just as you did on the left side. This leg does not go up as high because it has to cross over. Also adjust the Side-Side parameter (the top view is helpful here to estimate the spread between the knees). Apply some Twist to twist the thigh outward.

9. Continue down the hierarchy to the Right Thigh. This will be a slight bend. You're making sure the entire leg is not bent only by the right buttocks to avoid any unnatural bends in the body.

10. Next is the Right Shin. Although it says "shin," you really need to think about the adjustment of the body parts as adjustments of the joints, not the bones. So when we say shin, it's really the knee. Therefore, when you bend the shin, you're really bending at the knee. You also have to apply the Twist here to rotate the shin and foot into the correct angle.

11. Lastly, select the Right Foot. Remember, the adjustments you are currently making are the gross adjustments. After you get your figure into the general position, you'll have to go in and make some fine adjustments. Therefore, at this early stage of the posing, you don't need to try to get it absolutely perfect. Because you have the Poser figure in outline mode, you are not getting full feedback yet. You're just trying to get gross positioning based on the reference photos. From the top viewport, Sydney's legs should now look like Figure 2.25.

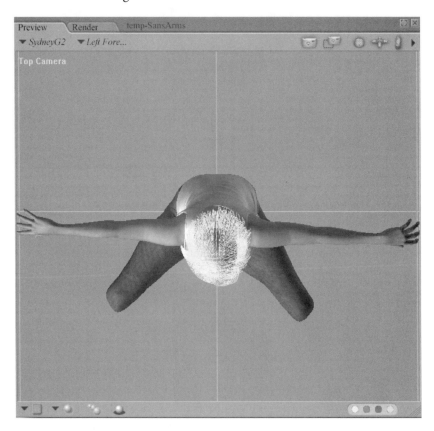

FIGURE 2.25
Both of Sydney's legs have been posed to match the reference photos.

12. Select the Right Collar, and using the Up-Down parameter, try to get it down to an appropriate angle before using the Twist.

13. Continue down the hierarchy to the Right Shoulder. Use the Up-Down and then the Twist to get the hand to rotate about 90 degrees. Although the figure outlines are very faint ghosts, you need to pay close attention to them, making sure fingers and so on are pointing in the right direction.

14. Next, you need to deal with the elbow bend. Select the Right Forearm. Just like when you select the shin, when you select the forearm, you are really manipulating the elbow joint. You may need to address the shoulder again to get the correct positioning of the elbow bend. Simply go back to the Right Shoulder, make the Twist adjustment, and then return to the forearm. This process does involve a bit of back-and-forth, but it's well worth it.

15. Select Left Collar to begin positioning the left arm. After the collar is aligned, move on to the Left Shoulder and the Left Forearm, making the appropriate adjustments to match up the figure with the reference photo. As you keep working, you will see the value of working in all four views because you can get a great deal of feedback on the positioning of each limb this way, as compared to working in only one view. Remember to go back or up the hierarchy as needed to get to the appropriate position. Leave the figure like this for now (see Figure 2.26). You will now go to the next stage where you actually work with the full texture shaded figure and make the final fine-tuning adjustments.

16. Now, to make the fine adjustments to the Poser figure, you'll work with the Main Camera in a single viewport and set the view to Texture Shaded.

17. Hide the reference images by selecting Ami_Front and going to Properties where you uncheck Visible and Visible in Raytracing. Unchecking Visible turns it off from being seen in your viewport as you're working. Unchecking Visible in Raytracing makes sure it doesn't show up in your render. Do the same with the Side reference. Now you're left with just the Poser model visible. You have some posing clean up to do here because there is some poke-through of the clothing.

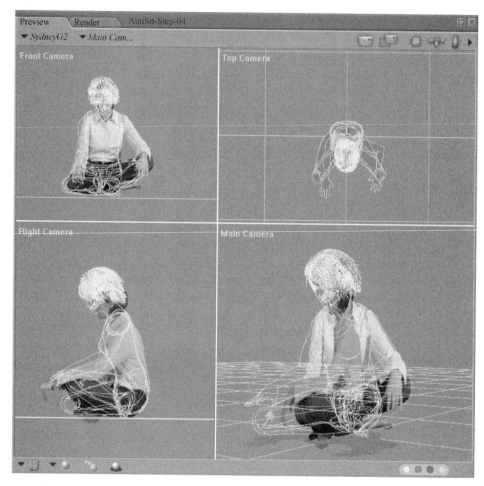

FIGURE 2.26
Rough posing of Sydney to the reference photos.

18. Make the final posing of the arms, beginning at the Left Collar, and then moving down to the Left Shoulder. Here you are mainly making tweaks to get rid of any deformations that make the body look contorted or unnatural. Next, tweak the Left Forearm and lastly the Left Hand. You want the hand to be gently grasping the kneecap (see Figure 2.27). Do this by opening the Hand Controls and adjusting the Grasp (also shown in Figure 2.27). Adjust the forearm as needed to make sure that none of the fingers cut into the kneecap.

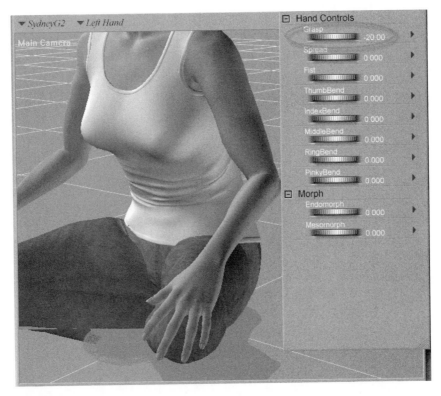

FIGURE 2.27
Left Arm and Hand tweaked into the final pose.

19. Orbit around to the right side to work on the Right Arm.

As you may have noticed, you are doing all these adjustments in a single view, intentionally not using the other views because now you're getting into an extremely organic fine-tuning process in which having the orthogonal views of top, right, and front could end up giving you information that is confusing. It's not just that you need to see a certain view; you need to be able to orbit the view and see the spatial relationships. As you orbit around in the single view, you can see what the true position is between the hand and the knee, for example. So at this point in the workflow, you're working with only the perspective view for these reasons.

20. Adjust the Right Collar as needed, and then move down to the Right Shoulder. Use the Up-Down, Front-Back, and Twist to remove any unnatural twisting and deformation and to position the Right Hand close to the Right Knee. Select the Right Forearm to adjust the wrist joint. Work with

the Hand Controls to fine-tune the hand. Adjusting the Bend and Grasp of the Hand gives you better control here than the Bend of the Forearm (see Figure 2.28).

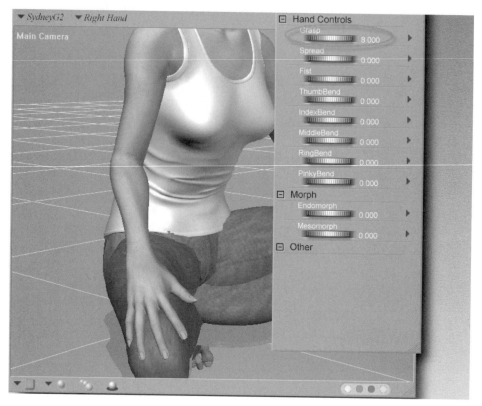

FIGURE 2.28
Right Arm and Hand tweaked into the final pose.

21. There is also some poke-through on the left breast (see Figure 2.29), which you will fix next. Select Left Breast, and turn off the visibility in Properties. Notice that there's still poke-through. In this case, you need to select the Chest and open the Breast Controls. You will adjust two controls, the Squeeze and the Flatten (as shown in Figure 2.30). This is to keep the body from forcing the limits of the clothing. As you adjust the BreastSqueeze to 0.240 and the BreastsFlatten to 0.380, you'll notice the clothing coming together, closing the gap (see Figure 2.31). Depending on what body part, what condition, and what clothing is involved, you'll need to have more than one solution for correcting poke-through errors.

FIGURE 2.29
Poke-through on left breast.

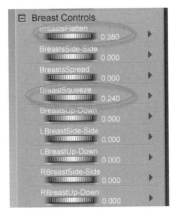

FIGURE 2.30
Breast Controls used to correct
clothing poke-through.

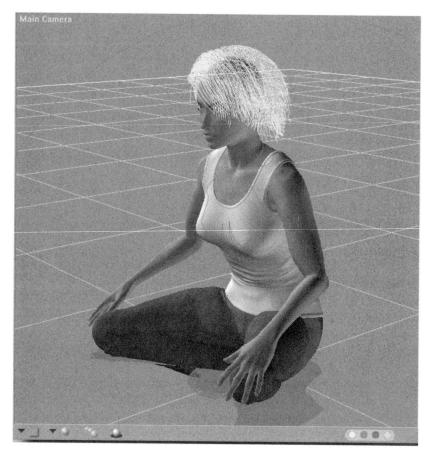

FIGURE 2.31
Clothing poke-through corrected.

22. Adjust her neck by selecting the Neck and adjusting the Bend to pose her neck in a more natural position as shown in Figure 2.31.
23. After she is in the final position, go ahead and render to see what the final result looks like (see Figure 2.32).

FIGURE 2.32
Poser figure Sydney is now posed based on the reference photos of real-world
model Ami.

SUMMARY

The figure posing is now natural because it matches the reference photos to a great
degree. Remember, "a great degree" is basically what you're after here because the
photos are of a 3D real-world object (the model), but they're stored in a 2D
medium (photographs, not 3D objects). These references will never give you a
100% match of how you position the 3D figure. However, they provide a very good
way to get some natural, believable poses in your Poser figures. And depending on
your animation workflow, this can be a great way of getting believable transitions
and positions for your Poser figures for character animation. If you want to check
your work against the actual project that you see here in the video, be sure to look
at your project file. There are five saved steps of this project so you can see how
yours compares to the final result.

3 Basic Poser Character Animation

In This Chapter

- Introduction
- Making Characters Walk Using the Walk Designer
- Making Characters Walk on a Path with the Walk Designer
- Importing Motion Capture Data to Animate Characters
- Using the Animation Editor and Curve Palettes to Edit Animation

INTRODUCTION

3D character animation is traditionally a tedious and strenuous technical process. This chapter takes a look at some of the methods provided in Poser Pro to simplify and reduce the difficulty of creating some character animation.

We'll explore the Animation Editor and Graph Editor to provide a much-needed basis for understanding how to achieve the project goals of later chapters of this book. Be sure to pay close attention and remember to review the accompanying video tutorials for this chapter on the DVD-ROM. Sometimes seeing the process in motion can help you get through a block in comprehension of a particular animation issue.

ON THE DVD

MAKING CHARACTERS WALK USING THE WALK DESIGNER

Poser Pro provides a very powerful tool for making your figures walk called the Walk Designer (see Figure 3.1). The *Walk Designer* is a highly intuitive walk synthesizer that provides walk design controls with names that are more like how we describe a person's walking behavior than how we would normally describe technical 3D animation controls. This makes for a fun and easy experience when designing a walk for your Poser figure.

By clicking the Walk button, the outlined preview figure on the left of the interface starts walking based on the setting of the sliders in the Blend Styles and Tweaks areas. Clicking Apply transfers this preview of the walk animation to the currently selected Poser figure.

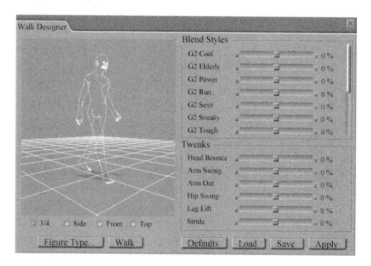

FIGURE 3.1
Poser Pro Walk Designer interface.

ON THE DVD   To learn how the Walk Designer is applied, you will start by working with the project file Exercise files/chapter 03/01-Walk_In_Place-start.pz3. All you have here right now is Ben standing on the stage (see Figure 3.2). You'll apply the Walk Designer to him to bring him to life. (You could also work with any Poser figure of your choice.)

1. From the main menu, choose Window>Walk Designer.

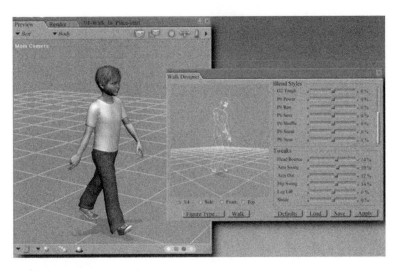

FIGURE 3.2
Ben walking.

The first time the Walk Designer is opened within a session causes a delay during the initialization period.

2. With the Walk Designer window open, you can click the Walk button to see the preview figure walking. You can choose perspective (3/4), Side, Front, or Top to watch the figure walk in those views. The perspective (3/4) view can show more information about the overall walk. On the right, you have the Blend Styles and the Tweaks control sliders. The Blend Styles are overall controls of the walk. This is where the walk design animation process is intuitively driven, as opposed to being highly technical. So, to make a "cool" walk, you literally drag the slider of G2 Cool toward the positive percentage (right) of Cool. Of course, this is e frontier®'s definition of a cool walk and not necessarily your cultural perception of a cool walk. It is extremely subjective and very controllable. You also have such a thing as a "negative cool" walk, simply by dragging the slider in the negative (left) direction. Depending upon the performance of your video card, you will have smooth or jerky playback of the preview motion on the left.

3. Now, it's time to create a walk animation for Ben. Begin by clicking Defaults to cancel any slider adjustments you may have made.

4. Click Apply. In the Apply Walk window (see Figure 3.3), select Walk in Place because you don't have a path to apply this to yet. Leave everything at their default settings. Click OK, and then close the Walk Designer. Ben is already in position to take a step. Click Play to see Ben walking. To make it smoother, switch to Fast playback (see Figure 3.4). To get a better sense of what's really happening, go to the last frame, orbit around, and click Play again.

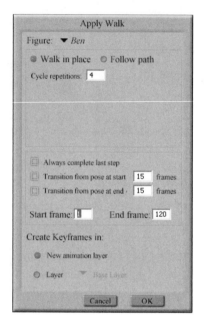

FIGURE 3.3
The Apply Walk window.

Ben - Full Tracking   Ben - Fast Tracking

FIGURE 3.4
Frame 1 of Ben's new walk animation shown here in Full and
Fast Tracking display modes.

ON THE DVD

5. Now, to create an animation of Ben running, once again open the project
   file Exercise files/chapter 03/01-Walk_In_Place-start.pz3. We're back to
   Ben with no animation applied. Open the Walk Designer again, and apply
   G2 Run. Be careful not to over-drive (go beyond 100) the slider, as you'll
   get some intense, overexaggerated results that will look more like defective
   animation than like a strong run. When you're satisfied with your selection, click Apply. Select Walk in Place, and leave all default settings as they
   are. Create this keyframe in the Base Layer by selecting Layer, and then
   choosing Base Layer from the drop down to the right (see Figure 3.5).

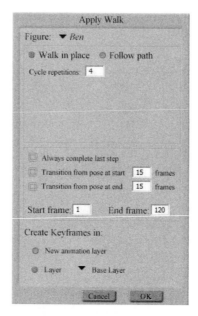

FIGURE 3.5
Choosing the Base Layer.

You have the choice of letting it generate a new layer or the base layer. In a later video of this chapter, you will see what the great significance is between these two options.

6. Select fast feedback for smoother playback, then go to the last frame, and orbit the camera around to view Ben from the other side. This automatically creates a keyframe for the camera's view of Ben. Click the Play button to see Ben running while the camera orbits around him to give you a good sense of how each of his limbs has been animated by the Walk Designer to create the animation as shown in Figure 3.6.

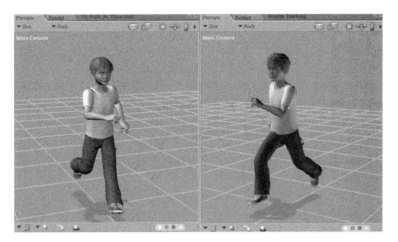

FIGURE 3.6
Orbiting camera while Ben runs.

7. You're going to create one more Walk Designer animation. Although you could reload the project file, this time, Undo (Ctrl + Z) the Camera rotation, and Undo the Walk Designer animation to reset Ben to his initial unanimated state. Open the Walk Designer, but this time to work with the Tweaks instead of the Blend Styles. Click Defaults to reset any previously adjusted sliders, and adjust the walk by using the Tweak sliders. These are focused on specific areas of the figure, whereas the Blend Styles work on the overall figure. When you're satisfied with your walk, click Apply. Leave all current selections as they are, and click OK. Again, orbit the camera to get a better view, and click Play.

You may notice that the Walk Designer allows you to create some strange looking animation. Because you have so much control, you can make walks that cause the Poser figure to animate in awkward or impossible ways. Remember you have more than 100% (positive and negative) available in each of those sliders, and many of those sliders interact with each other.

8. To see how the animation created by the Walk Designer actually looks in Poser, open the Edit Keyframes, and set the Layer to Walk Ben. This shows a keyframe for everything that is animated (see Figure 3.7). The green rectangles represent keyframes.

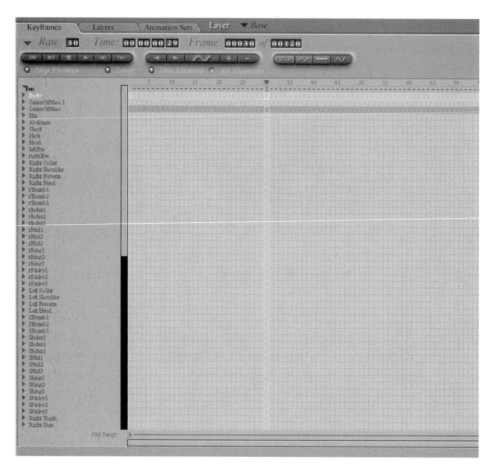

FIGURE 3.7
Walk Designer recorded keyframes for Ben.

So the flood of green rectangles of every body part indicates that the Walk De-signer has recorded a keyframe for every body part on every frame of the anima-tion. You can also view the animation channel hierarchy of each body part by clicking the arrow to the left of the body part (actor) name. For example, look at the animation channels for Right Thigh. You will see recorded keyframes for Twist, Side-Side, and Bend. The Walk Designer has recorded no keyframes for the other animation channels for this actor. You see the animation of Ben because you are currently on the Walk Ben layer. By default, the Walk Designer created the anima-tion on a new layer and named it Walk Ben. If you look in the Layers, you can see several different layers: Base Layer, Walk Ben, Layer_1, and so on. These are really from the different elements of this animation. The real animation is happening in the Walk Ben layer. You can see that it has the full 120 frames. Later on, you'll be getting into how this really is used to edit your animation. But for now, you just need to know where this information is stored.

MAKING CHARACTERS WALK ON A PATH WITH THE WALK DESIGNER

Now you'll create an animation of Simon walking. He'll walk along a path in the first floor of a furnished living room in a loft apartment, without bumping into things. You'll have to give him a realistic path similar to the path a real person would follow at home.

1. First, you'll use the Poser Library to build the room. Go to Library> Props>Poser 7>The Pad. Here you can add as many of these interior elements as you wish. They are designed to work together, so as you add them in, they will magically land in the correct places. To get a better spatial sense of how this all fits, zoom out, and rotate the view.

NOTE

Bear in mind that Poser has to go find the objects and load them in. They are not stored in the application; rather, they are stored on the hard drive and may even be in compressed file formats. So when you double-click an object, you may need to give it some time to be found and loaded in.

2. Make sure to add all of the walls.

TIP

For the front wall, go to Object>Properties and turn off Visible, but leave Visible in Raytracing checked. This way, when it renders it will be visible, but now, while you are working, it will not block your view. When you actually render, the camera will be within this space, so that you are right in there with Simon. If you don't make these allowances, you either have to create the animation without this wall, or not see what you are doing for a while.

NOTE

You can model your own props or import from libraries that you purchase online, from places such as contentparadise.com, cornucopia3d.com, or turbosquid.com. These are all places where you can look for content to import for Poser use. You do not model these props in Poser because that is not the function of Poser.

ON THE DVD

3. You can either continue adding elements on your own or simply open the project Exercise files/chapter 03/02_Walking_With_A_Path-Step-01.pz3, which has complementary elements assembled from this pad loft environment.

4. Now with the pad assembled, you have all the elements needed to make an interesting living space. Simon is in his original position (see Figure 3.8), and he needs to be repositioned to follow a path that will go around the outside of the furniture grouping.

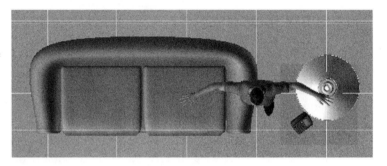

FIGURE 3.8
Simon still in his original position with his right leg inside the couch.

5. If you try to use the Translate/Pull tool, you will encounter some difficulties, no matter which element of Simon you select. So, the most effective way to move him is to open up the Object Properties (make sure you have Simon's Body selected) and, in the Parameters, use the Translate tools. Use the zTran to move him into position, and then rotate him around using the yRotate. For this exercise, set the yRotate to 90 degrees (see Figure 3.9).
6. Now you are ready to create the walk path. Go to the main menu, and choose Figure>Create Walk Path. This creates a curving walk path for the selected Poser figure. Adjust the view so that you can see all the points (knots) on that path to move/edit them.

When selecting points on the path to edit them, make sure the plus sign in the cursor goes away before you move the path point (knot) to be sure you are moving a point, not creating a new one.

TIP

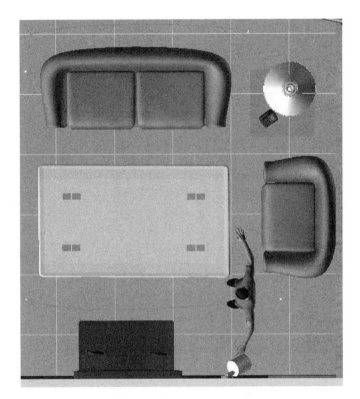

FIGURE 3.9
Simon in his corrected position and orientation.

7. Working in the top view, position the points of the walk path as shown in Figure 3.10. You need to add points to the path to reproduce the path shown in Figure 3.10. Make sure you have some sort of curve at the corners—it shouldn't be too sharp of a turn, otherwise, it will look unnatural when Simon takes those corners. When that is in place, it's time to have Simon walk along the path you've set up.

The continuity points determine the following out of the first point on the path and leading into the last point on the path. This is because the angle of the walk path curve at any point is determined by three points: the point before, the current point, and the next point. Positioning the continuity points gives great control over the behavior of the start and end points of the walk path.

NOTE

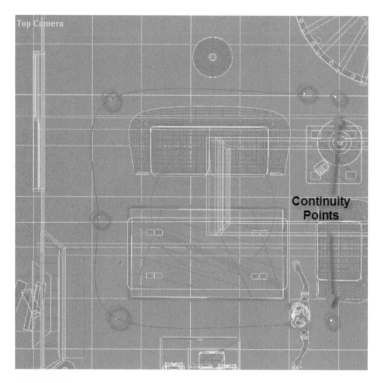

FIGURE 3.10
Simon's walk path.

You can save and compare your progress by loading Exercise files/chapter 03/02_Walking_With_A_Path-Step-03.pz3.

8. Select Simon's Body as the actor, and then launch the Walk Designer. Give Simon a Cool walk, and click Apply. Select Follow Path. Select Align Head to Next Sharp Turn, select Create Key Frames in: New Animation Layer, and click OK.

Align Head To One Step Ahead means that the character will always be facing the next step. End Of Path means the character's head is facing whatever the end of the path is. Next Sharp Turn means the character is always focused on where he is about to turn next.

NOTE

New Animation Layer should be used when you want to edit the walk animation separate from other animation within the current project.

9. You have now created a little more than 200 frames of animation. Variables such as the exact length of the walk path and the position of the walk path points impact how many frames of animation are needed to make the figure walk from the start of the path to the end. The initial number of frames (default) was 30. Click Play to see the result of your choices. Look at the corners to make sure they are not too sharp as he turns them. If the corners are too crisp, go to Edit>Undo Walk>Props>Path_1 in the actor list, and then pull the offensive corner points into a softer curve. The curve is smoothed if you spread the points out further from each other. When you're finished, select Simon's Body as the actor again, go back to the Walk Designer, and click Apply, using the same parameters as before.

NOTE

One reason to work with Fast Motion Tracking rather than Full is that when you work in Full, it may (depending on your video card's capabilities as well as the complexity of your project) skip so many frames in the animation that it may be difficult to find an error such as too sharp of a turn. If you do not see enough frames of the actual playback animation, you will not see where the error occurs. In Fast mode, you can quickly see whether you need to go back and edit the walk path.

ON THE DVD

10. Now, open the project Exercise files/chapter 03/02_Walking_With_A_Path-Step-04.pz3 to see the same scene. Look at it from the top view, with textured shading on. The visibility of the roof is turned off so you can see through it. If you drag through the keyframes, you will notice that the Top Camera is animating. Because you don't want this to happen while you're working, click the Key icon (in the Camera Controls) to turn off the camera animation (see Figure 3.11). This way, when you play the animation, the camera stays in place so that you can better observe the animation.

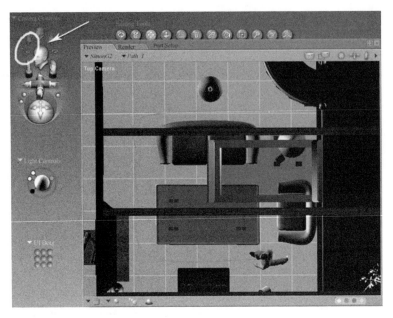

FIGURE 3.11
Locating the Camera Controls.

11. You need to observe your animation from several viewpoints, looking for points where your figure might be going into other objects. Also, take test renders at different points in the animation and from various camera angles.

TIP

Making use of area renders during this fine-tuning process can greatly speed up your workflow by providing rapid feedback because only the relevant area in question will be rendered (see Figure 3.12). For example, take an area render of the point where Simon walks past the entertainment center to ensure that he is not walking through any part of it. Take the time to do these little area test renders as you go along because problems are far easier to catch here, than at the end when you have finished rendering the entire animation (which takes some time to do.)

FIGURE 3.12
Locating the Area Render control.

12. You also need to test render entire frames to check for lighting, transparency, and reflection—the parameters that have a way of changing the way they appear in different parts of the animation. Even though playback at this quality would be a bit jerky on your video card, you do need to drag through the animation manually to make sure everything is okay. Although you cannot tell everything about the scene from this kind of color resolution, you can see things such as intersections. You also need to render preview animations of your projects because when you have cameras tracking moving figures, you should be concerned not only about where the *figure* is going to be, but also about where the *camera* is going to be. In an example like this, you could have the camera accidentally going through walls. If that happens, you will not see your figure or anything else for that matter.

ON THE DVD

13. Play the movie Exercise files/chapter 03/02_Walk_With_Path-1-Camera-Error.mov, which was rendered from a poorly set up scene. As you can see, the camera goes through the wall as it follows Simon around. For this reason, you need to render preview animations because when you look at the top view in wire frame, it's difficult to notice these kinds of mistakes.

ON THE DVD

14. Now play the movie Exercise files/chapter 03/02_Walk_With_Path-1-Camera-Preview.mov. This is the same animation but with the camera motion corrected. Again, this quality is just the preview quality. You can set this to render with all of your shadows, reflections, and gorgeous lighting to see just how wonderful your work really is so far.

To recap, when creating walk animation on a path, you need to add a walk path to the selected figure, edit the path so the figure will walk avoiding obstacles as desired, design the walk with the Walk Designer, apply the walk to the Walk Path, and check and edit your camera positions. This just touches the very basics of what you can do with this type of character animation in Poser Pro. Try adding multiple characters to the loft in this project to have each figure walking independently without overlapping each other. It's amazing what you can do with this!

IMPORTING MOTION CAPTURE DATA TO ANIMATE CHARACTERS

Now you will work with motion capture data to create animation in Poser Pro. *Motion capture* sometimes refers to the process by which the motion of an actor who is moving in the real world, wearing sensors in a studio space, is able to be recorded by cameras, magnetic sensors, or light sensors. The motion of the actor is then stored as 3D animation data. Motion capture can also be created with software that synthesizes human motion with biomechanical response.

This chapter looks at working with one flavor of the file format in the motion capture world known as BVH (Biovision hierarchical data). BVH is derived from the Biovision motion capture technology file format for storing 3D motion capture data. It's one of the original, oldest, and most proliferated motion capture formats. Most applications that can accept motion capture data today can accept Biovision or .BVH files.

You can find many of these .BVH files online free. Even though some motion capture files are included in Poser Pro, you can go online and find motion capture files in many places. One resources is *http://bvhfiles.com.* Another (my favorite) is *http://mocapdata.com,* which breaks down the motion capture files by easy to understand categories. As you go into these categories, it further breaks them down into subcategories. For example, Walk is broken down into Normal, Drunk, Sneak, Fast, and so on. This is from a Japanese university so their spelling is a bit creative, but they have some interesting styles, which can help you get close to what you actually need for the story you are building. The subcategories are then further broken into even more subcategories with a variety of different file formats, such as .FBX (Autodesk MotionBuilder), .C3D (Vidicon), .BVH (Biovision), and .BIP (Character Studio Biped). Again, when working with Poser Pro, you're looking for .BVH files.

Depending upon where you get your .BVH files, you may experience that some files work as you would expect in Poser Pro, whereas others might give you some twisted limbs and such. The good news about *http://mocapdata.com* is that most of its data comes in ready-to-use in Poser Pro, which means you have fewer cleanups to do when you get these files in. With that said, let's start working in Poser Pro and make some character animation from motion capture data.

ON THE DVD

1. Begin by loading the Exercise files/chapter 03/03_Motion_Capture-Step-01.pz3 file. Here Simon is in an empty version of the loft.
2. Before you add the motion capture data to Simon, make sure you have the correct figure selected. A scene can have any number of figures, so you must be sure you are bringing in the motion capture onto the correct one. In this case, select SimonG2 and Body. Import the BVH motion. You only have one motion capture file in Chapter 3, which is Exercise files/chapter

ON THE DVD

03/fighting-provocation-takiguchi.bvh. Accept all the defaults.

NOTE

At times, you may get a requester that says "No figure element to match BVH node Chest2." This happens because in figuring BVH or Biovision for motion capture, you can have more than one chest node (see Figure 3.13). This will be discarded by Poser Pro because the skeleton in Poser Pro really doesn't have anything to do with this. This requester is not a problem, only a notification.

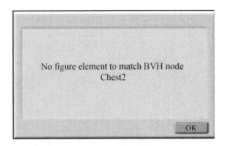

FIGURE 3.13
Missing element notification.

3. At this time, the motion capture is building keyframes for the skeleton that controls Simon, so that he will then move like the motion capture. It may take a minute or two for the motion capture data to load in, as it must make a keyframe for every frame of the animation. Depending upon the number of seconds in the motion capture data, this could take a while. If you open up the Transport, you will see there are 751 frames from this motion capture.

4. You can see that Simon is floating in the air (see Figure 3.14). You need to bring him back down to the ground to make it believable (for this project). But before you try to bring him down, let's take a look at the keyframes to understand what will happen when he comes down and how to best bring him down.

5. Open Edit Keyframes. Motion capture comes in on the Base Layer, and you're looking at the Base Layer by default. The main thing you want to look at here is the Body. As you see, the Body has only one keyframe. That's great news! Because there's only one keyframe, you can go ahead and bring him down. Close the Animation Editor. Select Simon's Body, and using the Parameter Controls, use the yTran to bring him down to the floor.

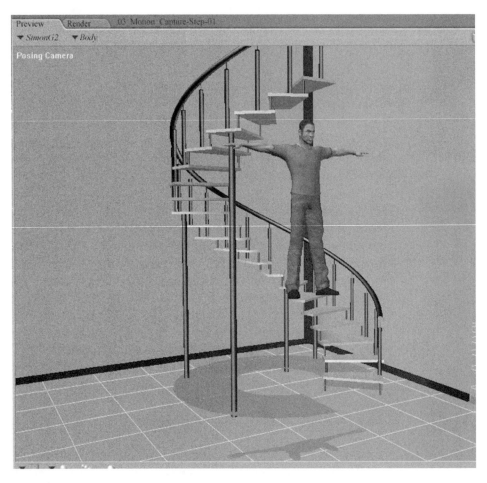

FIGURE 3.14
Simon floating in the air after motion capture data is imported.

6. After he is placed on the floor (see Figure 3.15), drag through the animation to see how it looks. Keep an eye on his feet to make sure they do not go through the floor, or float above it, at any point during the animation. If you find that the feet go through the floor, you can edit his body to bring it upward, but you might start creating erratic behaviors in the motion. A better solution is to take him back off the ground just a little, using the yTran, and then use a Python script.

FIGURE 3.15
Simon on the floor after the Body yTran has been adjusted.

7. From the main menu, choose Scripts>Utility>DropFigToFloorAllFrames. It will take a while to calculate because the Python script will go through all of the 751 frames to figure out where it needs to drop the figure to ensure that the figure will always be on the floor. It's a far more intuitive way to handle the problem than to go frame-by-frame manually adjusting the yTran parameter.

Python scripting is a popular script language used by many 3D applications to allow the user to add functionality to the main application and to perform repetitive tasks.

ON THE DVD

8. Now load the Exercise files/chapter 03/03_Motion_Capture-Step-01.pz3 file. As you may remember, when you first imported the .BVH motion capture file, you had 751 frames, and now you have 651 frames because 100 frames were trimmed from the animation. You have to deal with this when using motion capture animation files because of something called the T-pose. As you saw at the start of the imported motion capture data playback, Simon stands straight up with arms out to the side like a "T." It's a calibration stance where you start the motion capture data. As useful as that is when recording the motion capture data, when you're telling a story, you can't have all your actors starting in the T-Pose, so, you have to edit that out.

ON THE DVD

9. Load the Exercise files/chapter 03/03_Motion_Capture-Step-01.pz3 file that has the original 751 frames. You can see that the first 100 frames are actually used to get him into position. Open the Edit Keyframes, where you'll get rid of the first 100 keyframes. Be careful not to select the Body, as there is only one keyframe there for the entire animation.

10. Drag from the Center Of Mass, down and across, and make sure you go to 100 frames. When you have everything selected (except for the Body) within those 100 keyframes, delete the selected keyframes. The dark green areas now show where keyframes were deleted (see Figure 3.16).

11. Go to the end of the animation, and select all keyframes, starting from the lowest keyframes (Right Foot frame 751), going up and over to the left (Center Of Mass frame 101). Again, make sure you do not include the Body channel.

During the preceding selection process, it is very important not to release the mouse button until the selection of all needed frames is made.

NOTE

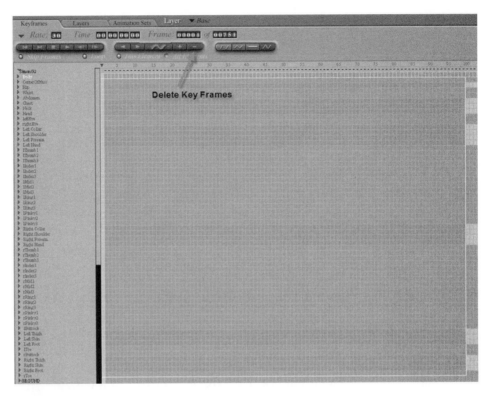

FIGURE 3.16
The first 100 keyframes have been deleted.

12. Release the mouse, and carefully drag those keyframes to the beginning of the animation, staying in the correct channel. Poser will need a few minutes to think about this before the action is completed. Now you have moved the useful animation back 100 frames. This does not yet make the animation become 651 frames long, however, it simply moves the animation back 100 frames. As you scroll through the keyframes, you will now see that nothing appears after 651 frames, which means that the animation would simply go on hold after frame 651. To solve this, close the Animation Editor, and manually enter 651 as the end frame (see Figure 3.17). You'll see a warning that this is an undoable action, but it's exactly what you want, so click OK. The end result is that the motion capture is now applied to the Poser figure. Play it back to see the finished result.

FIGURE 3.17
The end frame is now set to 651 to trim the animation
playback length by 100 frames.

That's the basics of how you bring motion capture data into Poser Pro and apply it to a figure, as well as a bit of the editing that you need to be aware of. You should go to *http://mocapdata.com* and download the free motion capture files. Bring them into Poser, and familiarize yourself with how the motions look and how they work on the figures, so that you can plan productions and short films. Knowing what's available to you at this great free resource can help you shorten the character animation production process.

Using the Animation Editor and Curve Palettes to Edit Animation

When working with animation data in Poser Pro, it's sometimes necessary and very helpful to know how to edit the animation after you've created it. Editing the animation refers to working on (or editing) the entire body of keyframes, rather than just working on one figure's actor (body part) on one frame. Instead, you would be working on the entire character's motion or working on the limbs of the character for an entire animation.

Next, you'll learn how this is done by applying animation-editing techniques to a Walk Designer animation that you build based on making the figure walk around an imported prop.

ON THE DVD

1. First, you'll need to create a new project. From the main menu, choose File>Import>3D Studio, set the Import Options as shown in Figure 3.18, and click OK. Then import the prop Exercise files/chapter 03/rings.3ds. You now have the imported prop of two large rings around the figure (see Figure 3.19).

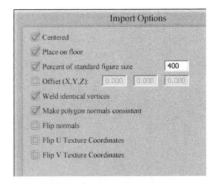

FIGURE 3.18
Import Options for the rings .3DS prop.

FIGURE 3.19
Large imported rings prop on the floor around Simon.

2. With the imported rings prop selected, you'll create a material for the rings. Go to the Material room, and open the library. Choose Materials>Procedurals>Metal, scroll down to select Knurled Metal (see Figure 3.20), and click Apply. This builds the material for the imported rings prop shown in Figure 3.21.

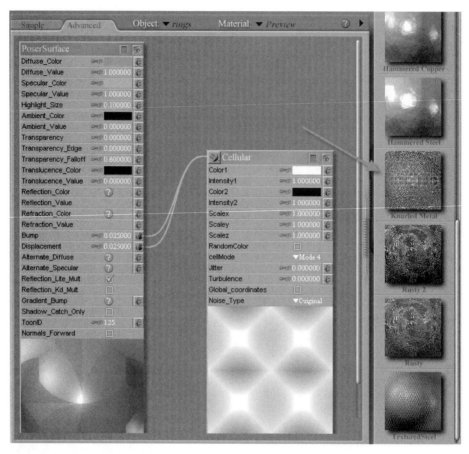

FIGURE 3.20
Knurled Metal material for the rings prop.

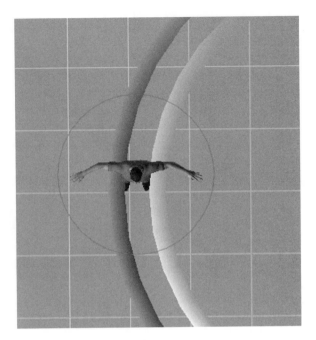

FIGURE 3.21
Simon positioned to the left, centered between the two
rings of the rings prop.

3. Back in the Pose room, set up Simon to walk around this prop. You'll work
   in the top view. Move him to the left side of the screen so he is positioned
   in the center of the two rings (refer to Figure 3.21).

4. Now you will create the path that he will use to walk on the rings. Create a
   walk path from the Figure menu. Position the walk path points as shown in
   Figure 3.22.

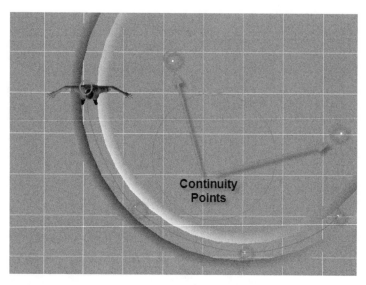

FIGURE 3.22
All points of the walk path are circled. Note the position of the
continuity points.

As you move the mouse across anything on the screen, it will try to highlight objects in the scene. Poser is helpful in that way, but sometimes it can be too helpful. Make sure you are actually working on your curve and not simply highlighting something you're passing over. Secondly, when you are working on the curve, the cursor will change depending upon whether you are directly over a point or not. You'll want to be directly over the points in this exercise. When you see a small plus sign on the bottom right of the curser icon, you are NOT over the point but rather, if you click down, you will now create a new point. Move the cursor over the point until the plus sign disappears. Now you are over the point. Simply hold down and move the point.

5. Now you're ready to make Simon walk. With the Body selected, go to the Walk Designer. For now, just apply the default walk. In the Apply Walk window, select Follow Path, and leave all defaults, except for the keyframes. Here, select the Create Keyframes in Base Layer. The reason for this is that in this current version of Poser Pro, if you create keyframes in the new animation layer, you will have difficulties editing the entire range of frames, whereas in the Base Layer, you can do that easily. This may change in future versions of Poser, so keep track of Poser Pro updates from *http://www.e-frontier.com*. Now, play back in Fast Tracking mode to see the figure walk along the path created. That's nice, but this is not the end of the process. You now have to edit it.

6. Change over to the Main Camera view. Currently, the figure is walking down inside the rings; however, you really want the figure to walk on top of the rings, with the feet spread apart. If you try to move the figure up on frame 1, it would move up on frame 1 but then immediately move back down. So, you need a better editing solution.

7. Go to Edit Keyframes. Here you can see that the Body has all these keyframes. If you twirl down, you can see all of the channels that have keyframes for the Body. There are keyframes for the x-, y-, and z-rotation and the x-, y-, and z-translation. Because you need to be able to move the body up, you need to use the yTrans. Although you can see that you have keyframes in the Keyframes Editor, you can't change their parameters there. If you open Object>Properties>Parameters, you can adjust the yTran there, but that will only affect the current key.

Using dual monitors is very helpful when working on Poser, so that you can keep the editor windows over on the second monitor, which makes for a more practical workflow.

NOTE

8. Instead, with the Body/yTran selected in the Animation Editor, go to the Graph Editor (see Figure 3.23).

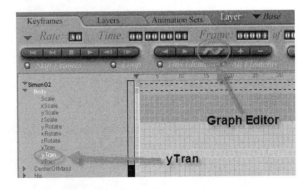

FIGURE 3.23
Simon's Body/yTran selected and the Graph Editor icon indicated.

9. You have all the keyframes of the yTrans of the body. Each black line represents a keyframe, so if you were to drag one of these lines up, you would literally drag the figure up or down on that selected frame of the animation. You now need to move all the keyframes up. You're currently only seeing a subset of the keyframes in the Graph Editor, depending upon the size of your editor window. Drag the slider at the bottom of the Graph Editor to

the right to see more frames, or resize the scroll bar to see a larger, or smaller, number of keyframes in the window. For this example, resize the scroll bar to see the entire animation. By putting the cursor either above or below the line, you can click and drag to select the keyframes. Holding the Shift key down, you can drag the selection in the other direction, to select them all. With the Ctrl key held down, notice how the icon changes from horizontal arrows to vertical arrows. This allows you to change the parameters of all those selected keyframes. Drag the keyframes up to adjust the Body yTran values of all selected keyframes. For a better view of the figure's location, select the front view camera, and position it so that you can see both the front view and the Graph Editor.

10. When you see that the figure is well placed (as shown in Figure 3.24), go back to the main view. Scroll through the animation. As you can see, he is now on top of the rings, but he is walking on air in some areas (see Figure 3.25) because his feet are not spread apart appropriately.

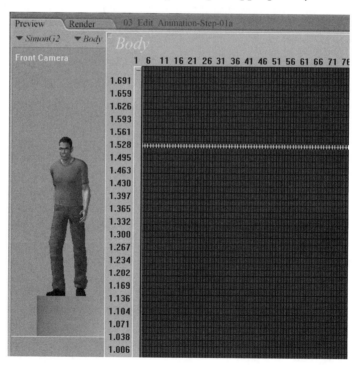

FIGURE 3.24
Simon's Body yTrans edited in the Graph Editor to raise him up to walk on the rings.

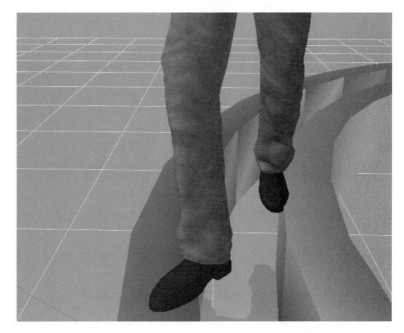

FIGURE 3.25
The Main Camera shows that because Simon's feet are not yet spread
apart, he unnaturally walks on air, for now.

11. Select the Auxiliary Camera to take a closer look at the feet. Select the Right
    Foot from the Body Parts list to see the keyframes for the right foot in the
    Graph Editor. Next, select the xTrans in the Graph Editor. All of the
    keyframes are still selected, so simply move all the keyframes down to move
    the right foot more to the right so that it is on the outer ring. When the foot
    is well positioned on top of the outer ring, select the Left Foot from the
    Body Parts list to view the left foot keyframes in the Graph Editor. With the
    xTran selected, and with the Ctrl key pressed, move those selected
    keyframes up to move the left foot more to the left so it is placed on the
    inner ring (see Figure 3.26).

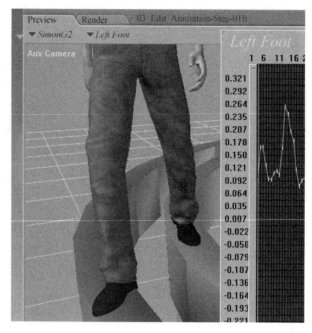

FIGURE 3.26
The left and right feet are now edited into place using the
Graph Editor.

*When switching between the preview and editor windows, make sure to click some-
where on the editor window to select it. If not properly selected, you may not get the
correct cursor change with the Ctrl key held down to move the keyframes vertically.*

12. With the left foot properly aligned on top of the inner ring, switch to the
Main Camera, and scroll through the animation. If he is sinking into either
of the rings anywhere along the way, go back to the Graph Editor, and select the entire Body in the yTran. Hold the Ctrl key down, and drag all the
keyframes upward until he looks well positioned. Here it's a good idea to
do an area render to see exactly how the feet are landing on the prop.

13. Lastly, you need to look at the adjustment of Simon's head. You'll introduce a slight head turn, to look at the camera, around frame 50, followed
by turning his head away from the camera by frame 100. To do this, open
up the Graph Editor again, and select the Head from the Body Parts list.

Many channels are available to work with, and one of the easiest ways to access them is to choose Object>Properties>Parameters, and then choose the property you want to work on. As you choose it in the Parameters window, it's displayed for you in the editor. So, if you are unsure which parameter to work with, you can select it with Object>Properties>Parameters and interact with it to see what effect each parameter has.

14. Now, go to frame 50, and as you adjust the Twist, you can see that it is the parameter to use in this case. Look at the Graph Editor now to see that you have just made an adjustment causing a keyframe to be out of step with the others. Simply drag that single keyframe back up to align with the rest of the graph. You can also see that there is a keyframe on every frame. If you are going to edit the head turning, that could be a bit of a pain. So, with the Head selected, go to the main menu and choose Animation>Resample Key Frames. Select to modify Current Element and select to Make Key Frame Every 10 Frames (instead of 4) because not much is happening with the head in the original animation. Now you can see that the animation in the Graph Editor has been greatly simplified, which makes it much easier to work on.

If you select another actor, the Right Forearm, for example, instead of the Head, and look at the Twist parameter, you can see a keyframe on every frame again. But if you select the Head, you only have a keyframe on every tenth frame. That's the value of the Animation/Resample Key Frames.

15. With that done, you'll now work on frames 50 to 100. Adjust your Graphic Editor window to see frames 50 to 100. On frame 50, his head should be in its original state. (As you move the mouse over the green line in the Graph Editor, the cursor changes to a horizontal, wide, double-headed arrow. You can now drag the green line to scrub through your animation.) Likewise, at frame 100, you want the head to be returned to its original direction. This means you have four keyframes in the middle, and you'll now get rid of three of them.

16. After frame 50, select and delete the first, third, and fourth keyframes. Holding the Ctrl key down over the remaining keyframe, slide it over to frame 79, and drag it downward until the head is turned appropriately.

17. Now, as you scrub through the animation, you will see that as he walks, he turns to look at you, and then turns back to watch where he's going. Imagine if you didn't resample the keyframes—you would have to edit each one of those frames! That would be a royal pain. So simplifying keyframes is sometimes a very practical way of dealing with animation editing needs.

This technique is also often used when working with imported motion-capture animation data because it too places a keyframe on every frame of the animation timeline. Figure 3.27 shows the completed Graph Editor curve for Simon's Head's Twist channel, and Figure 3.28 shows Simon mid-animation while he's looking at the camera.

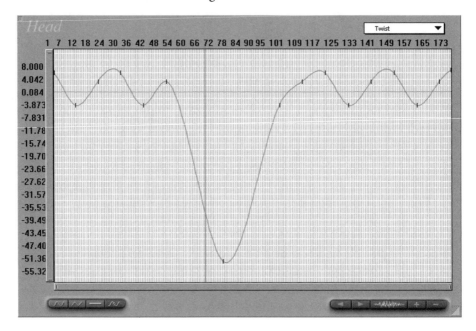

FIGURE 3.27
The final corrected Twist channel Graph Editor curve for Simon to turn his head to the camera at frame 50 and turn away by frame 100.

FIGURE 3.28
As a result of editing the Twist channel for Simon's Head in the Graph Editor, he looks at the camera mid-animation.

You've just learned the basics of editing your animation data. Also note that if you go to the keyframes again and look at the Head, you'll see a keyframe every tenth frame here as well—even that has been updated. And, if you twirl down and look at the Twist, you can see the edit you just did from frame 50 to frame 100. If, while going through the animation, you decide that the keyframe for the Head turn should come earlier, you can simply drag it to the frame where you want to see the turn. Just remember that it's affecting a curve, so be careful not to overshoot, or his head will turn in an exaggerated way. As you can see, Poser Pro gives you real control over keyframes and curves for editing animation.

SUMMARY

You now have the foundation to create character animation in Poser Pro based on the use of the Walk Designer and motion capture data. You should explorer the Animation Editor and Graph Editor further on your own now that you know how they are used. Any such additional preparation will serve you well as you progress to the next chapters in this book.

4 Walking and Running

In This Chapter

- Introduction
- Animating a Basic Walk Cycle
- Tweaking the Walk Cycle
- Variations of a Walk Cycle
- Animating a Happy Walk
- Animating a Run
- Transforming Walks and Runs

INTRODUCTION

In this chapter, you'll learn to animate a Poser figure manually rather than by using the Walk Designer. You'll build animation based on animation principles, and look at how this is advantageous compared to using the Walk Designer.

One of the benefits of animating this way is that you have much greater control over the actions of the animated character. For example, when animating manually, you can more easily transition to other animations for the selected character. If you have animation from the Walk Designer and you want to make the figure sit, stand, or slow down, creating such compound animation is definitely more of a challenge than if you had animated manually. Another benefit of animating manually is that you can add irregularity to your animation. This can break up the mechanically predictable patterns seen in animation generated by Walk Designer.

The repetitive nature of walk cycles is that they tend to be regular to the point of being mechanical. We are familiar with seeing people walk, and people don't walk in mechanical, predictable, cyclical ways. Along with a certain rhythm and cycle to their walk, there are nuances and irregularities that make their walk appear natural.

When creating animation manually, because of the reduced number of well-placed keyframes, you have the input to be able to add those irregularities and nuances as needed. Irregularity also comes by being able to break the routine of the walk cycle by adding changes such as making the figure's head turn or arm wave.

Imagine you have a figure animated in the walk cycle from the Walk Designer, and you want to have the head turn as you saw in a previous chapter. Because the Walk Designer places a keyframe for each of the figure's actors on every frame of the animation, the head turn requires a lot of work. So doing things like head turns, having the figure step over something in its path, or waving a hand are all more easily done if you animate manually.

Additionally, you might be tweaking the animation to a director's instructions— let's say he's over your shoulder telling you to add a limp or give some personality to the walk and describing it based upon human behavior. Although you do have some nice Tweak controls in the Walk Designer, when you have manual control over well-placed keyframes in the animation process, you have more intimate control over the slight variances to achieve those behavioral expressions in animation.

ANIMATING A BASIC WALK CYCLE

In more than 20 years working in 3D animation, I've had the opportunity to speak to many 3D animators. You might be surprised to find out that most of the 3D animators I have met know how to create amazing CG imagery, but don't know how to animate characters. Most had not tried. Of those who tried, most had sad results.

Character animation is an area of CG that requires the understanding of some principles and techniques, if you want to avoid a lot of frustration.

To animate the basic walk cycle in this tutorial, you'll use the pose-to-pose animation principle.

In the next few tutorials, you'll learn to animate walk and run cycles. A *walk cycle* is the motion of walking without traveling, much like walking on a treadmill. This allows the animator to really study every aspect of the character's walk without having the view obscured by scene objects or changing camera views.

In pose-to-pose, you create key poses and then edit the poses in between. Rather than try to explain this further, let's animate!

Let's get started by animating the SimonG2 walk cycle:

ON THE DVD

1. On the accompanying DVD-ROM, open the Exercise files/chapter 04/ Walk_Cycle_1.pz3. Here you have Simon in his T-pose with a few accessories. To animate his walk cycle, start by creating the extreme poses (see Figure 4.1).

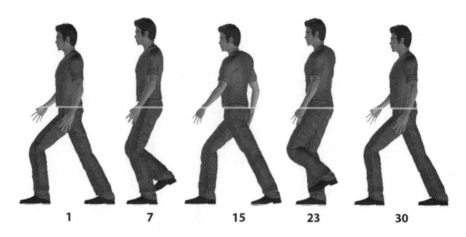

FIGURE 4.1
A Right Camera view of the keyframes (1, 7, 15, 23 and 30) of the walk cycle.

2. Make sure that his right and left hand have IK (inverse kinematics) turned on in the Figure menu and that you lock the hand parts (so that his fingers are not flying about), and then bring his arms down.
3. In the Main Camera mode, you can get a good spatial sense of where the hand is in relation to the rest of the body. Now, bring the right arm down. As you can see, although the arm is coming down, the hand stays in its original orientation. Use the Parameter controls to bend the hand into place. You can orbit around to check for any weirdness in the positioning. Use the Side-Side control to align the hand further into its proper place.
4. Use symmetry to reflect this over to the other arm. From the Figure menu, select Symmetry>Right arm to left arm. Select Yes to copy the joint zone's setup also.

TIP

Because this is a default Poser figure, the left and right joints are already set up to be symmetrical, so you don't need to go into any other options here.

5. After both arms are in their downward position (as shown in Figure 4.2), switch to the Right Camera view. Now you'll want to turn off the IK on both the left and right hand, as you will adjust the hips next (see Figure 4.3). If you forget to turn off the IK, when you adjust the hips, the arms will not move correctly with the chest. Move the hips forward and downward until the figure bends at the knees.

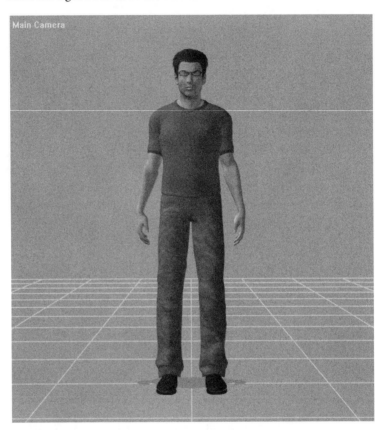

FIGURE 4.2
Both arms are down.

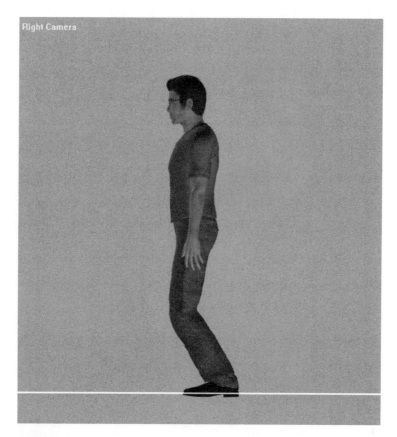

FIGURE 4.3
Right Camera view shows hips brought down to bend the knees.

6. Bring the left foot forward, and balance the body between the two legs, making sure there is a small bend on the right knee.

7. Turn on the IK for the left hand. It's easy to move the wrong hand here accidentally, as they are both in the same space. To make it easier, switch to the Main Camera, and orient the view so that you can tell the difference between the two arms. Then pull the left arm backward and down. Orbit around to see if it's in a good position. Switch back to the Right Camera view, and tweak the Side-Side parameter until the hand position looks natural (see Figure 4.4).

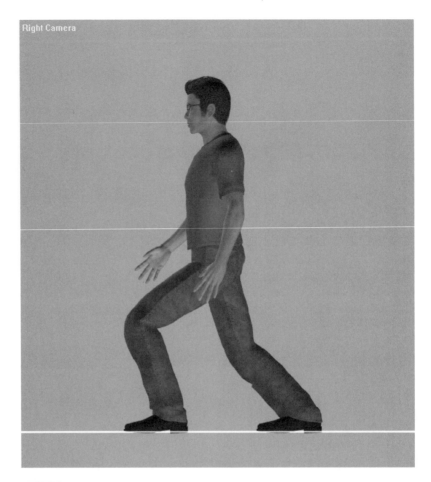

FIGURE 4.4
Right Camera view shows arms and feet posed.

8. Now that the arms and legs are in place, you'll make some fine-tune rotation adjustments to the waist and chest, which may not be obvious from the mechanical animation of the character but are important when you look at the real-world motion of people. Select the hip, and switch to the Main Camera. Because the left leg is coming forward and down, you'll want the waist to twist or rotate forward and down toward that leg. With the hip selected, use the yRotate (-13). You can see the whole body rotate in an awkward way. Don't worry, you're not done. But for now, you're simply focusing on making sure the hip is turning the way you want. Next, rotate it using the zRotate (-6). The figure is walking in the z-axis, so rotate

along that axis to have the hip turn down. Again, for now, this looks rather weird—he looks like he's not feeling well and is about to fall down—and it's supposed to. That's simply a step in the process of making him walk.

When you animate characters, get into the habit of going through the physical motions yourself. Get up and act, walk about, and go through the motions. So even though you're watching the video tutorial or reading this book, get up and take a few steps while paying close attention to your own body's biomechanics. That means paying attention to how your joints bend and twist. You might even want to walk slowly to see how the knees, hips, wrists, elbows, and shoulders come into play, so that when you animate, you can obviously recognize that some things should not happen, and some things should. Additionally, you may want to go online and search for "motion references" or "stock video footage" to see people in motion. Or, just grab your camcorder and get your friends and family to model the motions for you, so you can have various perspective views of the motions for your library. In other words, you really need to study "people in motion." You need to become a true student of human motion itself and not simply rely on looking at a 3D animation application and the positioning of a virtual figure. People know how people move, so you really need to be a student of people moving.

9. Select the Chest, as you now have to counter those rotations. Use the Twist parameter (15) and the Side-Side (8) parameter to straighten him back up. You also need to pull the left knee outward. The end result, although it looked pretty wacky at one stage, now looks more like a person about to take a step as shown in Figure 4.5.

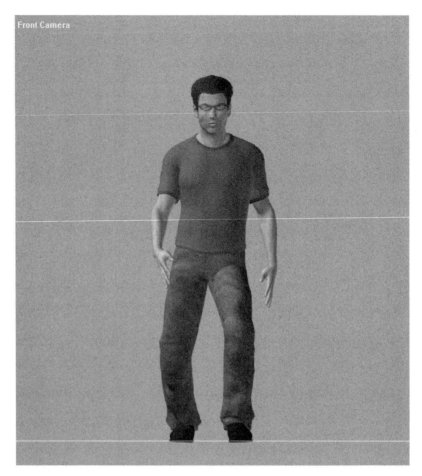

FIGURE 4.5
Front view of the first pose for the walk cycle.

10. With this done, it is now time to set some keyframes. You will animate from this starting pose, into a pose symmetrically swapping the left and right sides of the body, and back to this pose in a 30-frame animation.

11. Go to the end frame (frame 30), and then set a keyframe for those actors (body parts) that will be animated. Select the Right Foot, and add a key for it. (If you still have the IK on for the hands, make sure to turn them off at this point.) Select each hand, and add keys for them as well. Clicking the Play button on the Animation Controls will show no animation yet because the only two frames in the animation with keys (1 and 30) have the same pose.

12. Go to the midpoint (frame 15) of these keyframes. You will now swap the right and left side of the body, which is easy to do in Poser Pro. Make sure you have SimonG2 selected. From the Figure menu, select Symmetry>Swap Right and Left. You now have the figure left and right reversed, with the right leg and left arm in front. When you did this, a keyframe was automatically created because Poser works in an auto key mode, which means when you move objects, figures, or actors, Poser creates keyframes. When you play it now, Simon moves, but the animation looks like one of those old robot toys. So it's not soup yet.

13. To make this into a more believable walk cycle, switch back to the Right Camera view, and pose the legs at the point of crossover (frame 7). Here you'll change the pose where the right leg should be up in the air a little. You can easily see the right foot at frame 1, so select the right foot on frame 1. Go to frame 7 where you will raise the right foot up. Use the yTrans parameter to lift up the right leg (see Figure 4.6).

FIGURE 4.6
Right Leg lifted.

Rather than dragging the right foot with the Move tool, use the yTran in the Parameter controls to guard against accidentally selecting the left foot.

14. When you scroll through the animation, you will notice that the right foot sinks through the floor at around frame 16, which is obviously not desirable. To fix this, use the Edit Keyframes, and select the Right Foot (if it's not already selected).

If you happen to have a dual monitor, you may want to keep the Edit Keyframes window open, over to the side, while you animate.

15. As you slide through the keyframes in the Keyframes Editor, you can see the midpoint (frame 7) where the right foot is in the air, but there are no other keyframes after that indicating that the foot goes through the floor. The keyframes are not making the foot go through the floor, but rather it's the interpolation method. Before you correct it, let's look at exactly what is happening here. Expand the Right Foot channels, and make sure the yTran channel is selected as shown in Figure 4.7.

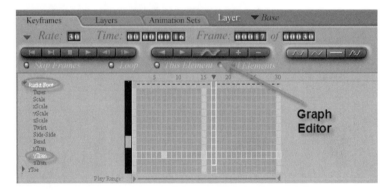

FIGURE 4.7
Right Foot channels in the Keyframes Editor.

16. Open the Graph Editor and see what's happening here by dragging the animation ahead, passing through the keys. Essentially, the animation is now negotiating the curve smoothly so that there are no abrupt changes to the angle of the curve. This is the default behavior of curves. The way a curve behaves when transitioning between points is called its *interpolation*. In Poser, the smooth default interpolation is called *Spline*. The type of interpolation needed to control the foot so that it no longer goes through the floor is *Linear*. Linear interpolation creates straight-line motion between points on a curve. To do this, select the midpoint keyframe on the yTran

channel. You will now set the interpolation of this keyframe to Linear. This is a quick and easy step: just click the Linear Section button (see Figure 4.8), which turns the linear keyframes brown.

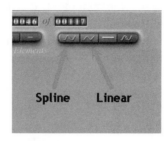

FIGURE 4.8
This is where you set the interpolation of the selected keyframe.

17. When you look at the Graph Editor, you can verify that it is now a straight line from frame 15 to 30 (see Figure 4.9). The end result in the actual animation behavior is that when the foot goes down, it does not go through the ground anymore. You are now set to continue the animation.

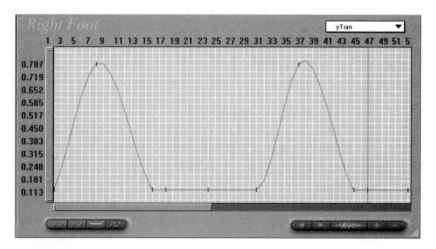

FIGURE 4.9
In the Graph Editor, you now see that frames 15–30 form a straight line. This is due to the linear interpolation previously set.

18. You now need to fix the left leg at its crossover point, just as you did for the right leg. Find the crossover frame (which in the tutorial occurs on frame 23). You could just drag the left leg up using the yTran, but it's actually helpful to take the value that the right foot had at its crossover point. To do this, go back to frame 7 (or the frame where the right foot was "up"), and select the Right Foot. Although you do want to have some randomness, it's also good to have some stable baseline values because that will prevent the figure from looking erratic or as if he has a limp (when you didn't intend for him to have one). The right foot has a yTran value of 0.788. Copy the value from the yTran, go to frame 23 (the crossover for the left foot), select the Left Foot, and then paste the value into the yTran. Again, due to Poser's auto keyframe function, a keyframe is automatically created on the current animation frame.

19. You will find the left foot has the same problem going through the floor here. As before, the solution again is to set linear interpolation for the relevant keyframe. Open the Keyframes Editor, select the first frame for the left foot, and set it to Linear. As you scroll through the frames, you should now see that Simon is no longer going through the floor at any point in time. It's not a perfect walk yet, but it's getting closer.

20. You now need to go to those crossover points again, starting with keyframe 7. Here, the figure needs to be raised up by the hip (refer to Figure 4.1). After you've raised him up at that crossover point, copy the value from the yTran, go to frame 23 (the second crossover point), and paste the value into that yTran to make the walk cycle even. Play the animation back to see the result. It's looking a bit better. It is important that the body rise up, at the point when the legs come together. Looking at the rotation of the limbs of the legs, you can see that in order for them to not be too bent, he has to move upward like a lever action.

21. Now you need to make his feet behave more realistically. One of the issues is that they do not appear to take decisive steps, and the toes are not bending. Let's deal with the first issue of decisive steps first. In the beginning of the animation, when his weight is on the left foot, you'll want to make him hold that position for at least another two frames, so that he will have gripped the floor. To do this, open the Keyframes Editor, select the Left Foot, and click on that first frame. You can copy and paste, or hold the Alt key (Option key on a Mac), and drag it out to frame 3. Then click the Play button to see the result (see Figure 4.10.) This adds a small amount of hold before he pulls away. Now, do the same thing for the right foot. On frame 15, the right foot goes down, so in the Keyframes Editor, select the Right Foot. First make it linear (so it doesn't create some strange action when you try to keep it in position on the floor), then copy frame 15, and paste into frame 17.

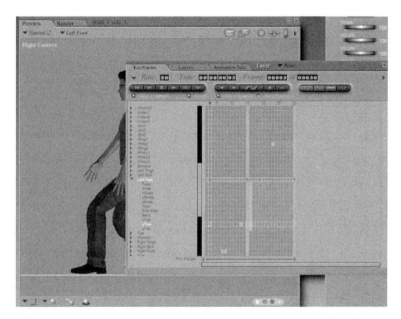

FIGURE 4.10
Pasting the keyframes to create a short "hold" time.

22. Next, you'll work on getting the toes to bend. Start by selecting the Right Foot. The toes need to bend as the foot begins to rise. So, on frame 3, use the Bend parameter to bend the foot downward, until the toes are below the floor. Next, you need to get to the toes. Rather than going through the whole drop-down list to find the toes, you can simply click on an empty spot on the Parameters palette to release the Bend parameter, and providing that the leg's IK chains are turned off use the keyboard down arrow to navigate to the next body part lower down in the hierarchy. For the left foot this will be the left toe.

23. Use the Bend parameter to bend the toes until they are once more on the floor. When you move forward on the animation timeline, as the foot leaves the floor, you'll notice that his toes stay bent. After his foot has cleared the floor, (around frame 8), straighten the toes back out using the Bend parameter.

24. When you scroll through the animation, you'll find that the toes are now "flopping" like molten plastic. This problem is, again, solved with the Linear interpolation of keyframes (see Figure 4.11).

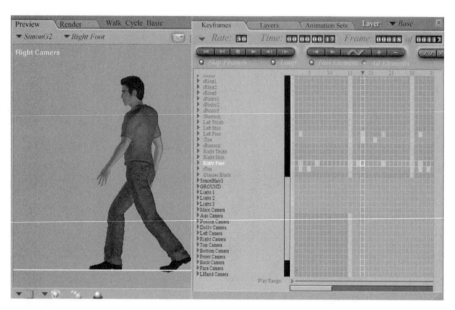

FIGURE 4.11
Setting the Linear interpolation.

25. You also have another issue. The angle of the foot needs to rotate back up. So, at the crossover point, select the Right Foot again, and adjust the Bend to rotate the foot back up as shown previously in Figure 4.1. Next, to take care of the toes, open the Keyframes Editor, select the first three keyframes for the Right Toes, and set them to Linear interpolation. Now, as you play back, you'll see the toes are no longer flopping like molten plastic as the foot is lifted. See the result in Figure 4.12.

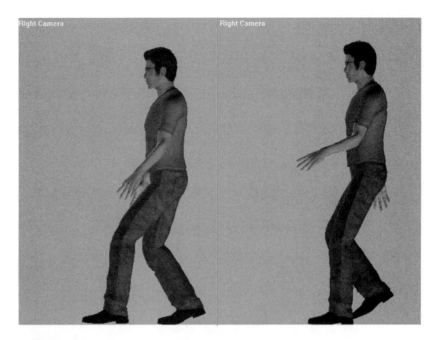

FIGURE 4.12
Foot and toes adjusted for a fluid movement.

26. Now it's time to do the same thing for the left foot. Starting at frame 15, let it go for two to three frames until you're at the point where you can see it should be bent. Select the Left Foot, and bend it down until the toes go through the floor. Select the Left Toes, and bend them up. Scroll forward a few more frames until the foot clears the floor, at which point you remove the toe bend.

27. Scroll to the crossover point, and adjust the bend of the Left Foot, as well as the interpolation of those toes. In the Keyframes Editor, select those frames, and make them Linear.

28. At playback, you may notice that the toes on the left foot go through the floor when the foot is flat on the floor. What's happening here is that even though the keyframes are added later in the animation, you need to make the beginning of the animation linear (which again is similar to what you saw earlier in this process). Open the Keyframes Editor, click that first frame for the Left Toes, and make it Linear. Now, toes are no longer going through the floor. Switch to the Main Camera view to get a better perspective and playback. You now have your basic walk cycle and can make creative choices on the personality of the walk.

29. Switch back to the Right Camera view. You can look at, for example, how low does he really come when he's at the extreme poses (frames 1, 15, and 30)? You can easily adjust that by lifting him up a bit by the hip. You'll want to make the exact height and position of the figure consistent. Therefore, the height should be consistent on frames 1, 15, and 30. The easy solution to that is to do it in the Keyframes Editor. If you adjust the hip's yTran and/or zTran parameter values, in the Keyframes Editor, with the hip selected, copy and paste frame 1 into frames 15 and 30, so that the walk cycle will not become erratic (see Figure 4.13).

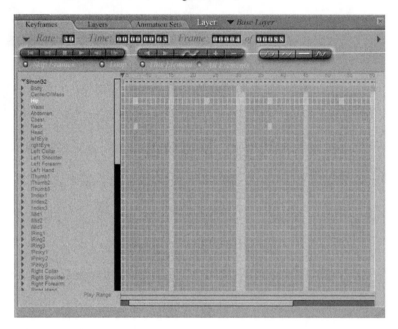

FIGURE 4.13
Keeping the hip position consistent in the Keyframes Editor.

30. If something weird happens mid-animation, that's probably because the rotation now does not match what you just did, when you raised the figure up. Switch to the Main Camera view, and orbit around to see where the adjustment is needed. Then, in the parameters, adjust the zRotate to straighten him back up. In this view, you can also see that the head of the character is turning unnaturally in response to the animation, as he's walking.

31. Switch to the top view, and zoom in to get a look at the orientation of the head. The easiest way to deal with that is to put tracking into Box mode (see Figure 4.14). The head faces forward at frame 1. At frame 15, it's

turned, and on frame 30, it's facing forward again, so your work is on frame 15. You need to adjust the neck. Select the Neck, and Twist it, so that it faces forward on frame 15. And, at the crossover (around frame 7), remove the head turn as well using the Twist tool. Do the same thing for frame 23 (the second crossover). Go back to the Main Camera, and set tracking to Full. Now the head stays facing forward as he walks, which is what you reasonably expect.

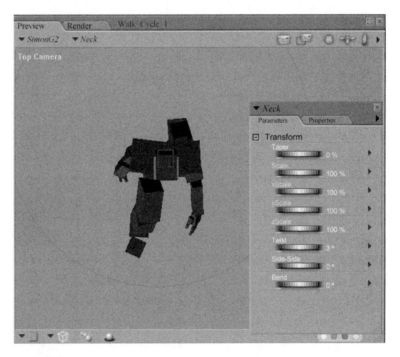

FIGURE 4.14
Top view of adjusting the neck in Box mode.

TWEAKING THE WALK CYCLE

ON THE DVD Now you'll see an example of how creating your own walk cycle gives you more creative control over the animation of the character's movement. We'll look at how to duplicate walk cycles and how to retime the animation. You will work with the Exercise files/chapter 04/Walk_Cycle_4.pz3.

1. Set the number of frames to 88. You'll want to make this have 3 walk cycles. So if you play the animation right now, it just goes through the first cycle and stops because there's no animation after frame 30. If you look at your

edit keyframes, you can, of course, see that you simply added empty frames. To fill those frames with actual animation, you go back to that Alt-drag method that you used earlier.

2. In the Keyframes Editor, select from frame 2 (it's important to not select from frame 1 because frame 1 is a duplicate of frame 30), and make a rectangle selection of all the keyframes, from frame 2 to 30 on all the actors (from Center Of Mass to Glasses Black). With that in place, go back to the top-left corner of the selected frames, hold the Alt key (Option key on Mac) down, and drag over to the empty frame 31 (see Figure 4.15). You've just duplicated a walk cycle. Go ahead and Alt drag the walk cycle to the empty frame 60 to create a third cycle. Easy! Play back in Fast mode to get a feel for what you have so far.

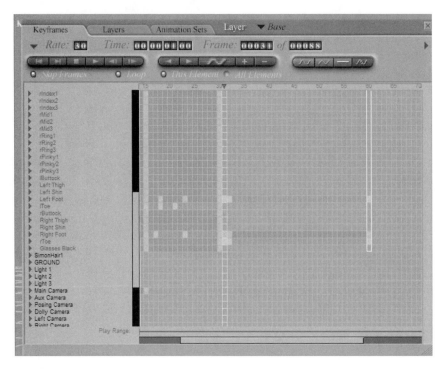

FIGURE 4.15
Dragging and dropping the walk cycle.

3. Now you'll add some camera animation so you can see what's really going on with this walk cycle. Change to the Main Camera view, and make sure that the Animation icon in the Camera Controls (see Figure 4.16) is not selected (not red). On frame 1, start with a side view, and then on frame 88,

orbit around so that when you get to the end, it's more of a front view. Close the editor, and play back again to now see the camera orbiting Simon as he walks.

If there's any previous camera animation already on that camera, get rid of it by going to the Keyframes Editor, selecting the Main Camera, and deleting any keyframes on the camera.

NOTE

FIGURE 4.16
Deselecting the
Animation icon.

4. To retime the animation, as you'll need to do in some future projects, you select the area of animation that you want to have applied to the whole length of the video. Now you'll make this animation slow down. To retime, you'll select the Body from the actors list, and then choose Animation>Retime Animation (see Figure 4.17). Set Source Frames to 1 to 30, and set the Destination Frames to 1 to 88. In other words, the information used in the first 30 frames will be spread across 88 frames. It will be about three times slower. As you play back, you'll notice how Simon walks much slower.

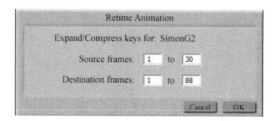

FIGURE 4.17
Retiming the animation.

VARIATIONS OF A WALK CYCLE

ON THE DVD Working with the basic walk cycle that you previously created, you'll now look at how you tweak a walk cycle to create variations. Open Exercise files/chapter 04/Walk_Cycle_Tweaked_start.pz3. You'll modify the walk cycle by editing existing keyframes mainly with the Graph Editor.

1. Start by selecting the Left Shin. By dragging it back and forth, you can see how you can affect the positioning of his leg. After you've experimented, go ahead and Undo. With the shin still selected, choose Window>Graph Editor. In addition to dragging directly in the viewport, the shin can be manipulated using the Side-Side parameter dial, as well as by manipulating the curve in the Graph Editor.

NOTE *It's important to know exactly which graph you're working with. When you look at the top of the Graph Editor, you can see you're working with "Left Shin" and with "Side-Side." The other way to get at this is to go through the Keyframes Editor. Here you would select the Left Shin and then choose Side-Side below it. If you are already in the Animation Editor/Keyframes Editor, you can select the correct channel there as well.*

2. For now, in the Graph Editor, you'll look at the entire range of keys for the animation of this selected actor (Left Shin). If the range of keys displayed at the top of the Graph Editor does not show from 1 to 117, drag the slider at the bottom of the Graph Editor (as shown in Figure 4.18) to display all available keyframes.

FIGURE 4.18
All keys for the Left Shin selected with the Side-Side parameter channel active.

3. With the Left Shin selected and the Side-Side active in the Graph Editor, drag to select all keyframes (use Shift-drag to add to the selection). With all the keyframes selected and the Ctrl key held down, drag the keys down to move the position of that limb, bowing it out further to the left for the entire animation.

TIP

In the Graph Editor, with keyframes selected, Alt-dragging (left or right) slides the selected keyframes forward or backward along the timeline. Ctrl-dragging (up or down) adjusts the value of the selected keyframes in the active parameter channel (that is, Side-Side, Bend, yTran, and so on).

NOTE

Because all keyframes for the Left Shin Side-Side are selected, moving the keys in the Graph Editor alters and bows the characteristics of the left shin for the entire walk cycle very easily.

4. After the left leg is sufficiently bowed, select the Right Shin (make sure Side-Side is still selected), and Ctrl-drag the keys up to make the right leg bow outward so both legs are now bowed as shown in Figure 4.19. Go ahead and play back. You now have a bow-legged walk. Because this animation is already duplicated 4 times, you have 117 frames and were able to edit the entire animation to bow the legs that easily. This is one of the significant and direct benefits of animating manually as opposed to working with the Walk Designer. This is not something you would attempt with animation from the Walk Designer!

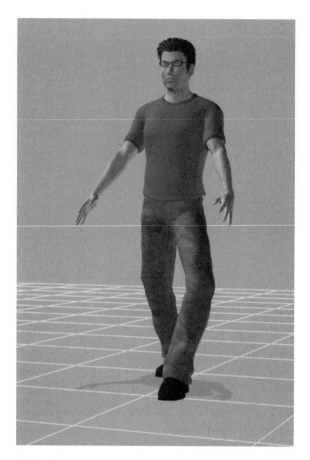

FIGURE 4.19
Both legs have been bowed by simply adjusting the
Side-Side keyframes in the Graph Editor.

5. Now, go ahead and tweak some more. Switch to the Right Camera view. Select the Chest and the Bend parameter. Because you want him to bend through the whole animation, you'll perform the bend in the Graph Editor. If you bend him simply using the Bend parameter, he will only be bent on the current animation frame. In the Graph Editor, select all frames (0–117) of the animation. Ctrl-drag down to bend him forward.

6. Select the Neck, and staying in the Bend channel, bend the neck up to raise the head.

7. Select the Left Shoulder, and adjust the Front to Back. In this case, it's interesting because there is a natural swing of the arm. Here you are offsetting the entire swing. To do the other arm as well, switch to the Right

Shoulder, and do the same thing. You can release the mouse and just hold the Ctrl key down if you need to go farther than the window view permits. Switch over to the Main Camera, and take a look at the tweaked walk. The figure should now look like Figure 4.20.

Main Camera

Right Camera

FIGURE 4.20
Simon's walk animation now adjusted to be a bow-legged hunchback walk animation.

8. To make this a bit more dramatic, change the number of frames to 234 frames. Select the Body from the actors list. Then choose Animation> Retime Animation. Make the Source Frames from 1 to 117, and the Destination Frames from 1 to 234, which will slow down the entire animation. You now have a bow-legged hunchbacked character lumbering forward.

This is a very simple example of how a walk cycle, which has been clearly defined, can be easily modified to create a significant variation in that walk. This should give you some clear guidance as to why you use this method instead of using the Walk Designer for everything. By creating your own keyframed walk cycles, you can very quickly and easily tailor the walk to tell your story.

ANIMATING A HAPPY WALK

Now that you've made a basic walk cycle in Poser Pro, let's look at other ways to modify the walk to show the moods of the character. You'll start off by making a "happy" walk. Before creating this happy walk, there are a few things to consider. In this next walk tutorial, you will create a stylized walk, which is very well suited for 3D characters or cartoon characters. This will not simulate real-life motion, which has thousands of points of nuance. When you need that kind of motion in animation production, it's best to use motion capture data because you can get to something realistic more quickly and satisfy your customer or the project director, as opposed to trying to animate a figure by hand to move as a realistic human. It's just not a wise use of time to try to achieve that by hand. Instead, we'll focus on how you can create useful, interesting, human animation that is really for showing 3D figures in motion. You will learn one concept of a happy walk.

"Happy," of course, is a very subjective term. It is even more so when it comes to describing the motion of a human in 3D. So, you'll see here basically one presentation of a happy walk with this figure. In your projects, you will likely need to give the happy figure slight differences or have a different display of personality or behavior. That's fine! The techniques you'll learn in this tutorial can be applied to any other observed expressive walks. The main point is, get the principle, and then apply it to your productions.

ON THE DVD

1. To begin, load Exercise files/chapter 04/Walk_Cycle_Basic. Be sure to set the number of frames to 30. You only need 30 to work with for now. Use the camera dots so you don't have to keep clicking to change the camera from the options. Set the first camera dot for the Main Camera view. Switch to Right Camera, and set the second camera dot. This way, you can switch camera angles back and forth quickly.

2. Using Figure 4.21 as a guide, you'll pose the Hips on frame 1. You need to arch the hips, which is easier in the side view. You'll rotate the hip in the xRotate (15°). The effect you're looking for by rotating the hip is to make the back curve. At the moment, the character looks to be leaning forward as though he's about to take a step or fall down, and that's fine. Next, select the Chest, and bend that back (-28°). The result is that there's a bend in Simon's back.

FIGURE 4.21
Five key poses in the happy walk cycle.

3. Using Figure 4.21 as a guide, pose the right arm. It is easier to pose if you use IK. When using IK in this type of posing, it's important to remember when to turn it on and when to turn it off. The controls for manipulating the limbs are definitely affected when the IK is on. Select the Right Hand, and turn on the IK for the Right Hand. You want to pose that arm to be up, so rather than bending the limbs individually, it's easier to just pose that arm up. Double-check the arm pose in the Main Camera to see if it's okay. In the Right Camera view, you can see the hand is deformed at this point. Just straighten it out with the Side-Side parameter. Now, turn the IK off. Select the Right Hand, and go to the parameters' advanced hand controls to adjust the Grasp and make it look more natural and relaxed.

4. Turn on IK for the Left Hand, and pull the hand back (as shown in Figure 4.21). Use Side-Side to straighten out the hand after the arm is in position.

5. Select the Neck, and bend it up.

6. Select the Left Foot, and bend it up.

7. Select the Right Foot, raise it up, and bend it down a little bit, until the toes go through the floor slightly.

8. Select the Right Toes, and bend them up. Now you have the basic starting pose set for the happy walk. Because you are working with a 30-frame walk cycle, you need to copy this information to the last frame (30) as shown in Figure 4.22.

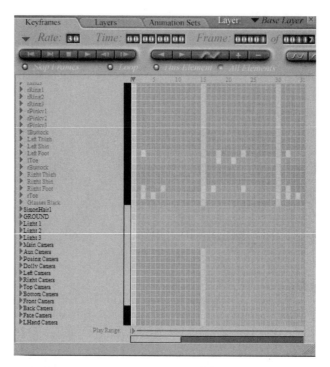

FIGURE 4.22
Copying and pasting the information to other frames.

9. To do that, open Edit Keyframes, and to make life easy, select all frames after frame 1 and delete them. Close the Keyframes Editor, and go to frame 30.

10. With each of the elements that must be posed (Left Foot, Right Foot, and so on), just press + (plus) to record a keyframe. If you're still using IK for posing the arms, turn IK off. This is because (due to the skeletal joint structure of the Poser figure) with IK turned off, you'll have control of the position of the arms based on the position of the chest. After you do this, you'll need to apply a keyframe to the individual elements of the arm. And, of course, you need to keyframe the hips, the chest, and the neck.

11. Now, go to frame 15, and select the Body. Make sure the IK is turned off. Go to Symmetry>Swap Right to Left. This automatically creates the in-between keyframe. Right now, if you play back, you'll notice he's like a robot, whose feet never leave the floor.

12. For the midpoint of the happy walk, go to frame 7. Here, you'll start by raising the Right Foot and bringing it back slightly. Use the Bend parameter to bend it down slightly. Make sure the IK is turned on for the Left Hand. Look at it through the Main Camera to make sure you're not creating a weird position.

13. Turn the IK off for the Left Hand, and turn it on for the Right Hand. The elbows of both arms stay up for most of this happy walk. They don't drop as much as in a basic walk. Next, adjust the curvature of the back to curve in the other direction. To do that, start with the Hip. With the Hip selected, use the xRotate, and rotate the hip forward (19°). Then select the Chest and Bend it forward (-31°).

If you notice one arm moving and the other not, the IK is on for one of the hands. If so, turn the IK off.

14. The arms may need to be readjusted again. If so, make further adjustments until you are satisfied. Just remember to turn the IK on and off. Also, don't forget to check your pose in the Main Camera view. Orbit as needed, to see the pose from all angles. Because the curvature of the back has changed, you also must readjust the neck so that the head is looking up and forward. This is essentially the completed crossover.

15. You now need to copy this crossover pose from frame 7 to frame 23, swapping right and left, but before you do so, you need to set keyframes for specific actors in the arms.

Even though you have the IK on the arms and the legs, you'll only set keyframes for the arm's actors. That's because the IK on the legs is always on, whereas the IK on the arms is only used for posing the arms, and you then set keyframes so that the actors' positions can be stored. So, first, make sure the IK is turned off for both hands. Then, you'll select the different actors for the arms and set the keyframes for the first crossover. All of this is because the position of the shoulders is being controlled by the angle of the chest (the shoulder's hierarchical parent).

16. Select the Left Hand, and add a keyframe. Do the same with the Left Forearm, Left Shoulder, Left Collar, and then Right Hand, Right Forearm, Right Shoulder, and Right Collar. Then open the Keyframes Editor. You don't need the keyframes for the body, so just select all actors below the body from frame 7. With the Alt key held down, drag frame 9 over to frame 23. Close the Keyframes Editor, and go to frame 23. Now, from the main menu, choose Figure>Symmetry>Swap Right and Left. Now you're getting closer to a happy walk. It's definitely different from the basic walk (see Figure 4.23).

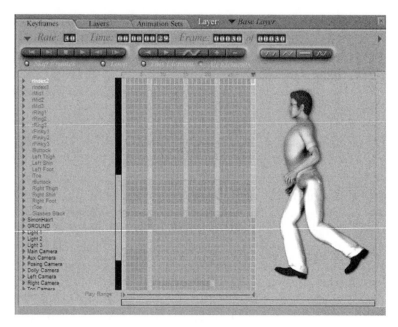

FIGURE 4.23
Adding frame 7 keyframes to frame 23.

17. Go to frame 5, select the Left Foot, and bend it, to be flat on the floor. You want that foot to stay that way up until frame 13 to appear as though the body weight is on that foot. Scrub the animation through to frame 13. Make sure the left foot is on the floor properly.

18. Slide through the animation to see what you have so far. Depending on the exact geometry of the figure you're using, you may have to use the linear interpolation on that foot to make sure it doesn't go through the floor.

19. Because you corrected the left foot to be flat on the floor on frame 5, and the halfway point of the cycle is frame 15, as you drag through frame 15, you see that the right foot is coming down. On frame 20, select the Right Foot and make sure it's placed on the floor. Next, bend the right foot down toward the floor, and then go to frame 28 to make sure it's still down and bent.

20. Just before the completion of the first half of the cycle, on frame 13 where the left foot is flat, look at the right foot and maybe lift it just a little bit higher up in the air. You're just giving him a little more pep in his step. Go to the opposing frame (28), and bring the left foot up in the same way.

21. Open the Keyframes Editor to look at the arms. You want to make them appear to be moving faster when they're toward the body and holding in place a bit while they're away from the body to give the sense of acceleration. The easiest way to do this is to take the keyframes for the Right Arm

actors at frame 1, and with the Alt key held down, drag them out two frames. Do the same thing with the Left Arm actors, at frame 15, dragging them out two frames.

22. Select those four actor keys and set them to Linear, on both the right and left arm. Look at the result, and orbit around the animation in the Main Camera view.

That's the essence of making the happy walk. As you can see, it is stylized. A lot of attention is paid to the curvature of the back, which is a serious key to this kind of strutting walk. You don't want a nice, upright, rigid pose for this. It has to be accentuated—something that really projects that this person has a unique attitude that is coming through every element of his being. Of course, if the character is happy, you would also give him a happy face (see Figure 4.24). We will look at the facial expression and the facial animation in a later chapter. But these are the basics of what you would need to know to create a happy walk in Poser Pro.

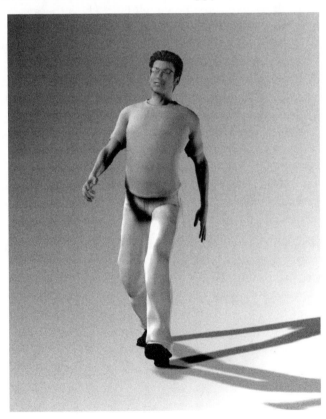

FIGURE 4.24
Simon enjoying a happy walk.

ANIMATING A RUN

Now you'll create an animated run cycle. It will be a stylistic animated run, not one of those motion captured, photo-realistic runs. The stylized run that you will learn in this tutorial is easily adaptable to other run styles you might need for your story. This run will be toward something, which means the body will be leaning forward as opposed to running away from something—let's say, a dog chasing you—so it will have unique characteristics. The run will, in essence, be a series of jumps, spending time in the air.

ON THE DVD

1. Begin by loading Exercise files/chapter 04/Walk_Cycle_1.pz3, which is Simon in the neutral T-position with a couple of props. Set the frame length to 23 frames. Because the figure is running, he's actually going to accomplish his cycle in a shorter period of time than a walk.

2. Because this run cycle will put Simon in the air, it could become a little difficult to determine how high he really is (because his feet will be off the ground). So, you'll add a guide line created from a primitive box prop. Switch to the Right Camera view, and open the Props library. Select the Box from the Primitives. Lift the box up, and position it so that it goes through his body at hip level. Adjust the xScale (150), yScale (10), and zScale (1000) to create a "line" out of this box, extending all across the view pane, and then raise it up to the bottom of his chest (approximately 4.2 on the yTran). Also, select a see-through material for the box to make posing easier (see Figure 4.25).

NOTE

This is kind of like a "training wheel" that you will not need later as you get comfortable and familiar with creating run cycles. But for now, it provides a reference point.

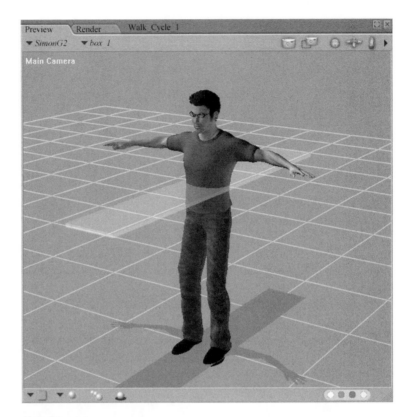

FIGURE 4.25
The box in position as a reference.

3. It's time to start creating the actual poses for the run. Begin with frame 1. You'll be setting your run cycle poses based on the reference of Figure 4.26. Switch to the Main Camera. Turn on the IK for both hands, and lock the hand parts. Then drag the arms down. Select the Right Hand, and use the Bend parameter to bend it down. You don't need to manually do the other hand; you can just choose Symmetry>Right Arm to Left.

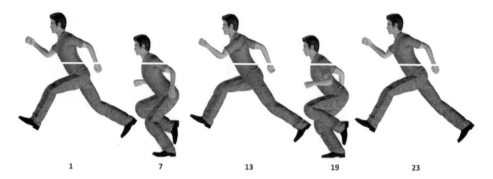

1   7   13   19   23

FIGURE 4.26
Key poses for the run cycle.

4. Open the Advanced Hand Controls, and set the Fist to 0.6 in both the left and right hands. He now has two closed fists as shown in Figure 4.27.

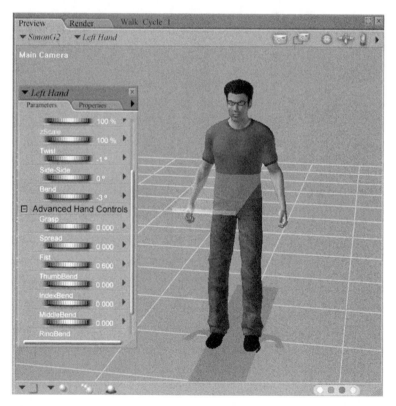

FIGURE 4.27
Simon's fists set in the Advanced Hand Controls.

5. Switch to the Right Camera to work on the arms next. The right hand needs to come up, and the left needs to go back. You'll use the Parameters dials for this to have as much control as possible. But first, turn off the IK for the hands. With the Right Hand selected, use Front-Back to raise the hand. Then select the Right Forearm, and use Side-Side to position the arm. Switch between views to see what the pose looks like from different angles.

6. Select the Left Shoulder, and use Front-Back to bend the entire arm back.

7. Go down the hierarchy to the Left Forearm, and bend it into position. These are just initial adjustments to the arms. You'll make adjustments again after the chest has been rotated.

8. Rotate the Hip with the xRotate (30). Then, select the Chest, and bend it back slightly (-8).

9. Tweak the arms to have them match the pose for frame 1 of Figure 4.26 (shown previously). Start with the Left Collar. Use the Front-Back and the Up-Down parameters. Then scroll down through the hierarchy, and select the Left Shoulder to get the left hand to move back. Continue to the Left Forearm to bend it back as shown in Figure 4.28. Now, let's revisit the right side.

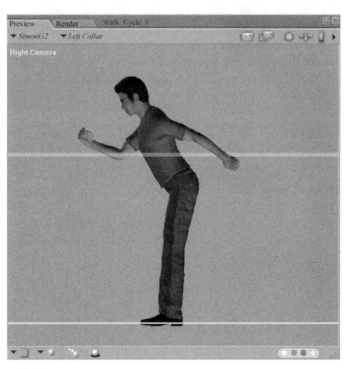

FIGURE 4.28
Adjusting Simon's arms.

This tweaking and adjusting process has an iterative nature. You adjust one body part, adjust something else, and then come back around to the initial spot again. It's because the hierarchical interactive flow—the way the joints in the Poser figure are connected—affects how the limbs bend and how they crease the body.

10. So, now, make the final adjustments to the right arm, starting at the Right Shoulder, and then going down to the Right Forearm. These poses of the arms are just for the style of running in this exercise. You can take creative liberties and make different arrangements of the angles to make your own run.

11. Now you will lift the Hip because after you begin to pose the feet (because they are using IK), their behavior will be very different if you pose them before you lift the figure into the air. Lift him off the ground by the hip until the bottom of his buttock is on the line (created earlier in step 2).

12. Now it's time for the legs. Based on frame 1 of Figure 4.26 (shown previously), drag the Left Foot out front because the right arm is out front. Leave a slight bend in the leg. Bend it up a bit. Next, drag the Right Foot back, leaving a bend in the knee. Bend the foot down.

13. Adjust the Hip to make sure it's centered between the feet.

The choice of how far you spread the legs out affects not only the dramatic impact of the style of the run but also the distance the figure will travel per step, and therefore the speed at which he runs. The farther apart, the faster the run and the greater the distance over time.

14. The neck also needs to be adjusted. Bend it so it's facing straight ahead (see Figure 4.29).

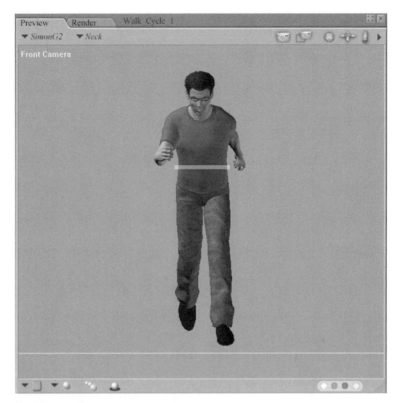

FIGURE 4.29
Simon's neck is facing straight ahead.

15. With all this in place, it is time to copy these keyframes to the end. Go to the last frame (23), and set keyframes for each of the actors you've positioned on frame 1 (neck, chest, and hip, both feet, both hands, and all parts of the arms) (see Figure 4.30).

In addition to doing it this way, you can also use the Keyframes Editor. If you want to edit keyframes here, you could, for example, select the four frames for the left arm from frame 1, hold the Alt key down, and drag them over to frame 23.

NOTE

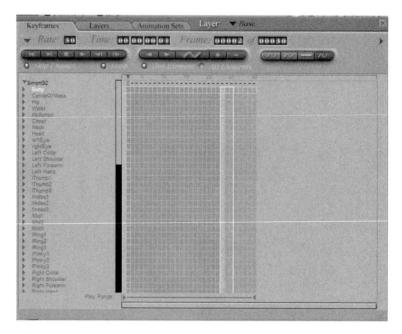

FIGURE 4.30
Copying the keyframes to frame 23.

16. Now go to frame 13, which is the midpoint. Here you want the figure to be in the diametrically opposed pose. Select Figure>Symmetry>Swap Right and Left. This sets a keyframe automatically.

17. It's now time to create the remaining poses for this run cycle. You'll do them in the order of first creating the crossover pose keyframes, and then filling in the remaining keyframes, from the earliest to the latest, in pairs. This means you have frame 1, frame 13, and 23 already posed. You will now pose the first crossover, which is frame 7, and its pair, frame 19 because frame 19 is frame 7 with the symmetry swapped, left to right. You will then go to frame 3, and its pair, which is 15; frame 5 and 17; and finally frame 9 and 21.

18. At first, this order of keyframe adjustment may seem bizarre. There are two factors that contribute to the need to tweak the poses in this order. (1) The hierarchical structure of the Poser figure joints causes body part siblings to sometimes require readjustment. (2) The interpolation between keyframes causes a liner or smooth transition between keyframes that requires a change in the interpolated motion curve.

While posing the figure for the run cycle during the next few steps, be sure to also take a look at Exercise files/Chapter 04/Run_Cycle_1-Main Camera.mov and Exercise files/Chapter 04/Run_Cycle_1-Right Camera.mov to get a motion sense of how the various poses go together.

19. Based on Figure 4.26 (shown earlier), let's start with frame 7. Here you want to have the figure down on the floor. Begin by dragging the feet downward. Then drag the hip down. You want the right foot in the air and the left foot on the floor. The figure needs to appear to have weight and impact, as it's coming down (basically from a running jump).
20. Bend the Left Foot to be flat on the floor. The right leg should be sticking up with the knee showing in the front and the foot bent back to a vertical angle to the floor.
21. Bend the back backward a little to create a bit more of an arch.
22. Take the left arm back. The right arm should be brought forward and up slightly. Select the Right Forearm, and use the Bend parameter. Also, rotate the Hip slightly on the x-axis to give more of a sense of motion—that he's really going somewhere. Check Simon's run in Figure 4.31. Double-check the pose by orbiting in the Main Camera.

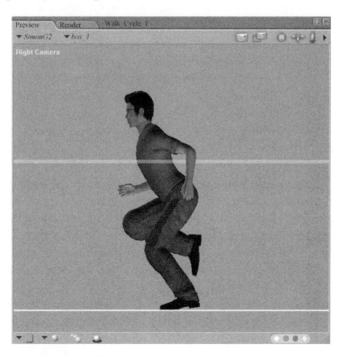

FIGURE 4.31
Simon's running pose.

23. Slide through the frames to see the motion so far. Using Alt-drag in the Keyframes Editor, copy the keyframe for actors posed in the past three steps from frame 7 to frame 19. On frame 19, go ahead and swap the symmetry Right to Left, and play back. You now have a rather primitive run in the making, although not too interesting yet.

24. Go to frame 3. This is where the figure has hang-time. He's in the air in a run cycle and may appear not to be moving. Bear in mind that when the run cycle is transformed (so that the figure is actually running across land or running across the room), though the hang time occurs for these couple of frames, the figure is still moving forward toward the end destination. This hang time is easy to achieve by going to the Keyframes Editor. Simply copy all the frames, except the Body, from frame 1, and drag them over to frame 3. Do the same with frame 13, moving them over to frame 15. Delete the keys for the Body.

25. Go to frame 5. Here you want the left leg extending downward. Lift the Hip a bit. The right leg should be bent up, as well as the right foot. The left arm needs a slight adjustment. Select the Left Shoulder, and bend back slightly with the Front-Back parameter. Check the right arm in the Main Camera to make sure it's not twisting out. Adjust the Right Shoulder to raise it up a little bit. In the Keyframes Editor, take the keyframes from frame 5 and copy over to frame 17. On frame 17, swap the symmetry.

26. Go to frame 9. On this frame, you want to see him leaping off the ground, so for one thing, you'll need to raise his hip up until the "line" is at chest height. Bend the left foot a bit until the toes go through the floor. Select the Left Toes, and bend them level with the floor to give the sense that the left leg is propelling his body.

27. Raise the left leg toward his chest, until the thigh is approximately horizontal.

28. Bring the left arm forward and the right arm back a bit more. Go down the hierarchy to the Right Forearm, and bend it out, so you have that classic freeze-frame of a run. Orbit around in the Main view to make sure nothing is out of order such as an arm twisting too far in or out.

29. Copy frame 9 to frame 21 in Edit Keyframes, and swap the symmetry on frame 21.

30. Set the frame length to 67 frames. Choose Animation>Retime Animation. Set the Source Frames from 1 to 23 and the Destination Frames from 1 to 67.

You may wonder why we are using 67 frames, as 3 x 23 is 69. Bear in mind that as you look at your keyframes, frame 1 and frame 23 are the same frame. So in order to not have a hiccup due to that duplicate frame, we subtract 1 frame every time we duplicate the length, which leaves 67 frames.

31. Play the animation. Right now, there's a little hiccup in the animation, so open the Keyframes Editor, and adjust the Play Range to end on frame 66 (as shown in Figure 4.32), so it will only cycle through 1 to 66 upon playback. Click Play again. Frame 67 must exist for the keyframing to work properly, but when you preview or render the animation, if it is to repeat continuously, it's helpful to have that last frame turned off.

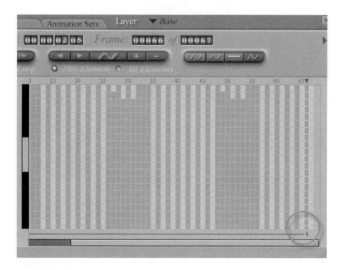

FIGURE 4.32
Adjusting the play range.

This is how your run cycle will look from now on until you transform it (see Figure 4.33). When you transform it, he will actually be traveling, whereas right now, he looks like he's on a running treadmill. That's the basics of creating your run cycle in Poser Pro, and later we'll look at transforming these cycles.

FIGURE 4.33
Your run cycle at this stage.

TRANSFORMING WALKS AND RUNS

Now you will transform your walk cycle, which means you will move the walk cycle so that the figure will not be simply walking in place as though he's on a treadmill. This is how you get the Poser figure to walk around a room, or walk down the street. Essentially, this is how you transform a cycling figure into a traveling figure.

ON THE DVD

1. Load the Exercise files/chapter 04/Walk_Cycle_Basic.pz3. You will add a box, as before, but this box is placed just beneath the floor and is just for maintaining the correct position of the foot on the floor so the foot doesn't slip. By preventing the foot from slipping, you can create the believable illusion of the figure walking forward.

2. Add a Box from the Library props. Scale this box smaller on the yScale (40), and move it down with the yTrans (-0.310) below the floor, centered underneath the foot. Scale it out on the zScale (130) to fit the foot lengthwise.
3. Duplicate this box by choosing Edit>Duplicate Box1. Use the zTrans to position it underneath the other foot (see Figure 4.34). You may notice a slight difference between the box mode of the figure and the fully texture shaded mode, so make sure the box is lining up with the fully texture shaded mode of the figure.

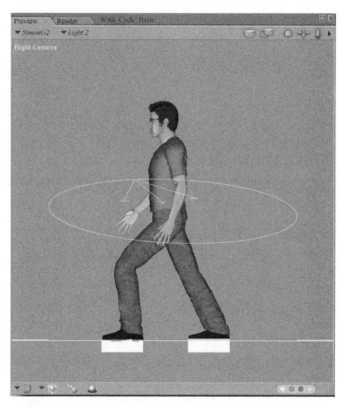

FIGURE 4.34
Boxes are positioned under Simon's feet.

If you look at this from the top view, you can see that the boxes are not positioned to be necessarily directly under the feet. Because he's walking in a straight line, that's okay. But if your story calls for the figure to make turns or walk around corners, you need to also line this up in your top view.

4. Now you need to calculate the distance between these two blocks using a very simple method. Click on the first block. You can see its zTran is 2.589. (Your actual value may be different, so note the value you have here.) Using a calculator, calculate 2.589 minus the other block's zTran (which is 0.301). Put the result in the memory (M+), and then clear the calculator (C). Click on the first block, and enter its value again (2.589) plus memory recall (MR) equals 4.877. That means your next block should be at 4.877.

5. Duplicate the first box, and in the zTran value for this (third) box, enter 4.877. You've now added a third box in front of the figure, which is his next step. Based on this principle, go ahead and lay down seven additional blocks.

6. A helpful tool for setting the distance for the blocks is to use a spreadsheet (see Table 4.1). You have the Exercise files/chapter 04/Transform_Walk_Blocks_xls in your exercise files, and you'll see how to build one now. For the first block, in column C row 3 (C3), you have the zTran distance (0.301). The second block's z distance is 2.589 (cell C4). In the D column, enter =SUM (C4-C3), which means the second block minus the first block. Continue to the third block. Its value in the C column is =SUM (C4+D4). The string symbol means that all future calculations will refer explicitly to cell D4, even though you will be moving down the list of blocks in the C column.

Table 4.1 Excel Spreadsheet with the Calculations

Block	1	0.301
Block	2	2.589
Block	3	4.877
Block	4	7.165
Block	5	9.453
Block	6	11.741
Block	7	14.029
Block	8	16.317
Block	9	18.605
Block	10	20.893

7. Place the curser at the bottom-right edge of cell C5, until it turns into a small cross, and just drag it down to block 10 (C12), which fills in all the sums for the values of the zTran for the remaining blocks in column C.

8. With all the blocks laid out, you can now begin to transform your figure. If you didn't lay out your 10 blocks, you can load the Exercise files/chapter 04/Walk_Transform_2.pz3 project (see Figure 4.35).

FIGURE 4.35
The blocks are all positioned.

9. As you scroll through the timeline, you can see that the figure is still walking in place (as he should be). You will now transform the body. If you open Edit Keyframes, you can see that the body only has one keyframe—just the default keyframe at frame 1. Select that keyframe, and select the Linear section so the interpolation of all the keyframes on the Body channel will be linear. Close the editor. Make sure you have SimonG2 and Body selected. Now pay very close attention to where the left foot is on the block (as shown in Figure 4.36). Zoom in as needed to do so.

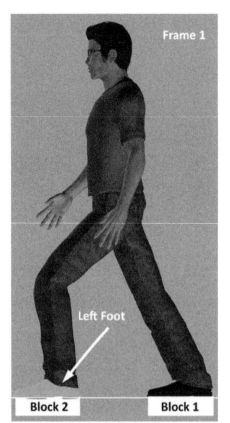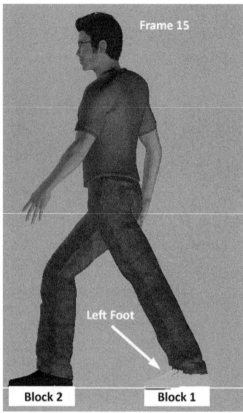

FIGURE 4.36
Before transforming Simon's walk cycle, his left foot is on block 2 in frame 1, and his left foot is on block 1 in frame 15. For him to move forward, his left foot will have to stay in place on block 2 at frame 15.

10. As you make that first step, make sure the left foot doesn't leave that block but stays fixed in the same position. Also, remember, the way it looks here in Block mode is not what you're really focusing on. You're focusing on how it looks in the full polygon, Texture Shaded mode. One thing to note is that the keyframe marks in Edit Keyframes will also give you an indication of where you need to set your key. Your next key for the Body zTran will be set at frame 15. So, drag the body forward by one block so the left foot stays on block 2. You may need to make a fine adjustment on that key with the Body's zTran to make sure the back of the heel matches up with the back of the block.

11. You'll also need to make another adjustment because the left foot shifts forward at one point. Make an adjustment keyframe at the point where the foot stops going forward any farther, which is frame 3. Don't make the mistake of dragging Simon manually (as this can cause his yTran position to change erratically). Use the Parameter dials, and drag the zTrans. Again, you're matching the back of the left heel with the back of the block.

12. From the time the right foot goes down onto block 3, you are no longer focusing on making sure the left foot stays put on block 2.

13. To complete the rest of the steps, drag the body's zTran forward to keep the foot that lands on the next block from slipping (as you've just done in the previous steps).

You may use the front of the foot or the back of the foot, but the rule is to be consistent.

NOTE

ON THE DVD Now your steps should be completed, and you should see an animation similar to the video tutorial's when you play it back. You can also load Exercise files/chapter 04/Walk_Transform_3.pz3 to catch up to this point. By using the block method, you now know how to transform a walk cycle to walk to any location. Because the walk is created by keyframes and not by using the Walk Designer (which creates keyframes for every single frame of every actor of the Poser figure), you have few enough well-placed keyframes to manipulate the characteristics of your walk in the Graph Editor, simply by selecting an actor and modifying its keyframes to cause the behavior you want to see.

Now, you'll transform the run cycle so that your figure can actually run along the floor. Again, this is very much like the transform of the walk cycle, in that this is how you get the figure to actually travel and not just run in place.

ON THE DVD
1. Start by loading the Exercise files/chapter 04/Run_Transform_1.pz3 project. Two blocks have been placed, just as you placed the blocks for the walk cycle. Their distance is a bit further apart because this is a run. You will position the body of the figure to match those blocks because they keep the feet in the correct landing position. Make sure SimonG2 and Body are selected. You are now on frame 1, and you have 23 frames in the cycle.

2. Drag to frame 7, which is the crossover point in this animation. As you can see, at frame 7, the left foot is on the floor. Because you have the Body selected, use the zTran to transform the figure onto the first block as shown in Figure 4.37.

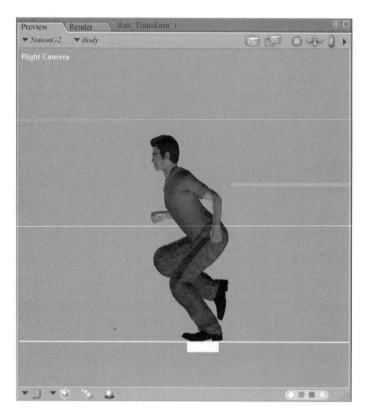

FIGURE 4.37
Moving Simon onto the block.

3. Go to frame 17, and transform the figure to the second block. The figure should be staying on that block until the foot really gets off, but he's not doing that.

4. Look at the Edit Keyframes. You are working with the Body, and the Body should be all linear keys. This is one of the aspects of keeping the foot from slipping, so make all those keys linear.

5. He really needs to go forward a bit still, so make sure the Body is selected, and drag forward on the zTran to get the final keyframe. Open the Keyframes Editor. The Body keyframes are linear, but as you can see, the foot is not staying where it should because it's trying to interpolate to the next key. Watch for where the toe gets off the ground, and then drag the Body with the zTran so that it brings the toe back onto the block. Play back in the Main Camera perspective, zoomed out so you can see the action as shown in Figure 4.38.

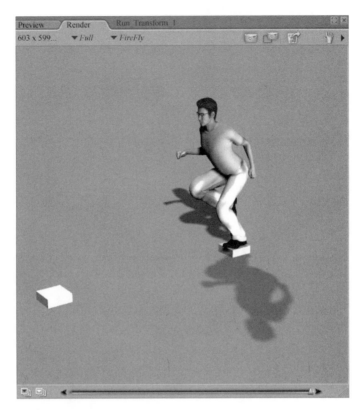

FIGURE 4.38
Simon runs from block to block.

Now the transformation of the run cycle is complete. Now that you've seen how both the runner and the walker are transformed, the process should be demystified so that you can easily set up run and walk cycles and get your figures moving about the room to tell your stories.

SUMMARY

Now that you've learned how to animate and transform walk and run cycles, you're on your way to becoming a true character animator. What you've learned so far is transportable to other major 3D animation packages after you learn the appropriate interface and relevant applicable tools.

Gaining this intimate knowledge of how characters actually come to life prepares you for the next chapters where action gets more challenging.

5 Animating in Environments

In This Chapter

- Introduction
- Walking Up Stairs
- Walking Down Stairs
- Object Avoidance

INTRODUCTION

In the previous chapter, you learned about creating walk cycles from pose-to-pose animation, and you learned to create run cycles and how to tweak all cycles to achieve different results. Now we'll increase the challenge by creating a walk animation up the stairs based on the same principles of pose-to-pose animation you learned in the previous chapter.

We'll start by creating a walk cycle, then translate that walk cycle to walk across the floor, and then raise the walk cycle up to complete the walk up the stairs. When creating a walk cycle animation up the stairs, some of the challenges to be aware of are that the cycle is going to be affected by the length of the step and the height of the step. The style of the stairs will include some stairs that are spiraling, some will have a landing, and some will be just basic, standard stairs. A landing is where you have a flight of stairs followed by a flat area, and then more stairs. It could be a turning point, or it could continue going straight.

Also, you have to decide how you're going to raise the figure to go up the stairs. Then, you must choose between straight-ahead or pose-to-pose animation. You're familiar with pose-to-pose now, where you create the extremes of an animation and you basically adjust the in-betweens. Straight-ahead animation means you don't have any predetermined extremes, but rather as you move forward in time, you simply animate more of the figure. This gives you the greatest creative freedom, but it also requires great animation skills and much more time.

The animation we'll create walking up the stairs will be similar to a familiar character in a video game walking up the stairs. This will not be an example of motion-capture character animation but rather more like cartoon or 3D character animation.

Poser has a built-in stairs prop in the Props library (see Figure 5.1), but we chose not to use that prop in this tutorial for a few reasons. The stairs prop is a single color, and rather than going through the whole exercise of identifying each of the polygons and assigning them different materials, we imported a stair object created in a different 3D application. In this case, it was simply a matter of distributing some cubes in CINEMA 4D and giving every cube a different color (see Figure 5.2). You can use any 3D application to do this. If you don't have a 3D application, and you want to replicate these kinds of stairs for your project, you can simply create a series of cubes. By using the box object in Poser's Prop library, you can create the varying step sizes and assign every box a different color so you can have the same result that we have here.

FIGURE 5.1
The stairs prop in Poser Pro.

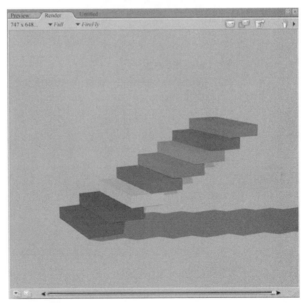

FIGURE 5.2
Our stairs object imported into Poser Pro from CINEMA 4D.

After the stairs object is imported, you need to decide whether to treat it like a prop or treat it like a figure. It might seem most obvious that you would want to treat it like a prop, but in this case, you actually want it to be a figure. You may think "figure" always means a 3D character, but "figure" is just a different class of 3D object in Poser.

To make the object a figure, follow these short steps:

1. Select the imported object, and go into the Setup room.
2. When the pop-up window appears with a question (see Figure 5.3), click OK.
3. From the Setup room, go back into the Pose room.
4. Click Yes when the next question appears (see Figure 5.4).

It's really that simple! It's how Poser interprets an object that has gone into the Setup room. After you have the figure, you may also want to go ahead and save it in your Figures library. In this case, save it under your own new folder under Figures, as shown in Figure 5.5.

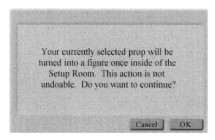

FIGURE 5.3
Warning message when entering the Setup room.

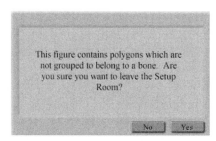

FIGURE 5.4
You will choose "Yes" at this warning.

FIGURE 5.5
Saving your steps to the
Figure library.

When it's a figure, instead of a prop, you can control the height of the stairs from its base. When it's a prop, it's controlled from its center. You'll need to make these stairs 5% as tall as it naturally is in the y-axis when you're animating. And, if you were to use it as a prop, it would simply create an object floating in the air. Using it as a figure causes it to go down to the ground, and then it easily comes back up later when you need it. So, you can see that using it as a figure creates an easier workflow.

WALKING UP STAIRS

ON THE DVD

1. To begin the project of having Simon walk up the stairs, open the Climb Stairs-Step-1.pz3 project from your Chapter 5 Exercise Files folder. Select Figure 2, which refers to the staircase. You have SimonG2, his hair, and the stairs. With Figure 2 selected, adjust the height of the stairs to be flat so that Simon will be able to walk across as you build his walk cycle.

NOTE

It may seem insignificant, but you need to consider one issue because it will affect how you go forward. When one foot is on the second step, the other foot should be on the step below it. This distance between the feet will be something to consider when you add your box. The box will define the spacing between the feet in the walk cycle.

2. With the stairs still selected, go to the y-scale, and set it to 5%. This, as you can see, still gives you the color distinction so you know how to position his steps (see Figure 5.6).

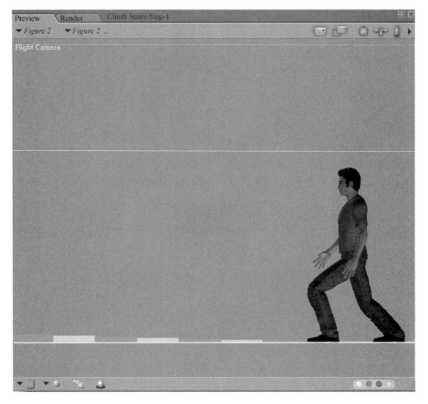

FIGURE 5.6
The steps have been scaled down on the y-axis.

3. Go to the Props library, and get a box. Add the box to your scene, and close the library. You want to move and position the box to achieve the equivalent of one step. To do this, drag the box underneath the step, and zoom into the area. Use the Scale tool to manipulate the size and shape of the box, until you have something that looks like a very thin rectangle, fitting right underneath the step.

4. As noted earlier, one step ends at the first arrow, the second step ends at the second arrow, and so on (see Figure 5.7). Use the tip of the toes as your guide. The length of this rectangle signifies the distance between the feet. Now bring the box backward, to underneath his actual foot, lining up the front of the box with the front of the toes as shown in Figure 5.8.

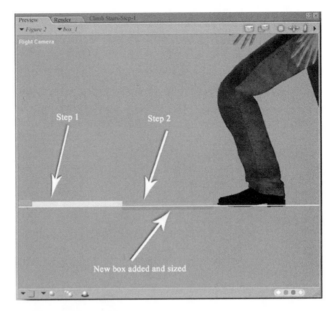

FIGURE 5.7
Arrows showing the placement of the toes on each step
and the new box underneath.

FIGURE 5.8
The new box is moved back and placed with the front edge
under Simon's toes.

5. Now you're ready to define the pose for your walk cycle. Select the Si-monG2 figure to set the pose. Switch to the Move tool, and position his hip and back foot forward. Take a look at it in the Main Camera. Remember, this is just the first pose in the walk cycle. One simple thing we'll do is to select each hand and give it a bit of a grasp. This removes some of the excessive artificiality from the pose, while having hands splayed just looks way too unnatural (see Figure 5.9).

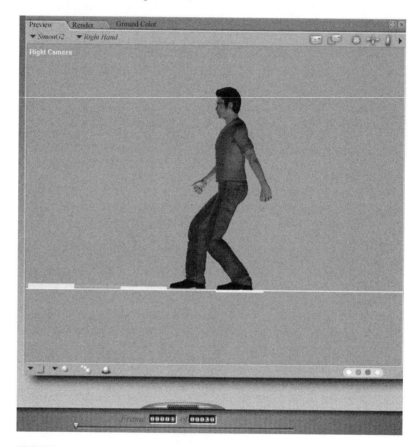

FIGURE 5.9
Simon's first step with hands in slight "grasp" position.

The grasp of the hands should definitely be done on frame 1, so make sure the timeline is not on some other frame. Otherwise, you won't get the great benefit for preparing frame 30 based on the keys of frame 1.

NOTE

6. Set the keyframe for frame 30 based on frame 1. Open the Keyframes Editor. You want to work with the SimonG2 figure. You don't need a keyframe for the body, so with the Shift key held down, select the keyframes from Center Of Mass all the way down to Right Toe. Then, with the Alt key held down, drag it across to frame 30. (If you drag across while having the hierarchy list scrolled down, it could be a little bit tricky to land on the right key. It may be easier to drag from the top.) (See Figure 5.10.)

7. Now you have frame 30 based on frame 1. Because you already have all the keys selected, hold the Alt key down again, and drag it to frame 15. Now frame 1, frame 15, and frame 30 are identical as shown in Figure 5.11.

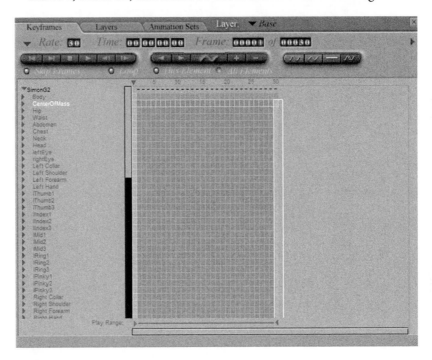

FIGURE 5.10
Dragging the keyframes to frame 30.

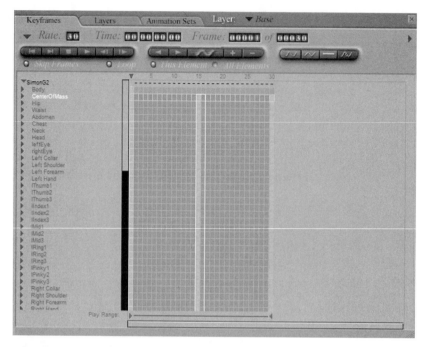

FIGURE 5.11
Keyframes set at frames 1, 15, and 30.

8. Go to frame 15 on your timeline, and with SimonG2 and Body selected, go to the Figure menu. Select Symmetry/Swap Right and Left. Now frame 15 has the alternate pose as shown in Figure 5.12. Now you're ready to fine-tune the walk cycle.

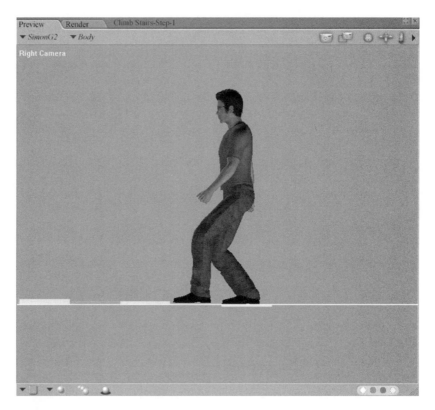

FIGURE 5.12
Right and Left Symmetry have been swapped at frame 15.

9. Switch to the Right Camera, and scroll to frame 7. On frame 7, the right
    foot should be raised up. Select the right foot (it's easier if you select it
    while you can see it on frame 1 so you don't have to try to select it through
    the left foot), and then use the Parameter controls to raise it up with the
    yTran to about 0.8. You may notice the foot is going through the floor as it
    steps down, so you'll need to make that into a linear keyframe. Open the
    Keyframes Editor, select the Right Foot keyframe on frame 7, and make it
    linear (see Figure 5.13).

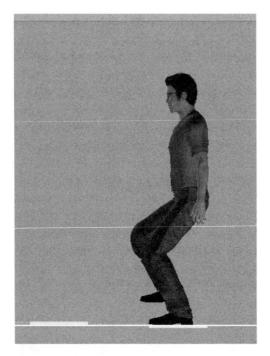

FIGURE 5.13
Simon's right foot is raised at frame 7.

10. Raise the left foot at frame 23. Select the left foot, and raise it to 0.8 on the yTran. The left foot also goes through the floor and needs to have a linear key. Place the linear key on frame 1 for the left foot.

11. Next, you need to adjust the up-and-down motion of the hip. The point where you have the crossover on frame 7 is the point where the hip should be in its highest position. The hip is currently at -0.32. Raise the hip, using the yTran, to about -0.133 as shown in Figure 5.14. Go ahead and copy this, and paste it into the yTran on frame 23, which is the other crossover point. Switch over to Fast Tracking mode to review the walk cycle. He's basically taking two steps: a left and a right footstep. You will now extend that to four steps, so that he walks four steps up the stairs.

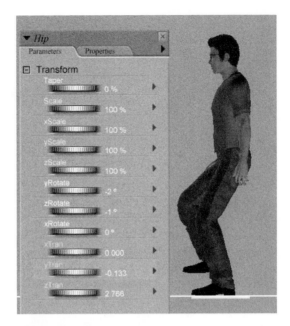

FIGURE 5.14
Setting the yTran value for Simon's hip.

12. Begin by setting the total number of frames to 59, to double your number of walk cycles. Do not make it 60 frames because this would copy the first frame and create a small glitch. Next, open the Keyframes Editor, and select all frames from the Right Toe up to Center Of Mass. (You don't need to copy the Body or the Glasses.) With the Alt key held down, drag and drop the copy into the final frame. The last frame is now 59.

13. When playing back the animation, his left foot may be dipping below the floor. To correct this, select the Left Foot and make the Left Foot keyframe linear on frame 30. (It will be rather obvious which keyframe needs to be made linear, by following the pattern of the other linear frames.) (See Figure 5.15.)

You can delete the keyframe for the body because it is not needed yet.

NOTE

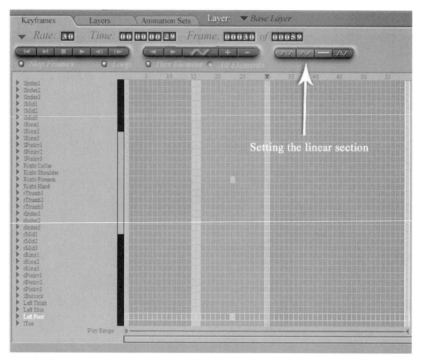

FIGURE 5.15
Setting the linear section.

14. At this point, you no longer need the box underneath his foot, so with the box selected, open Properties, and turn off all three visible options (Visible, Cast Shadows, and Visible in Raytracing). With SimonG2/Body selected, you will animate Simon walking across the flattened stairs.

15. Now you edit the zTran parameter of the body to keep the left foot in its current position for the duration of one step. One step is 15 frames, so you will zTranslate to make sure the left foot stays in its current position. In essence, the steps act as the guides that you used the boxes for in the previous chapter. You may need to make some slight adjustments, so make them as you find them. A foot may be too far forward, for example. When you play it back, you may see there's some slippage. The solution is to go to the Keyframes Editor/Body and set all the Body frames to linear.

16. The next step is to keep the right foot in place. But first, go ahead and move the right foot back a little bit. The reason for this has to do with the fact that the stairs will be coming up, so it may create a slight problem if the toes are right up to the raised step. The toes may go through the stair as the step is raised.

17. With the Body selected, go to frame 30. Then adjust the zTran, moving him forward, until the right foot is in the same position on the stair as when he put his foot down as shown in Figure 5.16. As you can see, you don't have to use two colors for the stairs. There are other alternatives to having this outline shading, but you can see the benefit here of having the two-color shading on the stairs.

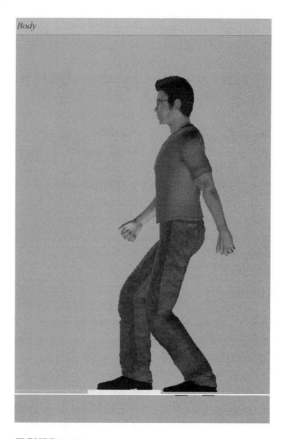

FIGURE 5.16
Simon's right foot is in the correct zTran position.

18. Go to frame 44. (Make sure you still have SimonG2/Body selected.) Drag him forward to the next step, using the zTran. If you are getting lost, as far as where the feet are landing because they're going through the stairs now, then you can set the figure style for the stairs (Figure 2) to Wireframe.

19. Go to frame 59, and zTranslate him forward one step. Now the walk cycle has been translated, and he's walking forward, across the flattened stairs.

20. Now you're ready to raise the stairs back to their original height. Return to frame 1, and select Figure 2. The yScale is set to 5%. Now set it back to 100%, which raises the stairs back to their original height. Because it's a figure and not a prop, select the figure and then select Lock Figure. This will prevent you from getting confused and accidentally selecting the stairs when you're selecting the actors for Simon. Now, as you go through the timeline, you will notice that adjustments are needed to take it from a simple walk cycle to walking up the stairs.

21. On frame 15, select the Right Foot, and raise it up. You may be tempted to drag the foot because you have the Translate tool selected, but you should use the yTran to raise the foot instead because you want to maintain that exact distance from the raised step. Also be careful with the difference in placement of the foot. When looking at it in Box mode, it appears as though the heel is not down. That's because that is the true deformation of the human body, but remember, a shoe has a heel, so you must go by the visual of the full texture-shaded figure, not the box view.

22. Set the tracking mode to Full so that when you're scrubbing through it, you can see all the little issues, such as whether the foot is going through the stair or actually going on top of it. If you're not in Full tracking mode, you won't see it.

23. The figure's height position is a little different on the first step compared to the rest of the steps because he's coming from the floor. Therefore, the height position is not as adjusted as the ones that will follow. Still, you'll need to set a keyframe for the hip and the body at this frame. Select the Hip, and press the + key to set a keyframe for the hip (see Figure 5.17). Select the Body, and repeat to create a reference for the next set of frames so they can relate to how high the figure was on frame 15 (instead of looking back only to how high the figure was on frame 1). Again, if you didn't do that, you could have a weird interpolation, or averaging, of height between the stairs and the floor, which would cause an unnatural elevation problem for the figure.

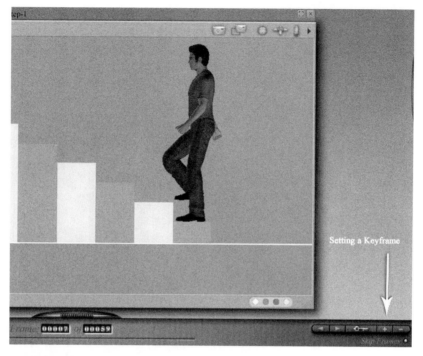

FIGURE 5.17
Adding a keyframe.

24. Go to frame 30. (If you were to raise the hips here to get him on the stairs, his legs would be stretched out and become useless.) Raise the elevation of the figure using the body. Think of the body as being a container that contains the whole figure. So, with the Body element selected, raise the figure up so the pose remains intact. Raise it until the foot on the lower step is posed correctly.

25. Select the foot that should be up on the next step, and raise it using the yTran. Play it back (in Full mode). You may see the foot going through the stair on the way up. You will fix that issue for the whole animation later. For now, you just want to make sure your elevations are correct.

26. Go to frame 44. Remember to use frame 44, not 45, as you started from a base of 30 and copied frames 2 through 30, which is 29 frames. Add that to 30 and you get 59. Therefore, the midpoint in this second half of the cycle is frame 44. Again, select the Body, and adjust the yTran to place the foot on the lower step. Then select the foot for the upper step, and raise it with the yTran parameter. If the foot is too far forward, use the zTran to slide it back (see Figure 5.18).

FIGURE 5.18
Adjusting Simon's position on the steps at
frame 44.

27. Select the Body, and go to frame 59. Use the yTran to raise the body, placing the foot on the lower step. Select the foot, and raise it to the top step
with the yTran.

28. Now, let's go through the animation and look at where the feet are really
going. You're looking for the intersection of the feet with the stairs. When
you find an area where a foot needs to be higher, select the foot, and adjust
it on the yTran. (You want the foot just slightly raised as it's going over the
front of the stair step, and then placed flat on the back of the stair to look
natural.)

29. You'll also see that the feet are dragging through the front of the steps. In
this case, bring the foot up on the yTran, and adjust the bend of the foot as
it's rising up. To adjust the bend, you need to address it from when the foot

is leaving the floor. Go to frame 17, which is two frames after the foot leaves the floor. With the Left Foot selected, adjust the bend using the Bend parameter. Make sure the toes go through the floor a little bit, then select the Left Toe, and bend it up, level with the floor as shown in Figure 5.19.

30. Open the Keyframes Editor. You need to make sure the Left Toe has a linear key on frame 15 to keep the toe from getting floppy. Then, at frame 19, bring the Left Toe back to its default of 0 degrees. Because bending the foot affects how high the foot appears to be when trying to negotiate past the step, it's important to make sure your bend animation is completed before trying to complete the elevation of the foot to not intersect the step.

31. Back in the Preview pane, you'll see the toes are now flexing backward, which tells you that keyframes 17, 18, and 19 for the Left Toes need to be made linear as well.

32. The toes are still going through the front of the step. The easiest thing to do here is to go into the Keyframes Editor, and on frame 23 for the Left Foot, rather than dealing with this unneeded frame 22, raise the yTran value here. Also, go to frame 20, and raise that yTran.

FIGURE 5.19
Adjusting Simon's toes.

33. The left foot needs to be raised around frame 24. Raise the foot on the yTran, and adjust the Bend to 0 degrees. You can see how the elevation of the foot animation is quite different from a regular walk cycle. There's a dip on frame 22. Adjust the Bend of the left foot upward on that frame, and then look at it in the Graph Editor. It's fine to have a bit of a curve here, but you don't want to have a curve that fluctuates up and down because that will look like an anomaly when you play back the animation.

34. Look at the graph for the yTran. As you can see, there is a problem here. It should not be going up, then down, and then up. Navigate to the next keyframe, and adjust the yTran parameter to even out the dip, turning it into one curve only to smoothe out the motion.

Checking the curves in the Graph Editor is extremely helpful because it gives you a better sense of the relationships between the keys of the channels of the keyframe. That sounds like a mouthful, but you're dealing with the motion of the foot in the x-, y-, and z-axis. Each of these is a channel. Bending is also a channel. Scaling, twisting, side-to-side—all of those represent individual channels. The relationship of the keyframes in each channel, over time, is represented in the Graph Editor. Sudden dips, flat areas, or spikes alert you that this is where you should adjust the keys to fix very erratic animation.

35. Now, scrubbing forward, you'll see how the next foot also intersects with the front of the stair. Repeat the same steps as for the first foot. Bend the foot two frames after the foot leaves the step. Bend the toe up as the heel leaves the step. On frame 34, release the bend on the toe. Make sure the toe bend keyframes are linear. By looking at the pattern of linear frames, you can see that frames 1–14 for the Right Toe also need to be linear, as well as frames 44–59 for the Left Toe.

36. At frame 36, raise the right foot up using the Bend parameter, and zero out the bend on frame 41.

37. On frame 46, bend the left foot and toe so the toe touches the stair as the heel lifts off. Release the toe bend on frame 48. On frame 51, bend the left foot up to clear the front of the stair. Grab the foot at the extreme deviation point, and drag it up. Open the Graph Editor for the yTran. Again, you can see the problem in the double peaks. It may be tempting to simply click on the keyframe and drag it, but it's very risky to do this in the Graph Editor because you could inadvertently create a new keyframe right next to it. The safer thing to do is to use the Previous Key button and then raise that parameter. You can raise it directly in the Graph Editor, as well as in the dial on the parameter controls. The Graph Editor is also necessary in character animation

because you could very easily add keyframes in between keyframes when tweaking your animation and not realize it. And, the Graph Editor lets you adjust the relationship between the keyframes that you placed and the ones you didn't, so that the end result is a smooth animation.

38. Zoom out to look at what you've done so far. The animation is now complete. You can look at it from the Main Camera as well.

To recap, you simply imported some steps, created a walk cycle of a figure, translated the walk cycle across the scaled down steps, set the scale of the steps back to 100%, and key framed the elevation change of the figure to those steps. You fine-tuned the bend and elevation of the feet so that they were posed and placed appropriately.

Walking up stairs is not such a difficult thing if you can just master these basic steps of the process. It's something that becomes fairly obvious as you do it two and three times, and then you can apply it to your projects at will. However, in the beginning, it's crucial that you understand why you've done each step that you used in this process.

Now you'll create the animation of the figure walking down the stairs. The workflow is similar to that of walking up, with just a few inverted differences.

WALKING DOWN STAIRS

ON THE DVD

1. Open the WalkDown Stairs-Step-1.pz3 project file in the Chapter 5 Exercise Files folder. You will create an animation project of the figure walking down the stairs based on the walk cycle you created for walking up the stairs. We've simply removed all the translation of the body so that the figure will walk in place when you begin.

2. Look at the keyframes for SimonG2/Body. There's only one keyframe set for the body: frame 1. That's very important for what we do next. You want to be sure that while you're on frame 1, you turn the figure around. So, with SimonG2/Body selected, go to the yRotate, and set it to 180 degrees. Translate it back in the zTran until the right foot is on the fourth step (see Figure 5.20).

FIGURE 5.20
Simon rotated and moved back in line with step 4.

3. After he's situated on the fourth step, translate on the y-axis to bring him upward until he's standing on top of the stair step. To get him onto that fourth step, instead of elevating the entire body, elevate the body so the left foot is on the third step (see Figure 5.21). Then move the right foot onto the fourth step using the yTran because, as you can see, the left foot is leading (it's in the front), which means that's the foot that is on the lower step as shown in Figure 5.21.

FIGURE 5.21
Simon positioned on the steps.

4. Move forward to frame 15. You now want to maintain the position of the left foot to be on the third step. To do that, select the Body, and translate forward on the z-axis. Again, you're not going to do anything with the hips on this because it would cause a great amount of stretching in the legs. Scrub through frames 1 through 15, to see what you've done so far.

5. You now need the left foot to stay in place and the right foot to go down. The appropriate thing to do is to bring the entire body down because, as you may remember, the body is a container for the figure. Therefore, select the Body, and use the yTran to bring the entire figure down. Then select the left foot, and use the yTran to lift it back up to the step above. There will be a lot of unnatural bending at this time, which is fine because at this step in the process for the animation, you're simply getting the placement of the feet (see Figure 5.22).

FIGURE 5.22
Placing Simon's feet in position at frame 15.

6. Go to frame 30. Make sure you have the Body selected when you do these translations in the z-axis, rather than having one of the feet selected, which would cause a stretching in your animation. Use the zTran and yTran to move the figure's body forward to the bottom step, then with the Right Foot selected, raise it up to the step above using the yTran.

7. Go to frame 44. With the Body selected, translate forward on the z-axis, and then down on the y-axis. Select the Left Foot, and lift it to the top of the first step using the yTran.

8. For the last frame, just advance Simon's body so that both feet are off the steps. You now have a very crude animation of the figure walking down the steps as seen in Figure 5.23.

FIGURE 5.23
Simon depicted at the final frame.

9. Now it's time to go in there and make some adjustments, particularly to the feet. Start on frame 1, and zoom in to get a better view of your adjustments. Select the Right Foot. Transform it upward, bend the foot downward until the toes go through the stair, and then bend the toe upward. This is how the figure will start. By frame 4, the foot is starting to penetrate the step, so drag the foot up further to clear the step. Then release the bend from the toe.

10. On frame 11, the foot goes through the next step. So drag the foot up to clear that step. Here you will need to look at the graph because we can see there's a bit of an unnatural movement that causes the foot to bounce on the air. You'll want to look at the yTran, so select the yTran first and *then* open the Graph Editor to make the yTran the active channel. You can see that the problem is a dip in the curve that is coming down and has some hang time delay that's not needed. So, select keyframe 8, and bring it up to get rid of the hang time delay.

11. Close the Graph Editor, and take another look at the animation. There's still a little bit of hang time, so open the Graph Editor again. This time, select keyframe 11, and bring it down a little bit. You may also need to bring keyframe 7 up slightly to further even out the curve. (If you have a dual monitor, you can leave the Graph Editor open on your right monitor.) The hang time has now been removed, so that's fixed.

12. When you get to frame 15, and the right foot is planted, the left foot needs to be adjusted. Lift the left foot, bend it downward, and then bend the toe as shown in Figure 5.24. Here, let's also check something else. Go back to frame 1. You may see that the left foot is really at the edge of that step, so at frame 15, let's also make sure that even though you've bent it, that you also go back and put it back where the toe was to prevent foot slippage.

FIGURE 5.24
Adjustment of toe bend at frame 15.

13. Depending on the project you're in, you may need to keep a close eye on this, or if there are just a couple seconds and you can't clearly see where his feet are, you might be able to get away with it. Just be aware that it's easy to correct the foot slipping in these kinds of animation.

14. Continue forward. Around frame 27, you can see that the left foot is a little bit too close to the step, so go ahead and drag that left foot out to clear the step. Frame 30 is the next point where you will lift the right foot up, bend the foot down, and bend the toe upward. Make sure the toe is at the edge of the stair after it's bent. Scrub forward. There's obviously a bit more work to be done here because the right foot goes straight through the stair. Start by removing the bend on the toe. Let's also verify that we have the bend from the left toe removed on frame 18. On frame 34, lift the right foot up to clear the stair.

15. To correct the weird action going on here, you need to go into the Graph Editor. You want to look at the y-axis for the right foot. It's ending at the right place, but how it's getting there is too radical. You can adjust keyframe 37 upward. As you take it forward, introduce another keyframe at frame 40. The curve will need some work, but for now, you just want to get the foot out of the step. Adjust keyframe 37 upward again to smooth out the curve. Also, take a look at the Bend channel. The bend is set on frame 30. Introduce another keyframe at frame 40 to get that bend a little higher up.

16. Go back to the yTran channel. The dip on frame 37 is really showing up visually on the graph. It's going down when it should be going up, so adjust that point upward, smoothing out the top of the curve. Another channel you need to pay attention to is the zTran. As you can see, keyframe 36 is too low as well. Adjust this point by raising it up to create a straight line between the keyframes before and after it (see Figure 5.25). One of the strong values of the Graph Editor is that you can visually relate to the animation problem on a channel level. Now the foot clears the stair perfectly.

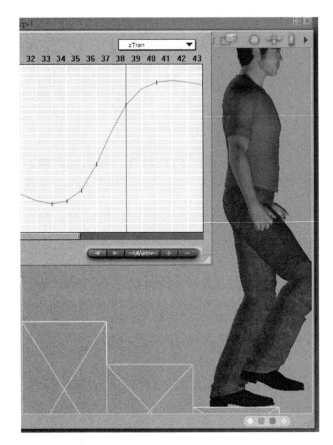

FIGURE 5.25
Adjusting the zTran in the Graph Editor.

It's going to be common to run into such problems in animation, especially when you get to free-form animation, such as fight scenes, dances, or very strong levels of expression, where you have gestures, so you need to be very familiar with your Graph Editor.

17. Correct the foot going through the bottom step by dragging it clear. On frame 44, lift the left foot, and set the bend on the foot and toe. Translate the toe forward to the edge of the stair to prevent foot slipping. On frame 47, remove the bend from the toe. Looks like there's some bend left in the right foot as well, so go back to where it lifts off on frame 34, and set the toe bend value to 0.

18. Open the Keyframes Editor, and set all keyframes for the toes of both feet to be linear. It will help to get rid of some of that floppy type motion. Scrub through the animation to check the current result.

19. Now you will work with the hip. Start by going to frame 7, which is the crossover point. You can see that this is the point where the hip should be a little bit higher. With the Hip selected, translate in the yTran to bring the hip up. Copy the yTran value, and paste it into the yTran on frame 23, which is the next crossover point, as well as on frame 36 and frame 52. On frame 52, when he's come down to the floor, notice what's happening to his right foot. The hip is actually a little too high here, causing the foot to not land squarely on the floor. Adjust the yTran visually here, rather than numerically.

Because he is stepping onto the floor and both feet will be at the same level, the value for the hip is set differently from the previous steps.

NOTE

20. Look at the result in the Main Camera. Select the Stairs/Figure 2. From the Display menu, select Figure Style/Document Style, to set the display of the stairs to the same as the document. Play back the animation to view the result as shown in Figure 5.26.

FIGURE 5.26
View of Simon going down the stairs from the Main View.

That's the workflow for creating character animation of a character walking down the stairs. Now you can see how walking up and walking down is basically a modification of a standard walk cycle, in which you treat the figure as though it's a body container, and you adjust the elevation of the body container. You then adjust the placement and bend of the feet and the toes and appropriately adjust the y-axis elevation of the hip at the crossover point.

OBJECT AVOIDANCE

Now you will create obstacle-avoidance character animation. This is where you take transformed walk cycles and adjust the 3D characters to not collide with objects in the scene.

When you're creating 3D story telling with walking characters, they won't always walk in a straight line. If your scene has a character walking down a hallway, the door at the end may not be directly in the center of the line of sight. It may be off to the side, or you may have a piece of furniture that you must navigate around to get to this door. Or, a pipe may be in your way that you must crouch under. All of these are examples of object avoidance.

We're going to look at how you modify transformed walk cycles to deal with object avoidance. Object avoidance animation can basically be broken down into three steps.

1. Build the obstacle scene by working with whatever 3D application you'll be using to lay out your 3D scene or by adding props within Poser to create your scene.
2. Merge the transformed walk cycle with the obstacle scene. Without this, there is no way to realistically keyframe or animate where the character should adjust to avoid contact.
3. Adjust the transformed walk cycle to avoid the scene obstacles. A few different techniques will be required to accomplish the realistic sense that the character is avoiding the obstacles.

In this tutorial, you will work with project files. These break down the process into five distinct areas, so you can check your work with milestones that allow you to track your progress.

ON THE DVD

1. Start by loading the first step, which is Object_Avoidance_Step 1.pz3 from the Chapter 5 folder in the Exercise Folder. It has a walking character and two simple obstacles. If you look at this from the Main Camera, you can see

there's a bar coming across, which the character will need to duck under. There is also a large cylinder in the walk path that the character will have to avoid and walk around (see Figure 5.27).

2. If you were to play this animation back, you would see that currently, it's like some kind of terminator character, or ghost, who just walks through everything. This is simply the starting point. Here you have the walk cycle merged with the props. Because these are just simple Poser props, you can quite easily create these on your own.

3. Now you need to create some special keyframes for avoiding this first barrier. From the Right View, the bar obstacle requires the 3D animated character to duck down.

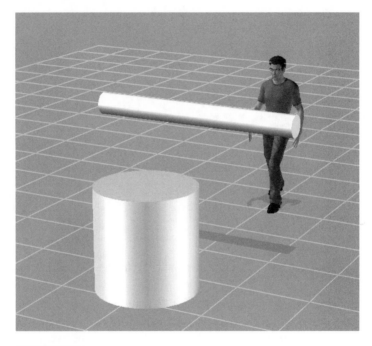

FIGURE 5.27
Simon will need to avoid these obstacles.

ON THE DVD

4. Working with the file Object_Avoidance_Step 2 - 1st obst Cleared rough.pz3, you'll be looking at the next steps in this process. Open the Keyframes Editor. As the character goes through the timeline, on frame 20 (which needs to be for our crossover), some keyframes seem to have almost no purpose. If you look at this in the Right Camera View, on frame 20, before you can actually bring the figure down, you're setting some keyframes to hold it in place. These keyframes are called barrier keyframes.

5. The character appears to be pulling a bit unnaturally (see Figure 5.28), which is something you'll be tweaking in the next steps, but the main purpose of those barrier keyframes is to prevent the action of avoiding the obstacle from starting too early, or, in other cases, from ending too late. So, you select the actors of the animated character that will be animated to avoid the obstacle. Then you set barrier keyframes for them before they will be animated and after they're animated. Of course, to avoid the obstacle, it's a matter of setting keyframes for the appropriate actors.

FIGURE 5.28
Simon at the point where the barrier keyframes are set on frame 20.

In this case, we animated the hip to bring the figure lower to the floor (because his entire body must duck), selected the abdomen, and we adjusted the bend of the abdomen. We also adjust the bend of the waist, and we adjust the neck. This is based on your story needs and also somewhat based on what people would realistically do. When you're bending under a pipe, if you're running for your life, you may not want your face looking down toward the floor, you may be looking ahead at your next challenge, or you may be looking back to see who's chasing you. This bending of the neck is really based on your story-telling needs. However, the waist, abdomen, and hip are based on the physical demands of the obstacle that you're going through. This is all assuming that we're discussing going through an obstacle of this nature, which is something you must crouch under.

Now we have transformed the walk by editing only the hip, the waist, the abdomen, and the neck. From this point forward, we're back to our regular animation, and as you can see, he simply walks through the next obstacle. If you look at this from the Main Camera, you can see he really does simply walk through it. There's no avoidance as of yet.

ON THE DVD

1. Open the next project, Object_Avoidance_Step 3 - 1st obst Cleared.pz3.
2. We're now looking at two things. First, we were at 117 frames until now. We're now at 125 frames because the time it takes to walk past this obstacle required him to slow down, so his body could realistically go through the motion of crouching. Without increasing the time, he would appear to unrealistically go through this obstacle too fast. To deal with this, rather than having the keyframe immediately after the first obstacle end on frame 30, the keyframe was dragged to frame 37, which is a key pose. So he's slowing down coming into this because he has to be careful not to hit his head. Then, we simply selected all the frames from frame 30 and pulled them back to frame 37, and then we could adjust where these frames exist, from being much earlier, to being much later. This is all a part of the slowing down to do something that is a bit more challenging and dangerous, which is to avoid this pipe overhead (see Figure 5.29).

FIGURE 5.29
Simon at frame 30 ducking under the bar.

Object avoidance animation is an iterative process. You have to animate, go back, and then look and tweak more. You have to go back and forth a bit. The guiding light of how much is enough will be the style of animation you're doing and your deadline. But be prepared to have to go over the animation you've done, as things adjust in the animation sequence before and after the place you've animated.

3. Continue by opening the next step, which is Object_Avoidance_Step 4 - 2nd obst Cleared.pz3. Here we'll look at the second obstacle—the large cylinder being cleared. You have a different set of challenges to deal with in the second obstacle.

4. One of the issues you'll run into with object avoidance animation is that sometimes, to be able to animate the characters (feet in particular), you'll need to change the display mode of some of the obstacles. So here, as the character tries to walk past the cylinder, it's very difficult to select the character's feet in the Right View. If your obstacle is set for the Figure Style, this becomes a bit difficult. Although it's still possible to select the figure's feet, as you can see from the outlining, it's a bit difficult, visually, to really get there. In that case, you may want to set the Element Style to Outline so you can be confident about not only what you're selecting but also where it is landing in the animation process.

5. Switch to the Top View. As you exit the first obstacle and start to plan for the second obstacle, there are a few things you have to accomplish. First, the body must start to rotate, which becomes interesting because in previous animations we would use the Figure/Body to transform the body. In this case, we don't do that because we would lose our ability to grip the floor. It would actually create the need for additional workflow steps to grip the floor. Therefore, rather than having to deal with creating an additional workload for gripping the floor, you can adjust the Hip instead (see Figure 5.30). Adjusting the hip then makes the body start to act more like a rag doll. The body is a container for the entire character. Adjusting the hip is interactive with the rest of the character's limbs, or actors.

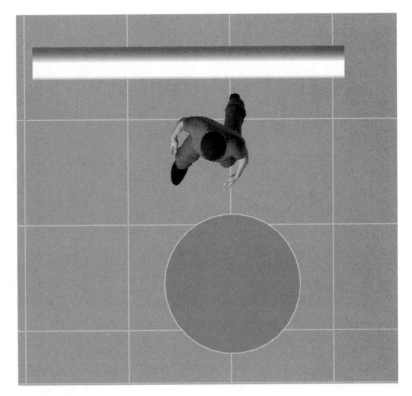

FIGURE 5.30
The beginning of adjusting Simon's hip at frame 57.

6. Also, we'll have to start thinking about the fact that we're clearing the first obstacle, so where does the foot land in preparation for the second obstacle? Originally, it would land going straight ahead. But if we were to avoid this obstacle, even from our very first step coming out, we need to be planning to walk around the obstacle. Therefore, the foot is planted more to the character's right, and as we go forward, we can see that the foot is also pivoting (on the heel) to turn. In addition to that pivot, we also have the rotation of the hip coming into play, so he's able to start making his avoidance.

7. During the process of animating object avoidance, the character may penetrate part of the obstacle. This is part of the process you'll be tweaking as you go through your iterations of the animation.

8. Here again, as Simon has gone by the first quarter of the cylinder, we're rotating the hip to get him back into the correct orientation going around the obstacle. Foot slipping becomes an interesting challenge in this kind of animation because if you simply transform a walk cycle—which is already

transformed linearly, going straight—but you transform it now to avoid an obstacle, the length of the steps will actually increase. And, as the length of the steps increase, you can have foot slippage on both feet. Therefore, pay close attention to this in both the Front View and Right View shown in Figure 5.31.

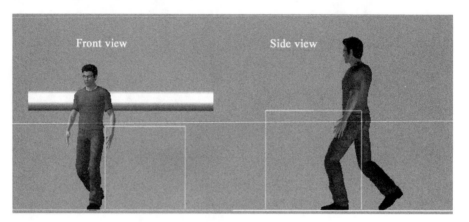

FIGURE 5.31
One quarter of the way around the second obstacle from both views.

9. In the Right Camera View, zoom in, and select the Right Foot. As you can see, it is slipping. Even though the original transformed walk cycle was not slipping, you will see new slipping introduced as you deal with obstacle avoidance. Rather than using the block technique, which can become a bit of a pain in this kind of animation and can have absolutely spontaneous path orientation, you'll want to use more analog, hands-on techniques.

10. My favorite technique is to put your hand to the screen and use your fingers as a reference for the posing of the foot. Go back and forth between the keyframes of that foot, and use your fingers as a reference of where the foot should be. Then use the Object/Properties parameters to adjust the placement of the foot. In this case, adjust the z parameter because that's all you can be really sure of in the Right View.

11. Switch to the Front View, and basically do the same thing. Go back to the previous key. As you go back and forth between these keys, the foot is not necessarily moving in the wrong way, but it is rotating and pivoting, which is fine. Our key reference here becomes the heel of the foot. Where is the heel? Is it moving to the right or the left?

12. Let's do a final check in the Main Camera View. You can see that the foot is planted. It's just simply pivoting. So, by using the technique with your fingers to the screen, on the Front View and Right View, you can get a quick workflow (see Figure 5.32).

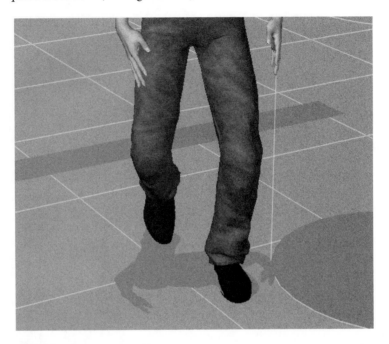

FIGURE 5.32
Adjusting Simon's foot from the Main View.

One of the reasons I mention things like using your fingers on the screen is that character animation can become quite tedious. You can have a sequence of having a character walk for 30 seconds. How many blocks are you going to create to make this character animation not have foot slipping? Using your fingers, creatively, on your screen as a reference can really speed up your workflow and engage you in your character animation work. As we continue the character animation, you'll see there are several places where the foot slipping needs to be corrected.

13. Open up Object_Avoidance_Step 5 - Camera & hands.pz3. Here the second part of the object avoidance has been tweaked. The foot slipping has been addressed, as well as some creative camera work as shown in Figure 5.33. It's not just a matter of being fancy and telling a story. Sometimes, you'll have to create camera work specifically to make sure you can see the

character as it's walking past all the obstacles, to check for errors, or to check for the obstacle objects intersecting with the character, to check for foot slipping, and so on. Sometimes, you may even need to put a texture on the floor.

FIGURE 5.33
Viewing the second part of the object avoidance.

14. Set the playback to Fast mode to view the animation. Bear in mind, even though you see some overlap right here, this is a bounding box of a cylinder, which means it's really not going through the cylinder at all.

This is a technique of object avoidance that you really should master and not just because your stories may call for it. If you're fortunate enough to get to work in 3D animation and get paid, you should be prepared that your customers may require very common things like object avoidance animation.

SUMMARY

After learning how and where to apply both the pose-to-pose and straight ahead animation methods (principles) in this chapter, it's essential that you see the increased creative power available to you by using these methods to create animation rather than simply using Poser's built-in Walk Designer.

Additionally, a great benefit of mastering these animation techniques is that you can easily adapt them to any major 3D application to animate characters there. Although the specific workflow steps such as how to edit and move keyframes or how you pose characters may be localized to the particular 3D application's methodology and style, character animation is character animation—no matter what application you use.

6 Lifting and Throwing

In This Chapter

INTRODUCTION

Creating lifelike 3D animation isn't the easiest thing to master because after you understand the principles involved and how to apply them, you must also become an astute student of human behavior and motion. Behavior is important because it drives motion. The projects that we'll go through in this chapter combine many of the principles of animation to create the illusion of human motion.

LIFTING

Now let's look at how to create the character animation of Simon lifting a heavy cylinder. Unlike when we animated walk cycles, we won't be using any pose-to-pose animation (having the extreme poses and the in-between poses set); instead, we'll be using straight-ahead animation. In straight-ahead animation, you animate simply by moving forward through your timeline and posing your character as the character needs to be for that point in time, and you don't have a beginning, middle, and end predefined.

Straight-ahead animation gives you greater spontaneous creativity; however, it does require a thorough understanding of the biomechanics involved. You should have fun with this because understanding how to do this kind of character animation helps you understand how to animate the character doing practically anything.

We'll look at the issues of weight, for example, the weight of the object, and how the weight affects the animation of the character. And in this expression of weight, we'll consider how a human would respond to a related weight. We'll also be looking at balance, between the object and the character. By balance, we mean that as the character has to lift an object of a certain weight, the body must balance itself, distributing that weight between the object being lifted and the weight of the body. You'll see from different points in the animation, the torso, the hips, and the legs will be balanced accordingly with the cylinder, based on its mass.

We'll also look at timing, overlapping motion, anticipation, and follow through, as well as how these principles are used in this kind of animation. We'll also pay attention to some small details that really help sell the illusion of the animation of lifting. This illusion improves the *appeal* of the animation, which is yet another important principle of animation.

The animation should convey effort, on the part of the 3D character, just as you would see effort from a real person. We need to make sure that it's not a Styrofoam object with no effort and no mental forethought going into the lifting. Simon must appear to really put an effort into lifting this cylinder. Mastering this kind of detail will help you make your animation projects come across in a way that can actually be felt by the people watching them.

Conveying weight is not just a matter of keyframing animation, but rather you should think of it as an actor on a stage. So if you have an actor in theatre, and the actor is lifting a prop, the prop is supposed to be heavy. In reality, the prop is actually quite light and probably made of some papier-mâché or Styrofoam, but the actor has to convey that he's lifting a heavy weight, through his own effort. We'll be doing the same thing with Simon.

In addition to what you'll do in this tutorial, when you want to demonstrate weight of the object being lifted, you need to follow through by adding the appropriate textures and image maps to convey that the object really is a heavy object.

Simon will lift this heavy, cylindrical object onto a shelf. To keep the view unobstructed, we won't start with the shelf in the scene. We'll work with several saved projects, which you can access from the DVD-ROM accompanying your book.

ON THE DVD

The projects are saved in 14 files that increment in levels of completion. A few projects are actually on the same frame, but they demonstrate some additional animation that is broken into separate projects. The successive saves, for example, from one step to the next step, could contain updates or tweaks in the later step to things done in the preceding step. This kind of recursive workflow is at times common when animating a character. As you go forward with the animation, you'll need to go back and make some minor adjustments to actors who have been previously animated.

NOTE

Actor is the Poser term for a body part.

To begin this animation project, follow these steps:

ON THE DVD

1. Load the Lift Step 01.pz3 project from the Chapter 6 exercise files. Here we see Simon in his default pose, before lifting, as he stands behind the heavy cylinder on the floor in front of him (see Figure 6.1). We're going to create a little bit of anticipation. Begin by going to frame 15. You will bend his knees, and then slump and center Simon over the cylinder, so he faces the cylinder.

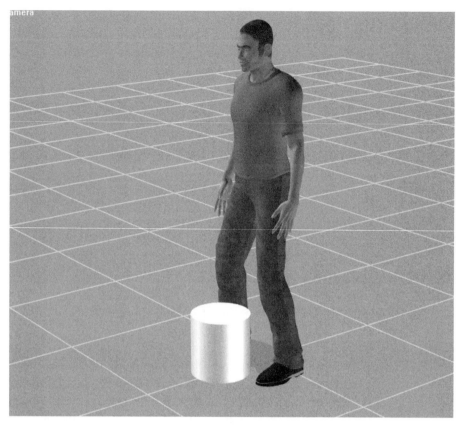

FIGURE 6.1
Simon stands behind the heavy cylinder.

2. Switch to the Right Camera view. First, bring his hip and his hands down. Make sure you have the Figure/Use Inverse Kinetics on for both legs and both hands.

3. Adjust the abdomen and the chest so they are slumped forward. In the parameter dials, with the Abdomen selected, adjust the Bend to 21. Select the Chest and Bend it as well (to 14). Select the Neck and Bend the neck down to 10 for the face to face the cylinder. Also Bend the Head to 16. It's very important that you distribute the slumping of the body throughout elements along the spine, rather than limiting it to a single body part, so that it appears as a *person* actually slumping and not just an object bending.

4. Go back to the hands again, and position them forward and down toward the cylinder (see Figure 6.2). It's important to make sure the hand parts are locked (Figure/Lock hand parts), so you don't get the "crazy finger syndrome" where his fingers start doing wild and uncontrollable things.

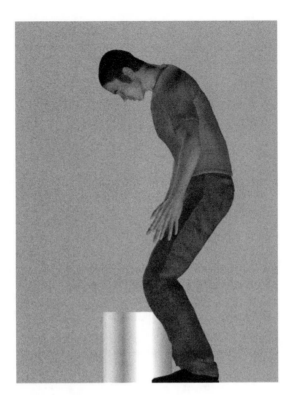

FIGURE 6.2
Simon stands slumped over the cylinder.

5. Depending on how much difficulty you experience when posing the arms (e.g., the body gets too twisted or bent), when you're posing a character in this scenario, adding some chain breaks can be very helpful. For example, looking at this from the front view, if you have a situation where pulling the arms down causes the body to move left or right, you can add chain breaks (on the shoulders and hip) as shown in Figure 6.3, so that when you pull the arms down, it doesn't cause the body to slump toward the side that the arm is on. If you do use chain breaks, you may want to turn them off when you're done with them by choosing the Chain Break icon and clicking on the added chain breaks.

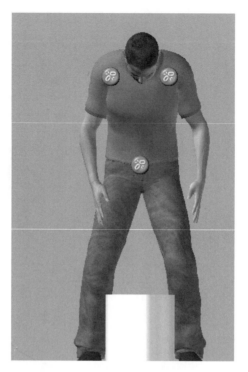

FIGURE 6.3
Chain Breaks are added for posing stability.

6. Switch back to the Right Camera view. All we're doing here is showing him anticipating the lift. He's not really lifting yet. Scroll through your animation, from frame 1 to frame 15, to see what you have so far.

7. Go to frame 30. On frame 30, Simon will crouch down, and his hands will hold the top of the cylinder. His knees will spread apart, his arms will be fully extended, his torso will bend over the cylinder, and his head will be facing the cylinder (see Figure 6.4). This is where he goes from anticipation to action.

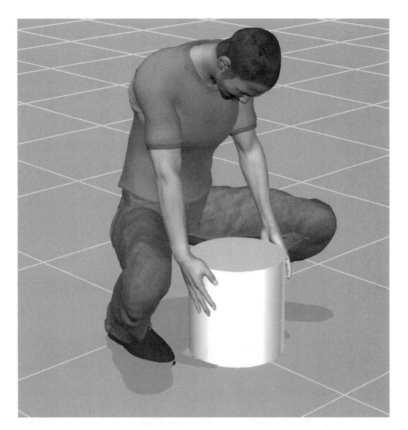

FIGURE 6.4
Simon crouches down with his hands on top of the cylinder.

8. Bring his Hip down until he's in a crouching position. Bring his hands down as well. When they're fully extended, much of the crease of the elbow will be eliminated. Remember that when working in the Right View, you can still use your hinting. Even though the right hand is on the other side of Simon, you can use Poser's natural hinted outline feature to know where to select the hand. As you can see, through the animation of this action of lifting, it's beneficial to leave IK on for the duration of this animation, rather than trying to use FK (which is the forward kinematics of adjusting each of the actor's arms).

9. Switch over to the Main Camera, and zoom in for a closer look. We have a couple of problems here. His hands are not really on the cylinder, and his knees are in the cylinder. Take his knees out by dragging the thighs outward until they clear the cylinder. If you try to use the parameter dials, you'll be there all day, so it's much more effective, in this case, to just go

ahead and drag the body part into position. Next, drag and place the hands around the cylinder with the thumbs on top.

10. You may have a couple of problems with the hands if they penetrate the cylinder and the arms if they penetrate the legs. So, go ahead and move the legs out, until they clear the arms. To adjust the hands, use the Hand Cam to get a better sense of what's going on. Starting with the Left Hand Camera, move the hand forward a little. Then, to pose the hand, adjust the Bend and Twist parameter dials. Make sure that the thumb is not going through the cylinder. You'll need to constantly adjust your view to check for problems. You don't need the hand to make a perfect grasp on the cylinder, but you want to get the illusion that he is lifting the cylinder with his hands. When you're ready with the left hand, switch to the Right Hand Camera and make the same adjustments so that your figure is now posed as shown in Figure 6.5.

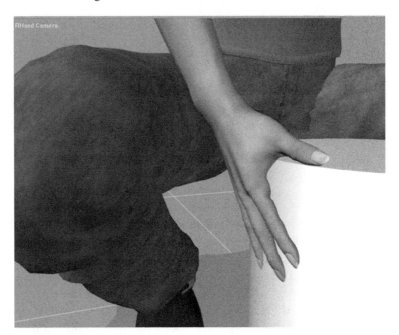

FIGURE 6.5
The right hand posed to hold the cylinder from the top.

11. In addition to the positioning and orienting of the hand, you can also add things such as Grasp adjustments in the Advanced Hand Controls parameter, which can help the fingers better hold the cylinder.

12. Switch back to the Main Camera, and go through the animation to see that so far, you have anticipation and Simon bending down and holding the cylinder.

13. Now, on frame 45, Simon crouches down some more, spreads his knees more, and bends his arms sharply at the elbows. This is all part of the anticipation that demonstrates the amount of energy and effort that Simon must make to lift this heavy cylinder. And so, because his arms are fully extended on frame 30, for him to get this heavy cylinder off the floor, he's going to have to really apply more muscles in a way that gives him better leverage. His leverage is not maximized when his arms are extended, so he bends his elbows to apply more pressure in his palms to the cylinder.

14. Switch to the Right Camera, center, and zoom in for a good view. His torso needs to bend down more. This also gives you room in the arms for the elbows to come out. Bring his hips down a little bit more, apply some Bend to his Waist, Abdomen and Chest, and bring his Neck slightly up.

We're taking the training wheels off here so that you can pose your Poser character to match the project. The inserted figure images and saved project files will provide additional guidance if needed.

15. Now work from the Main Camera. You can see that by simply bending his torso, you've created the bend in the elbows because of the IK in the arms. The legs are going through his arms again, however, so grab those and move them out. Orbit around to check the other leg as well. Usually (in a symmetrical animation such as this), if one leg is penetrating an arm in this kind of animation, the other leg is doing the same.

It is absolutely critical to keep track of which frame you are on in the animation. You'll want to kick yourself if you haven't advanced your frame appropriately, so keep a close eye on that.

16. Simon seems like he's in pretty good order now, for this step in the process. Go ahead and review what you have so far by scrolling through your timeline. Your work should now look like Figure 6.6.

FIGURE 6.6
Simon's ready for some heavy lifting.

17. Go to frame 60. On frame 60, Simon will start to stand up by raising his hips, his knees will bend less than they're bent right now, and his knees will also spread a bit less. His arms will fully extend, and his torso will be less slumped over the cylinder as he will start to balance his weight distribution between the cylinder and his body.

18. Again, be sure that you've moved to frame 60, and select the Right View Camera. Raise his Hip up until the hands are dangling just above the cylinder. Then, bring the cylinder up as well. It will be important to go back a few frames and set a keyframe for the cylinder because it hasn't had any keyframes set so far. This will prevent it from starting to rise before you want it to. Select the cylinder, go back to frame 45, and set a keyframe. Then, go back to frame 60. Here on frame 60, you'll start to raise the cylinder. You'll do this with the parameter dials because you just want to move in the y-axis—you don't want to create any additional motion in the x-axis and z-axis.

19. Next, adjust the arms by using the yTran to take them (both) up a little, so they're not sliding down so far relative to where they were before on the cylinder. (You may find you have better control doing this move in the Main Camera view. If we were to move it manually in the Main Camera view, you may be moving it in the x-, y- or z-axis, which gets a bit unwieldy.) As you see, it may take a while for the IK to agree to move.

20. You also need to bring the knees in because that extreme spread was only needed when he was crouched all the way down. Bring them back in to where they would reasonably be at this stage in the lift (as shown in Figure 6.7). Continue to make sure the legs are not intersecting the arms or the cylinder. Double-check it in the Right Camera view again.

21. Start to raise the head because he's basically gaining confidence that he has this under control and is starting to look up to look forward. As you drag through the animation so far, you see that the cylinder is doing its "going-through-the-floor" thing, so you need a linear key (shown in Figure 6.8). With the cylinder selected, open the Keyframes Editor, and set the linear key on frame 45. Now the cylinder no longer goes through the floor.

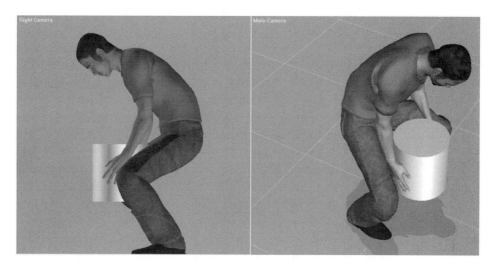

FIGURE 6.7
Simon's lifting the cylinder now.

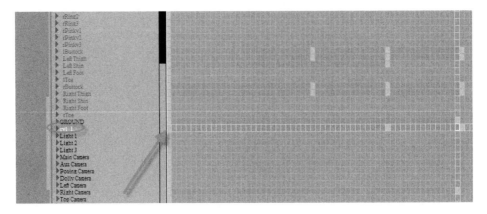

FIGURE 6.8
Linear key set to keep the cylinder from sliding through the floor.

22. To compare your progress so far to the related saved step in the exercise folder, save your work, and load Lift Step 05.pz3 (refer to Figure 6.7) to take a look at where you are in the animation. Compare that to what you've done, make adjustments, and, if needed, review the previous steps just to make sure you understand the principles we're going over.

23. Now we're going to animate on frame 75 (refer to Figure 6.7). Here Simon is going to stand a little higher, raising his hip. His knees will still be bent and spread. His arms will fully extend, but he'll be holding the cylinder out, away from his body. His torso will be straightened and pulled back, away from the cylinder, as he counterbalances his weight—distributing the weight between the cylinder and his body—and his head will start to lift and face forward, past the cylinder.

24. Begin by looking at the Right Camera view. Raise his Hip. I'm not telling you specific numerical values here because it's more important that you learn the flow and the principles than that you memorize parameters. When it's your character and your story, you'll use your own parameters.

25. Now you need to straighten out that torso by working up the chain of the torso and relaxing those bends a bit. First, relax the Bend in the waist, then the Abdomen, and then the Chest. You can see how that naturally brings the arms up and away from the body. Then, raise the cylinder using the yTran, and move it on the z-axis (zTran) away from the body (positioning it between his hands in his current position).

26. Let's look at the Main Camera. If the cylinder goes through one of the hands, the easy solution is to adjust the xTran of the cylinder to move it into place. Because of the animation of the hip, Simon's center of mass can shift during the process, giving you these slight deviations that cause you to

need to adjust the object being lifted. If your story requires the primary focus to be on the exact position of the object—that specific axis, let's say the character is lifting a ring off of a shaft, then you obviously can't adjust the ring in the x-axis—you'd have to adjust the entire character instead. Scroll through your animation, in Fast Tracking mode, to see what you have so far.

27. Now, still on frame 75, you need to raise Simon's right foot and move it back to place it at the crossover point at this particular frame. Here Simon is beginning to adjust his pose to compensate for the heavy weight of the cylinder. Just like when you lift something heavy, you'll often have to steady yourself by taking a step back to accommodate the additional weight. This is part of the distribution and balance of the combined weight of the person lifting and the object being lifted.

28. Select Simon's Right Foot, and move it back with the zTran. Then, from the Right Camera view, you can pose it more easily. We moved it first in the Main Camera, with the parameter dial, just so we can distinguish the right foot from the left in the Right Camera view. Now we're looking at choosing the crossover point.

29. You'll notice a problem with his foot, just like with the cylinder, in that it's rising from the very beginning. For the cylinder, we created a keyframe before the keyframe when the cylinder was up; however, in this case, we've already created that keyframe for the foot rising up, so you can go to Edit Keyframes and select the Right Foot. Go to frame 1, hold down the Alt key, drag a keyframe over to frame 60, and then make that keyframe linear. Close the Keyframes Editor, and look at the animation again. Now his foot stays on the floor until you need it to get up.

Linear keys are incredible solutions for these issues, but a linear key needs an actual keyframe to make linear. So we had to drag a keyframe out, from frame 1 to frame 60, because the keyframe on frame 1 contained the position information for the right foot, which would be needed on frame 60 before it began to rise up to frame 75.

30. Go to frame 90. Simon stands almost to his full height here, with a little bend in his knees, to communicate the heavy weight of the cylinder. His arms are bent at the elbows, holding the cylinder closer to his body. His torso is straightened.

31. Begin in the Right Camera view. Lift his hands and his hips, starting with the Hip. Also, bring his Right Foot down to complete his step backward. Then, drag his hands up. Because we're in the Right Camera view, we don't risk taking them away from the cylinder.

32. Next, bring the cylinder up. Scrub through your animation to see what's happening so far. Your project should now look like Figure 6.9. This is a good point to save you work and compare it to Lift Step 08.pz3 in the Chapter 6 exercise files on the DVD-ROM.

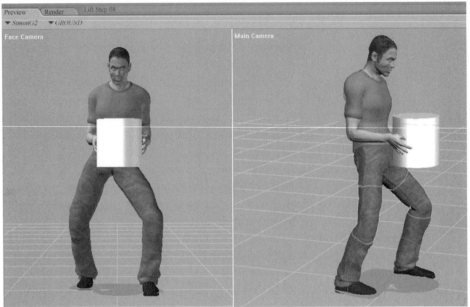

FIGURE 6.9
Simon now at the midpoint of the lift.

33. Now you'll be animating on frame 105. To place the cylinder on a shelf, Simon must raise his left foot and have his left thigh support the cylinder, so that his hands can move to hold the cylinder from below. This gives him better leverage and control of the heavy cylinder, as he raises it up onto the shelf. This is a regular stabilizing move that people often do when lifting heavy items, and conveying such familiar biomechanics makes it easier to sell the illusion of this animation.

34. Look at this in the Right Camera view. His left thigh is going to come up, so start by lifting his left foot and then lift the cylinder to match. Tip that cylinder a little by rotating it 10 degrees in the xRotate parameter. Bring the foot down to match the current angle of the cylinder.

35. Look at it from the Main Camera, and then bring the left leg in to be under the cylinder. Bring the left foot in as well.

36. Go back to the Right Camera view. Now, adjust the hands to hold the cylinder from below by dragging the hands down. Use the Hand Cams to get this right. Use the zTran dial to make sure the hand is at the z center of the left side of the bottom of the cylinder. Your left hand should now be posed as shown in Figure 6.10.

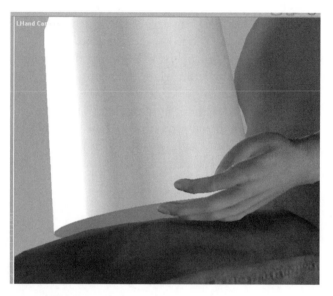

FIGURE 6.10
Left hand posed for frame 105.

37. Twist the forearm, and then the hand, so that the hand can support the cylinder from beneath.
38. At this point, you will start controlling individual fingers, starting with the thumb. We're just looking at the individual bends, so that the fingers can make contact.

NOTE

This part of the work can be a bit laborious. How much of an intimate detailed view you'll have of the hand on the cylinder, or whatever object your character is lifting, determines the level of effort and detail you'll want to apply here. But here, you can control each finger, making sure each makes contact.

39. In the Right Hand Camera, do the same on the right hand (as you previously did to the left). Again, apply a bit of a Twist to the forearm, so that when the hand is twisted, it won't seem unnatural. Adjust the zTran of the right hand to get it under the cylinder. Again, in the individual finger controls, start by applying a Grasp, and then fine-tune each of the fingers. You

might also want to get into the spread of the fingers, using the Finger Spread parameters, because this can have an interactive impact with the bending and grasping.

40. As you scrub through the timeline, you can see that, again, that right foot is coming up too early. (This will be more obvious from the Right View.) It's coming up so early that at one point Simon is magically in the air. You want it to be up at frame 105, and it's coming up all the way through, so that means you need to drag a keyframe.

41. Select the Left Foot, open the Keyframes Editor, hold down the Alt key, and drag a keyframe from frame 1 to frame 90. When you can't see all the frames, just release the keyframe anywhere, drag, and then left-click to drag it to frame 90 (without holding the Alt key down). Then, make it a linear key. Now, when you scrub through the timeline, you can see the foot stays on the floor and comes up only when you need it. Your pose should now look like Figure 6.11.

FIGURE 6.11
Simon's really getting into the lift now. He's using his left leg to support the heavy cylinder as he lifts it higher.

42. We still have a couple of problems. One main one is that the leg is going up to support the cylinder, and the hands are coming down at the same time. This situation requires overlapping motion animation principle.

43. On frame 120, keep Simon's hands in place until his leg is supporting the cylinder. So, in the Keyframes Editor, create keyframes for both hands on frame 120. First, select the Left Hand in the Keyframes Editor, hold down the Alt key, and drag a keyframe from frame 105 to frame 120. Do the same for the Right hand.

44. Go back and replace the information that is on frame 105 with the information on frame 90. Simply Alt-drag the information on frame 90 on the Left Hand to frame 105. That will overwrite what's on frame 105. Do the same for the Right Hand. That keeps the hands in place. Also, make those keyframes—from frame 90 to 105—linear. The keyframes for the left and right hands should look like Figure 6.12 in the Keyframes Editor.

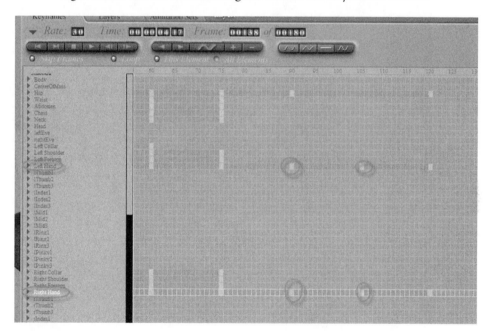

FIGURE 6.12
Corrected keyframes for Simon's hands.

45. Next, we have a little motion of the cylinder to address. With the cylinder selected, make frame 90 linear. Now you have the overlapping motion.

46. Now you need to check to see if the hands are going through the cylinder. Switch to the Main Camera. If one of Simon's fingers is going through there, switch to the Left Hand Camera for a close-up look. Use either the

Bend or Grasp to bend the fingers out. Again, we're not going to spend a lot of time on the exact finger placement, but you can actually control each finger manually in the Advanced Hand Controls so that his hand interacts with the cylinder the way you want. Check the right hand and do the same. Get back to the Right Camera view, and scrub through the animation. Now we have our overlapping motion. Your pose should now look like Figure 6.13 on frame 120.

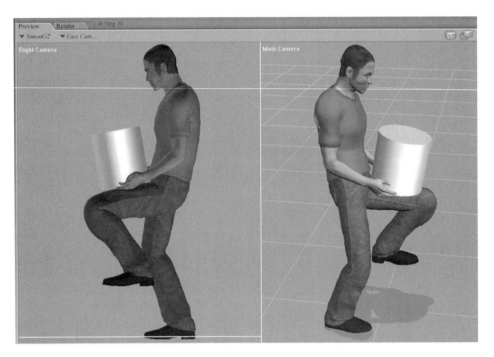

FIGURE 6.13
Overlapping motion is now in place.

47. Now you will animate on frame 135. You need to place the left foot back on the floor, in line with the right foot, and raise the hands and cylinder so that they're at the vertical level of the abdomen. The upper torso will also go back slightly in response to this lifting action.

48. Switch to the Right Camera view for this. First drag the left foot down, putting it in line with the right. Then, bring both hands up, followed by the cylinder. You need to adjust the hands a little because they're bending in an awkward way. Switch to the Left Hand Camera and use the Side-Side parameter to adjust the bend of the hand upward. Also, take the Twist out. You're placing the hands to hold the cylinder from beneath. Make the same adjustments on the right hand in the Right Hand Camera.

49. Scroll through the frames in the Main Camera view. You have some fine-tuning to do on the leg and cylinder, but you can do the fine-tuning when he steps forward. The main things to focus on in this step are that the left foot is going down in line with the right foot, the cylinder is going up, and the hands are following. You also want to have the upper torso going back. The method we chose for taking the upper torso back is to select the hip, and then use xRotate to rotate the torso back. Because of the way IK works, the hands stay in place, but the upper torso adjusts. Even the buttocks and legs will adjust a bit to accommodate that.

In this case, you're animating on frame 135, but the hips were adjusted on frame 137, so you can drag that back in the Keyframes Editor to correct it easily.

NOTE

50. Now the rotation of the hip is occurring a bit early. With the Hip selected, open the Keyframes Editor, and in the Rotate Channel, take the earliest keyframe of rotation before frame 135 (which turns out to be frame 90), Alt-drag that out to frame 120, and make it linear. That way, he's not unnaturally leaning back before you actually want him to.

51. Switch to the Main Camera, turn off the animation, and switch to Fast Tracking mode. Scroll through the animation. You're almost there!

52. At this point, load Lift Step 11.pz3 from the Chapter 6 exercise files on the DVD-ROM (shown in Figure 6.14). The very simplistic shelf (which is just a stretched cube) is in place. You can also compare your animation up to this point with the animation in this project file.

ON THE DVD

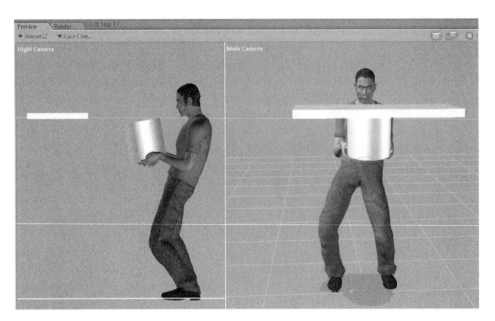

FIGURE 6.14
Shelves are added to the scene with Lift Step 11.pz3.

53. You will now animate on frame 150. The right foot is moving forward, in the crossover position, as Simon steps to place the cylinder on the shelf. You'll also be moving his hip forward to maintain his body's balance, and Simon will be holding the cylinder at its bottom, lifting his hands up and away from the body in preparation for placing the cylinder onto the shelf.

54. Working in the Right Camera, move the right foot forward, using the zTran parameter dial. When you can see the foot, lift it into place. As you put the cylinder onto that shelf, his hip is going to need to come forward as well.

55. For now, move the cylinder out of the way, and remove its rotation. Make sure a keyframe is in place to protect that rotation from leaking back to earlier keyframes. The previous keyframe is on frame 120 with xRotate. In the Keyframes Editor, Alt-drag the keyframe from frame 120 to frame 135, and make that key linear (see Figure 6.15).

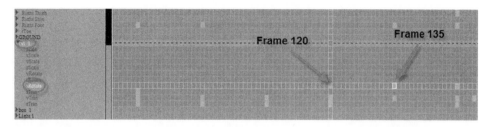

FIGURE 6.15
Frame 120 is Alt-dragged to frame 135 and made into a linear key for the xRotate parameter of the cylinder.

56. Move the hands up to support that cylinder, or, actually, to lift it into place. Switch to the Right Hand Camera, and although you won't spend an inordinate amount of time on the hands, you can at least make them not look so severely contorted. Do the same for the left hand.
57. Switch back to the Main Camera, and scrub through the animation.

Unless you have a seriously powerful video card giving you real-time playback of the full animated figure, it's important to still use Fast Tracking mode (rather than Full) at times, to get the fluid sense of the motion of the animation. Sometimes, having the animation jerk doesn't quite give you a sense of timing and realism.

58. Move on to animate on frame 165, in the Right Camera view. In this animation, the right foot lands on the floor just in front of the shelf, and the hip moves forward to accommodate this. The hands now place the cylinder on the shelf, and because of all this positioning, the left leg will be fully extended.
59. Start by moving the Hip forward; otherwise, it will be difficult to get the right foot planted properly, and then plant the right foot on the floor. Next, place the cylinder on the shelf, and move the hands to support that effort. To make this animation a little easier, we're allowing a bit of creative slide as the cylinder lands on the shelf. Switch to the Main Camera, and scrub through the animation. Frame 165 should be posed as shown in Figure 6.16.

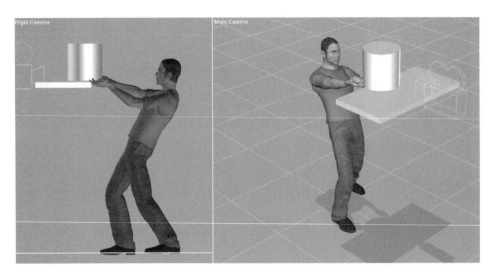

FIGURE 6.16
The heavy cylinder is placed on the shelf.

60. Set the final keyframe on frame 180. Here, you will bring Simon's hands down to his sides and lower his hips slightly, to relax his knees.

61. In the Right Camera view, bring both hands down. Switch to the Left Hand Camera. You can just zero out the parameters for Twist, Side-Side, and Bend. Also zero out the Advanced Hand Control parameters so you don't have any unexplainably bizarre hand posing. Lastly, Bend the hands down into a more natural state. You may also want to put a little bit of Grasp into the hands when the character is at rest, so the fingers don't splay out unnaturally.

62. Select his hip, and remove the rotation. Then walk up through the actors of the torso, looking for any rotation still in there, removing them as you go. You'll create a more natural pose of the arms when you set the end frame for the entire animation. So with the Left Hand selected, bring it up slightly on the yTran to create a slight bend at the elbow. Do the same on the other arm. You can also have him looking at the cylinder that he just placed on the shelf. With the Head selected, Bend it up a bit. Your final pose should look like Figure 6.17. Play back the whole animation now to see the result.

FIGURE 6.17
Simon's final pose with the cylinder on the shelf.

THROWING THE BALL OVERHAND

In this tutorial, you'll learn how to animate a character to throw a ball overhand.

ON THE DVD

1. You'll start with a character in a pose with the hands up ready to throw (as shown in Figure 6.18). From the Chapter 6 exercise files, open Throw-Step-01.pz3, which is the start pose you'll be animating from.
Simon has his hands up so that the ball would (later on) be in his right hand. The left is just posed as a natural support that a person would have to balance his body.

FIGURE 6.18
Simon's starting pose.

2. From here, you'll actually begin the animation process and advance the timeline to frame 20. You're working with 100 frames and putting key poses every twentieth frame. So, go to frame 20, and raise the left foot and move it forward and slightly to the left. Look at this in all four viewports. Select the Left Foot; and rather than trying to move it in the viewport manual, use the parameter controls (dials). Just move it forward. Notice that his body is tilted slightly to the right, which makes sense because his left foot is up.

3. You also want to rotate the z-axis of the hips. Select the Hip, and adjust the zRotate to 8 to help distribute the weight of the body so that you can center the weight on the right leg—so he can maintain his balance.

4. Next, you need to adjust the right shoulder and forearm to bring the right hand down to the right side of the right thigh. For posing the figure in most of what you're doing, you should use the parameter controls rather than IK or the editing tools, to have the greatest amount of control. Leave the Twist at 2. Set the Front-Back to 21, and set Up-Down to 57.

5. Now, you'll work on the forearm. Set the Bend to -6 to bring it down, which is basically how the right arm should be posed on this frame (as shown in Figure 6.19).

Note that for the majority of this animation, the ball will be in the right hand. This will be animated later. However, because of how you animate the ball with the character (the ball is never actually parented to the character) you first animate the character, and when that's done, you animate the ball. So you'll see his empty hands going through the motions for now.

6. Now, pose the left arm. Select the Left Shoulder. Set the Front-Back to -26. You basically want the left arm to be out and up. Set the Up-Down to -13; and then come down to the forearm. Remember you can just cursor down on your keyboard to get the next actor which, in this case, is the left forearm. Set the Bend to -31. At this point, the figure is posed appropriately on frame 20 for now as shown in Figure 6.19.

This is a bit of an iterative process to help give you a general sense of the posing and the motion of the character. At some points, we'll revisit frames and make adjustments or even go in between keyframes and make adjustments. Because the tangency of the curve of the motion that occurs between the actors as the character animates, it's sometimes easier to first set gross motion and then come and apply fine motion rather than trying to apply the fine motion linearly as you move forward. This is an element of the workflow that often occurs in most character animation.

ON THE DVD

7. To check your work so far, open Throw-Step-02.pz3, which basically catches you up to the work you've just done.

8. Now you'll create the pose for frame 40. Go to frame 40 to first move the hips left and slightly down to shift his weight. Select the Hips. Then set the zRotate to -1. At this point, you're using the weight principle of animation because you're starting to shift his weight distribution during the throw. You'll see that the upper body (at this point) starts to move in the direction in which the ball will be thrown.

9. Now you'll place the left foot on the ground because in the process of throwing the ball, the character is going to take a step forward. Select the Left Foot, move it to the left, and bring it down. By doing this, you've extended it to the point where the hips obviously need to adjust a bit as well.

10. The hips should be at about .7 in the xTran and about -0.23 in the yTran to help the knee bend properly. You don't want to have the knees too straight so that they look unnatural.

11. Now adjust the right shoulder. The right arm needs to be out and up forming a 90-degree angle in the arm. Start with the Right Shoulder. Set the Twist to -69, Front-Back to -9, and Up-Down to -4. At this point, the upper arm should be parallel to the ground.

12. Select the Right Forearm, and set the Bend to 53 to get the 90-degrees in the arm.

NOTE

As you look at the figure in different views, the right shoulder is rotated slightly back, hinting back behind the character. This speaks to the human rotation limits of the shoulder. The hand (the right hand) is also aligned with the head. So if you look at the figure from the Right View, the head actually obscures the view of the hand. These are cues to let you know the proper posing of the right hand.

13. Now pose the left shoulder to be down and slightly behind with the left elbow slightly behind the body. Start by selecting that Left Shoulder. Set the Twist to 47, the Front-Back to 15, and the Up-Down to -26.

14. Working your way down, select the Left Forearm. Set the Twist to 4, the Side-Side to 14, and the Bend to -16. So now, as you drag through the timeline (set for Fast feedback), you can start to see what's happening. He starts in the initial pose and goes through the motions of winding up to throw the ball. His weight is distributing through his body. The left foot is taking a step. It's all crude for now, but at least you can start to see the beginnings of a throw animation. Your pose on frame 20 should now look like Figure 6.19.

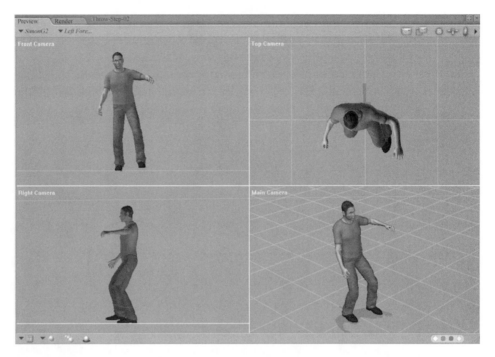

FIGURE 6.19
Simon on frame 20.

ON THE DVD

15. Your work should be similar to our Step 3, so to check your work against the exercise files, open Throw-Step-03.pz3 to continue on. Again because you are working in 20-frame increments, you'll now be working in frame 40. Begin by selecting his Hip. Rotate his hip to 50 in the yRotate, set the zRotate to -23, and set the xRotate to 1. You can see that the major thrust, the energy, for throwing the ball has been expelled. It was being wound up previously; now it's about to be expelled.

16. After rotating the hips, you'll also need to move the hips over to the left because the planted left foot is pivotal for this pose. The left foot is where the weight of the body is going to be placed, so you have to move the hips to allow the balance of the body to occur. Move in the x-axis, and you'll see that this causes the right foot to really get unplanted, and that's okay; you'll deal with that. You also want to make an adjustment to bring the body back down in the y-axis to get a good bend in the knee. You'll also be moving in the z-axis as part of the balancing of the body.

17. You also have to raise that right foot and pose it to trail and counterbalance the body. Now bring that right foot forward to avoid a very unnatural kind of twist.

18. Adjust the Twist, Side-Side, and Bend of the right foot (as shown in Figure 6.20). Set the Twist to 19, leave the Side-Side at -2, and set the Bend to 28 to create a little more natural pose for the foot.

19. That left foot has to be adjusted as well. Set the Twist on the left foot to 40, set the Side-Side to 2, and leave the Bend at 0. Your figure should now look like Figure 6.20. Drag through the timeline to look at what you have so far. The body is freely getting into that throw now.

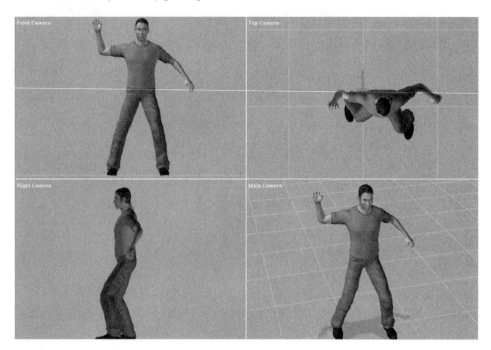

FIGURE 6.20
Simon posed on frame 40.

20. Continue working on frame 60 by posing the Right Shoulder to bring the forearm down and across the chest. Adjust the twist of the right shoulder by setting the Twist to 57, the Front-Back to 78, and the Up-Down to 53. Don't worry that it does look very crazy at certain points in the process.

If you're manually adjusting the position of the arms, or sometimes just dragging your dials to make adjustments, some combinations can get away from you and create some very bizarre and unattractive deformations. The simplest solution in those cases is to set your dials back to 0 and then make adjustments one at a time.

21. As you're animating a character going through a series of keyframes, you can get worked into a corner where it seems impossible to get a natural pose of the arm. If that happens, set your Twist, Front-Back, and Up-Down to 0 on the current keyframe you are animating; and then set the appropriate pose values with the dials for the selected actor in the arm.

22. Continue now working on the Right Forearm. Twist should be at 6, Side-to-Side should be at 0, and Bend should be at 71. The forearm is now coming across the chest, which is exactly what you wanted done with the right arm on this frame (as shown in Figure 6.21).

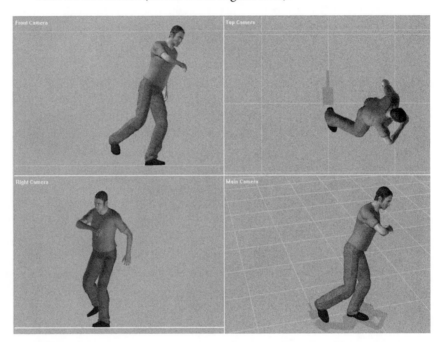

FIGURE 6.21
Simon posed on frame 60.

23. You now want the left arm to go down slightly, placing the left hand to the left of the left thigh. So again, working with the Left Shoulder, leave Twist and Front-Back as they are. Adjust the Up-Down to -53. Leave the Left Forearm as is.

24. Now look at your animation so far, and you'll notice a major problem with the right arm motion. That motion isn't going to throw a ball because in setting the gross keyframes, we've glossed over some critical keyframes that need to go in-between, mainly around frame 50 for now. So if your animation looks like this, you're doing exactly as you should.

25. In animating characters, there are points at which the animation often feels totally odd because the process is recursive and requires that you actually come back and fine-tune your work. So, to catch up to this point with the exercise files, if you want to compare your work, you'll be working with Step 4 (Throw-Step-04.pz3).

ON THE DVD

26. Go back now to frame 50 and make one of those fine adjustments to correct the arm motion for throwing the ball. You'll be working with the right arm, so start with the Right Shoulder. You want to pose the right arm to be outstretched to the front and above the body slightly to the right. Set the Twist to -81, the Front-Back to 70, and the Up-Down to -66. Continue down to the Right Forearm, and set the Twist to 6, the Side-Side to -15, and the Bend to 0.

27. If you go through the timeline now, you can see some improvement. However, you still have a little bit of a weird motion here, in between 60 and 50. Go to frame 55, and make another adjustment. Select the Right Shoulder, and set the Twist to -42, the Front-Back to 84, and the Up-Down to -35. Come down to the Right Forearm, and set the Side-Side to 2, and the Bend to 29. That should smooth out the motion some. At this point, your figure should look like Figure 6.22 at frame 50 and Figure 6.23 at frame 55.

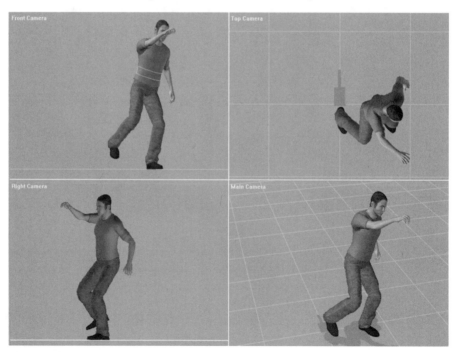

FIGURE 6.22
Simon posed at frame 50.

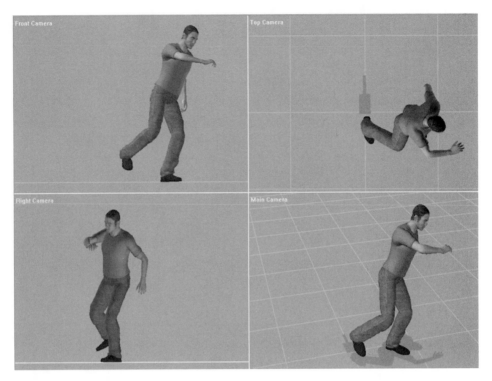

FIGURE 6.23
Simon posed at frame 55.

28. At this point, check the Graph Editor to make sure that the right arm motion is okay (shown in Figure 6.24). Check for any serious disruption of the continuity of the motion curves, which means you use the Graph Editor to check each of the parameters (Twist, Side-Side, Up-Down) that you animated for each of the arm actors, and make sure that there aren't any unexpected abrupt changes in the curve's shape. This is a great troubleshooting utility when creating character animation.

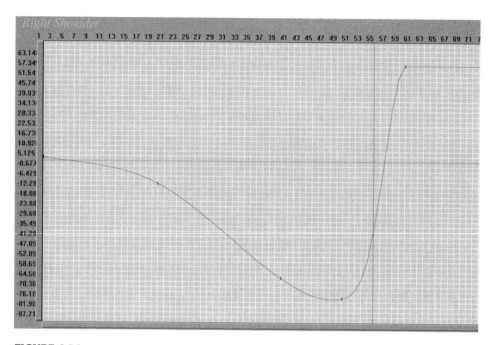

FIGURE 6.24
Graph Editor showing the motion curve for the Right Shoulder Twist parameter.

29. You should periodically check the Graph Editor whenever you are animating characters of any type. Look for bumps or strange spikes in the graph; if you find them, select these keyframes, and drag them up or down to edit those curves so that they end up being smooth. That will help you to get rid of very erratic motion.

30. Often, one thing that's most time-consuming in editing characters (if you aren't sure of what you're doing) is getting rid of unexplained twitches in motion. It could be that the hand, at one frame, just has a really funny motion; you just can't track it down. There is no keyframe at that point to make it move that way. However, if you understand that motion is expressed through curves in 3D animation and that curves have behavior that's between the keyframes, then you can see the benefit of using the Graph Editor as a way of adjusting the behavior of those curves so you can get smooth, attractive character animation.

ON THE DVD

31. Open Step 5 (Throw-Step-05.pz3) to move on to the next step. It's basically a culmination of all the work you've done to this point. Start by rotating the hip. Make sure you are on frame 80 before you do that. With the Hip selected, set yRotate to 19. The animation is coming out of the throw, so the body will try to balance back. Set zRotate to -7, and leave xRotate at 1.

Bring the right foot forward slightly left and then slightly down. Go forward, and adjust both arms to be forward of the body with the right hand at abdomen level and the left hand at waist level (as shown in Figure 6.25).

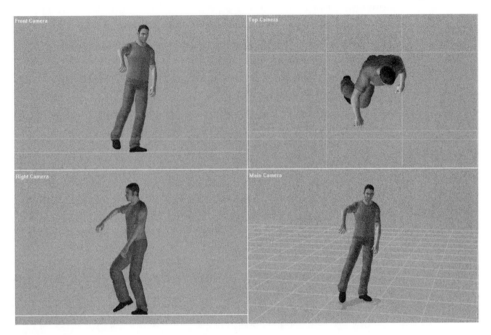

FIGURE 6.25
Simon posed on frame 80.

32. Working with the Right Shoulder to start, set the Twist to 59, Front-Back to 52, and Up-Down to 17. Work down to the Right Forearm, and set the Bend to 15.
33. Working with the Left Shoulder, set the Twist to 71, the Front-Back to -34, and the Up-Down to -51. Working on the Left Forearm, set the Side-Side to 1 and the Bend to -19. Your figure should now be posed on frame 80 and look like Figure 6.25.
34. Let's see how that's playing through for now. Amazingly, these series of poses are starting to form a throw.

As you go through frame 60, check the right arm and if you have any twisting or any kind of bizarre behavior between frame 60 and frame 70, make the required adjustments using the Graph Editor.

35. Now move on to the final frame, frame 100. You can load Step 6 (Throw-Step-06.pz3) as the starting point for that. You'll first remove all rotation from the hips to distribute the body weight on both legs. This will be the final pose of the animation; so you have him in his recovered pose. Remove the rotation by just zeroing them out from the Hip (xRotate, yRotate, zRotate). Also move the hip so that you can distribute the weight over both legs.

36. Now place the Right Foot on the floor behind the body, so he's taking a step back. Make use of different camera views to ensure this foot is actually placed behind the body.

37. Now pose the Right Arm with the elbow and hand just behind and to the right of the body. Start by selecting the Right Shoulder. Set the Front-Back to -13 and the Up-Down to 52. Then work on the Right Forearm, and set the Bend to -5.

38. Next make the left arm lower and down slightly. This is a very fine adjustment here on the left arm and is truly a matter of taste and style at this point. So on the Left Shoulder, set the Front-Back to -18, and on the Left Forearm, set the Bend to -10. Simon should now be posed to look like Figure 6.26 on frame 100.

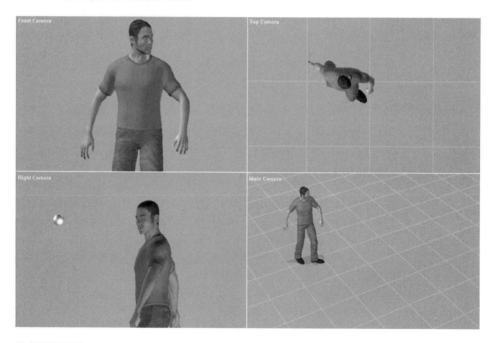

FIGURE 6.26
Simon posed at rest at the end of the throw on frame 100.

39. Go back to frame 20 to make an adjustment to the neck. If we play this back in full, you'll see he's throwing the ball, but he's acting like he has a stiff neck.

When animating straight-ahead as you are doing in this project, it's common to first pose the character on a wide range of keys and later return to previous keys to make adjustments as you're doing here. Because animation is not just key poses but rather motion relationships, the behavior of various body parts will only be re-vealed after several keyframes have been set. It then becomes easier to see what's out of place or moves unnaturally.

NOTE

40. Go to frame 20, and select the Neck. Give the Twist a 45-degree angle so that he's looking where the ball is going to be thrown. He starts out looking in front, and then as he gets ready to pitch, he starts looking in that direction. And now you are ready to animate the ball added on to the character.

ADDING THE BALL TO THE OVERHAND THROW

The character is basically set up at this time. You can see it in the fast preview. Open Step 7 (Throw-Step-07.pz3) so you can see all the keyframes that have been done **ON THE DVD** so far. Go to frame 0. To add the ball to the character animation sequence, you need to access the Poser library.

1. In the primitives, get simple ball. It's nothing fancy for now. Set the Scale of this ball to 36% in X, Y, and Z. Lift it up into position in the right hand as shown in Figure 6.27.

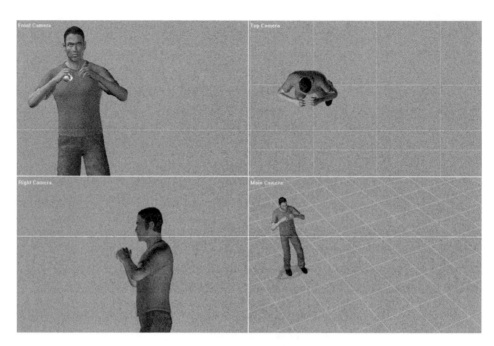

FIGURE 6.27
The ball is now placed in Simon's right hand on frame 0.

NOTE

One of the things that may seem tempting is to go ahead and parent this ball to the right hand. If you do that, for half of this animation, it will actually work fine. The problem comes when the ball has to be let go. If you parent it to the right hand now, the ball will still be influenced by the right hand. So, instead you can actually keyframe the ball to be in the right hand for a few critical frames.

2. When working with the ball in this part of the process, there's a little bit of workflow technique that you need to really be familiar with. It has to do with how you select and move the ball without accidentally selecting another body part. Switch to the Right View. Always make sure that you mouse-over the ball to see it outlined (as shown in Figure 6.28), which indicates that selecting now will select the ball and not part of Simon. That lets you know that you are able to safely move the ball—and nothing else.

FIGURE 6.28
The ball is now highlighted and ready to be selected to
be moved safely without selecting part of Simon.

When you first move to a viewport, it may be tempting to just select the ball and start moving, but if you've just moved to that viewport, you can accidentally do things like select Simon's hands and cause some really bizarre behavior. Also you want to work with your four viewports for this kind of work because it's very difficult to see the ball from certain viewpoints. So having all these viewports to work with is really helpful.

Also bear in mind that you may want to sometimes select the prop directly and then work with just the parameter dials. Don't trust any single view because, as you can see here, it looks great from the top, but from the front, you can see that you have some work to do.

3. Go to frame 20, and pose the ball to look like Figure 6.29.

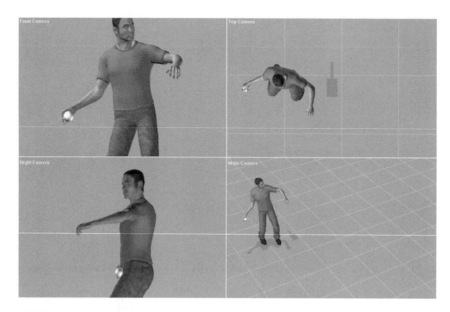

FIGURE 6.29
The ball posed in Simon's hand on frame 20.

4. Go to frame 40, and pose the ball to look like Figure 6.30.

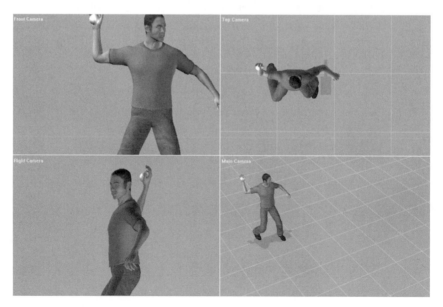

FIGURE 6.30
The ball posed in Simon's hand on frame 40.

5. Go to frame 30, and pose the ball to look like Figure 6.31.

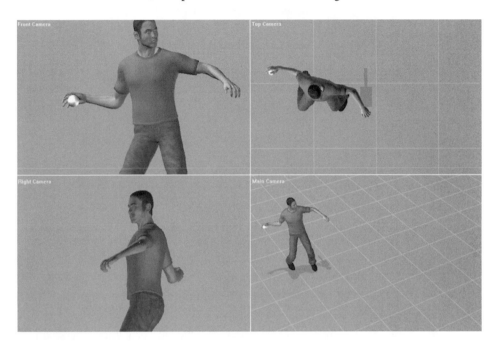

FIGURE 6.31
The ball posed in Simon's hand on frame 30.

NOTE

Remember that animation motion happens on curves. So the interpolation of the ball's motion between frames 20 and 40 would be a straight line; however, there are arcs of motion in the arm for throwing the ball that are not circles, so the interpolation is not as easily predicted. You actually have to set several keyframes at times for the ball, which is why you put a ball keyframe at frame 30.

ON THE DVD

6. The process shown so far is how you animate the ball to the character. Look at the final animation in Step 8 (Throw-Step-08.pz3). This is what your motion should look like for ball and character. If you look at the Graph Editor for the ball, which you should always do when animating, always be sure that you know if you're looking at the whole animation or not. (I generally tend to make it show the entire sequence.)

7. Look at the xTran (this is the direction the ball is really being thrown). Look at areas where there are a few keyframes because, quite frequently, that's where you'll find trouble, where the curve may actually go up and down, which indicates a problem. You generally want the curve, having a smooth relationship in the Y. Here, you have the point of release. At the

point of release, the curve generally stops changing elevation. Until then, the curve is following the hike of the right hand. Your ball's xTran curve should look like Figure 6.32, yTran curve should look like Figure 6.33, and zTran curve should look like Figure 6.34.

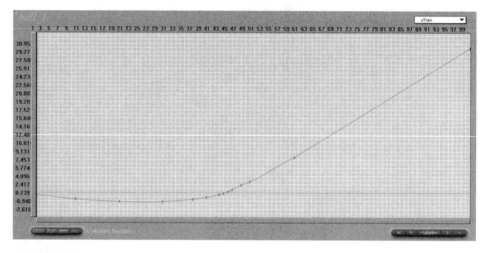

FIGURE 6.32
The xTran Graph Editor curve of the trajectory of the ball being thrown by Simon.

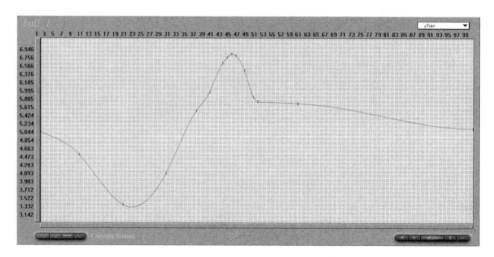

FIGURE 6.33
The yTran Graph Editor curve of the trajectory of the ball being thrown by Simon.

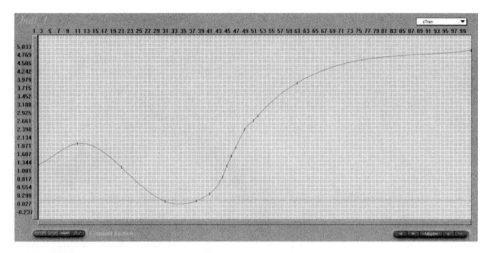

FIGURE 6.34
The zTran Graph Editor curve of the trajectory of the ball being thrown by Simon.

So, there you have the basics of how to animate a character throwing a ball. This is only the beginning of the process for you with throwing animation because this simplistic animation really needs to be built upon with nuance and behavior to tell your story. But at least this should give you a foundation from which to create some more interesting animation.

THROWING THE BALL UNDERHAND

In this exercise, you'll animate this character throwing a ball underhand using several principles of animation in the process. This exercise will actually be two separate animations that combine to form the illusion that a man is throwing a ball.

In the beginning, you'll spend almost all of your time animating the man throwing, and then you'll animate the ball. You'll see how to actually keyframe the ball being placed in the man's hand as it goes throughout because this version of Poser doesn't yet have the tools for animating parenting. So you can't parent the ball to his hand, have him animate throwing, and then unparent at the appropriate time. Instead, you'll use an easier and more direct method of animating the ball.

1. The figure is in the default pose, and nothing has been done. You'll be working with 100 frames, so set the end frame to 100. Also turn your Camera Animation off so that as you go through to look at your animation (as you progress), the camera won't be moving. This gives you greater control over observing what you are doing as the animator, rather than as the final viewer.

2. Starting on frame 1, pose the right arm at rest. Turn on IK for the Right Hand to pose this, and then turn the IK off. Make sure that the hand part is locked so the fingers don't go crazy. Bring the Right Hand down, and make sure there is a little bit of a bend in the elbow (as shown in Figure 6.35). Correct the odd rotation of the Right Hand using the Bend parameter. Also, give him a bit of a grasp in his right hand so that he's holding the ball. This is the starting position for the right hand (as shown in Figure 6.35).

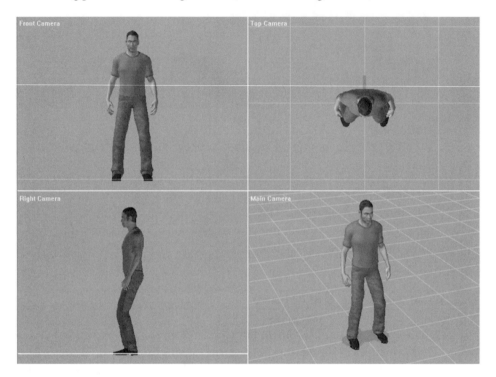

FIGURE 6.35
Simon posed on frame 1.

Whenever you move the hand with IK, you really need to check it from a few of the views to be sure that it hasn't been disoriented.

3. Now that this is posed with IK, turn the IK off for the right hand. From the main menu Figure/Symmetry, choose Right Arm to Left Arm to pose the left arm as well, and then adjust the grasp in the left hand. The left hand isn't holding the ball, so just try to get the fingers to rest in a relaxed and natural way.

4. Now you need to work on placement of the feet so that they spread a little bit. His stance is a little too upright for the throw. You want to make them equidistant so that the distance of the right foot from the center will be equal to the left foot from the center. Set the Right Foot xTran to -0.14. Copy that by pressing Ctrl + C. For the left foot in the xTran, use .14.

5. Now you need to adjust the Hip because with the feet spread apart, he's standing too upright. In the yTran, bring him down to -0.138.

You need to bring Simon down due to the weight principle of animation. To demonstrate that his upper body has some weight to it, he distributes that weight as his feet are spread apart. His body has to come down to represent that. The bowed knees help to sell the idea as well. Simon should now be posed to look like Figure 6.35 on frame 1. You can open up the Throw-Underhand-Step-01 Rest.pz3 from the Chapter 6 exercise files to compare your work.

6. Now move on to posing the next keyframe, which is the recoil for the throw, on frame 20. Start by sliding the Right Foot back by setting the zTran to -0.472 to show that as he is recoiling for the pitch.

Based on what your story is calling for, at this point, you would either have him slide his foot back or step his foot back. You may need to, for example, go to frame 10 and raise his foot up, if he is doing a step back. There are several ways of getting to this point.

7. You need to lower his hip because if you first move his right leg more to the right, and now move back, he'll have to come lower to support himself. With his Hip selected, set the yTran to -0.138. Make sure that you're working in the Front and the Right Views to keep the hip centered.

8. As you are positioning the legs of a character, it's very easy to focus on the legs but not distribute the weight of the body to center over the legs. So be sure to use the Right View and check this as you animate the character.

9. You also have to start to apply some rotation to the Hip xRotate so that the recoil can appear to really be happening. Set this parameter to 3 degrees. Although this rotation may seem to be very slight, it's the start of the rotation in a torso.

10. Go up the torso chain to the Waist. Apply a Bend here of 2 degrees. Go to the Abdomen, and set the Bend to 20 degrees.

11. Position the arms to demonstrate the recoil because the whole purpose of the recoil at this point is to build the energy for the throw. So, pull back the right arm. Working with the Right Collar, adjust the Front-Back to -15. Again this is all very subjective, based on the kind of throw you want to make.

12. Walk down that arm to the Right Shoulder. Again, just as a reminder, to streamline your workflow, click in the empty area of the parameter dials palette and then curser down to the right shoulder. Apply a few adjustments to three parameters: Twist to 26, Front-Back to -6, and Up-Down to 64.

13. Continue walking down that arm to the Right Forearm. Give a very slight Twist of 1 degree, set the Side-Side to 0, and set the Bend to 7.

14. On the Right Hand, set the Twist to 7, Side-Side to 9, and the Bend to 14.

While following the exercises on the video tutorials on the DVD-ROM or from the book, feel free to make adjustments on the posing of the different elements of the character to mimic ideas that you have for the characters in your story, as long as you can keep the concepts and the workflow together. It's okay if your figure poses a little bit differently and carries his weight a little bit differently, as long as you demonstrate weight, energy being stored, and the principles of animation in use.

15. Now move over to pose the left arm to act as a counterbalance to the right because, as the right arm is moving back, it's not only moving but it actually has some mass. Mass in motion causes the body to become unbalanced, so to counteract this, the left arm is going in the opposite direction to bring balance.

16. Starting with the Left Collar, set the Front-Back to -6, Twist to 0, and Up-Down to 0. Walk down that arm to the Left Forearm, and set a very slight Twist of 1 degree, set the Side-Side to 19, and set the Bend to -33. Come down to the hand, and set the Twist at 6. Orbit around a bit to better see what that really results in. The Sack Saddle is -9, and the Bend goes from a -4 to a -14. Now the arms are posed appropriately.

17. Before completing this step, you have one more thing to do. Adjust the neck because, as you go from frame 1 to frame 20, you can see he is looking ahead and then he is looking down, which doesn't make any sense. Go to frame 20, select his Neck, and bend his Neck so that his head continues to look at the target—whatever the target is. Set the Bend to -22. When you scroll from frame 1 to frame 20 now, you can see something that is a bit more useful. Simon should now be posed on frame 20 to look like Figure 6.36. Now you're ready to move to the next step. If you need to get caught up from the exercise files in Chapter 6, you can open the Throw-Underhand-Step-02 Recoil.pz3 project file.

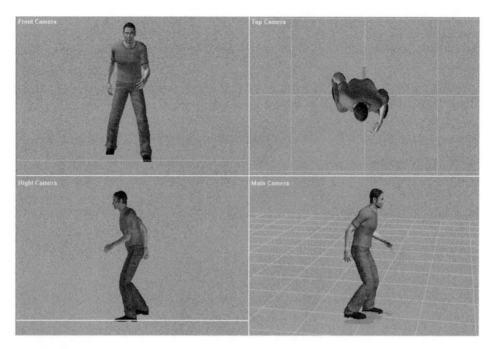

FIGURE 6.36
Simon posed on frame 20 to show the recoil for the throw.

18. Go to frame 40. Now we'll be building the anticipation into this animation. We'll be posing the right arm all the way back. This is going to be the farthest extent of the arm holding the ball for the throw. We'll be bending the body forward in the hip, waist, and abdomen. This will be able to create that realistic sense that he's really getting into his pitch. This is where we'll really be bending the skeleton of this character. This will be very dynamic and very expressive and will look like Figure 6.37 when we've got it right.

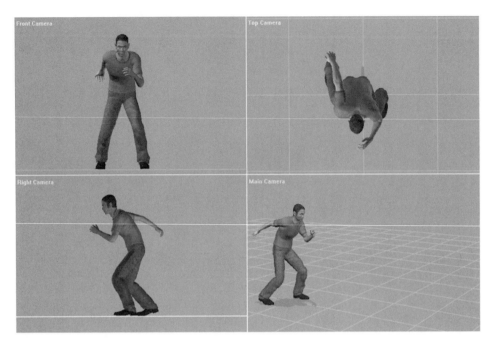

FIGURE 6.37
Simon in now bent over in anticipation of throwing the ball.

19. Start with the Right Collar, and make sure it has a Twist of -5, a Front-Back of -1, and an Up-Down of 0. Set the Right Shoulder's Twist at 26, bring the Front-Back to -18, and leave the Up-Down as is. Adjust the Bend of the Right Forearm to 9.

20. Select the Left Collar. Set the Front-Back to -6 and the Up-Down to 0. Now select the Left Shoulder, and set the Twist to -2, the Front-Back to -61, and the Up-Down to -36.

21. Now if you look at this from frame 20 to frame 40, you can see that although it does move, it doesn't move the amount you might expect to be at the full extent for the throw. That's because, even though this is the correct and final position for the arms, the appearance of the full extent of the throw is based only partly on the posing of the arm. The other part is at the posing of the torso. So when you get to the Bending of the torso, then the position of the arm will be a bit more extreme.

22. Start by setting the xRotate of the Hip to 7. Go to the Waist, and set the Bend to 10. Bend the Abdomen to 29. Now as you scroll from frame 20 to frame 40, you can start to see that a great deal more effort is involved.

23. Next, you need to complete the slide of the right foot. You began the slide earlier, but now you will take it to its final position to the back and to the right. On the Right Foot, set the xTran to about -0.650, and adjust the zTran to about -0.840. Simon should now be posed on frame 40 as shown earlier in Figure 6.37.

24. Now you are moving up to the throw part of the animation. If you are just catching up, you can load the Throw-Underhand-Step-03 Anticipation.pz3 exercise file from the Chapter 6 folder. This will get you to the starting point for this step in the exercise.

25. Start by raising and moving his hip forward, leaving only the toes of the right foot on the ground. This is where the actual throw is starting to occur (not the anticipation, but rather, the actual throw). Go to frame 60. Select his Hip, and move forward in the zTran to about 0.4. Move down slightly in the yTran to about -0.45.

26. Start to raise the Right Foot off the ground, leaving only the toes touching the ground by raising the foot up in the yTran to about 0.3. Come down to the Right Toes, and Bend to -19. Because the right foot now looks a bit out of place, Bend it to 20.

In your exact character for your story, the degrees here are going to be whatever it takes to make it look good. Don't become very attached to the actual numbers and the parameters you enter as you're going through this exercise. It's much more important that your characters look correct than that these numbers be the same.

NOTE

27. Continue by straightening his torso, leaving rotation in only the hip. Go back to the Hip to make sure the rotation is appropriately set. In this case, set the xRotate to 15. Then, go to the Waist, and set this Bend to 0. Go to the Abdomen next, and set the Bend to 15.

28. If you look at the difference between frame 60 and frame 40, you can see that you are shaping the spine as you are transitioning between those frames. The right arm is now coming forward and straightening as it crosses the right thigh.

29. Start with the Right Collar, and set the Twist to -5, Front-Back to -1, and Up-Down to -16. Go down to the Right Shoulder, and set the Twist to 26, Front-Back to 3, and Up-Down to 64. Continue to the Right Forearm, and set the Twist to 24, Side-Side to 0, and Bend to -16. On the Right Hand, set the Twist to -39, and leave the Side-Side at 9 and the Bend at 14.

Again the purpose of the left arm is to be the counterbalance. Bear in mind that the counterbalance is not simply to balance the weight but also to balance momentum because you have weight in motion. The right arm is to the rear, the left arm is to the front, and the motion of the right arm is coming forward with the body leaning, so we counter the weight and the momentum shift by also posing the left arm.

30. Continue on to the left arm by starting with the Left Collar. Set the Twist to 0, Front-Back to -6, and Up-Down to 0.
31. Go to the Left Shoulder, and set the Twist to 11, Front-Back to 8, and Up-Down to -56. Go to the Left Forearm, and set the Bend to -50. Simon should now be posed on frame 60 to look like Figure 6.38.

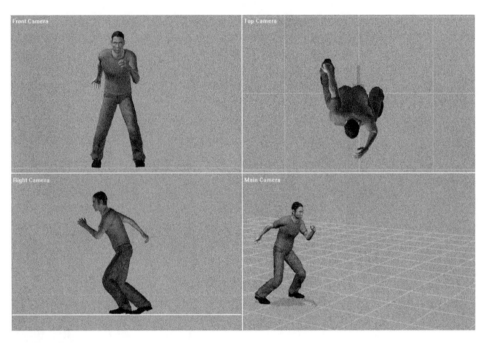

FIGURE 6.38
Simon posed on frame 60 of the underhand throw.

32. To continue with the follow-through, you'll be working on frame 80. If you are catching up, you can look at Throw-Underhand-Step-04 Throw.pz3 from the Chapter 6 exercise files.
33. Now you need to raise and move the hip forward further to fully extend the character into the throw as he follows through. This will further extend the right leg. Start by working on the Hip. Move the zTran to 0.59, and raise up a bit in the yTran to -0.2. Looking at this from the side, you are trying to

reach full extension (as shown in Figure 6.39). The right leg will reach its extension for this animation here. Leave the rotation in the hip as is to allow the body to be straightened on this angle and still be leaning forward.

34. Now you need to deal with some intermediate frames. Go to frame 66. (As in previous exercises, you return to set an earlier keyframe after first setting a latter one.)

Again, this has to do with all the splines created (and shown in the Graph Editor) when keyframes are formed, so that you can define the points through which the motion must occur before you set other keyframes, which then are affected by the previous and next keyframes.

35. Let's create this intermediate keyframe (on frame 66) to make sure that as he is going to throw the ball, he is continuing to hold the ball, but then opens his hand to release the ball. To achieve this, on frame 80, with the hand selected, make a slight adjustment on its grasp.

Because of Poser's auto keyframing, by making just a slight adjustment to the grasp of the hand on frame 80, you set a keyframe for just that hand's grasp on frame 80.

The reason you should not simply click the plus button (Create Keyframe icon) to make the keyframe is that it will make a keyframe for everything (all actors in the selected figure), which can seriously tamper with your animation motion curves in the Graph Editor.

36. Go to frame 66, and make another keyframe for the right hand by just making a slight adjustment. With the right hand's grasp now stored on frame 66, go back to frame 80. Now, you need to have the hand open to free the ball. Of course, the whole arm will be in motion, but by setting the earlier keyframe at 66 for the right hand, you have a reference that is the start of when the right hand begins to open to free the ball.

37. Work on that right arm now, starting from the Right Collar. Set the Twist to -34, Front-Back to -17, and Up-Down to -16. Work down to the Right Shoulder, and set the Twist to -16, Front-Back to 70, and Up-Down to 64. Go to the Right Forearm, and set the Twist to -46. Finally, go to the Right Hand, and adjust the Side-Side to 2 and Bend to 5.

38. Work on the left arm now, and again be sure that you are working in frame 80. You can leave the parameters for the left collar as they are. Move on to the Left Shoulder, and set the Twist to 20, Front-Back to 31, and Up-Down

to -70. Go to the Left Forearm, and adjust only the Bend to 6 so it's really extended back out there. Simon should now be posed on frame 80 to look like Figure 6.39.

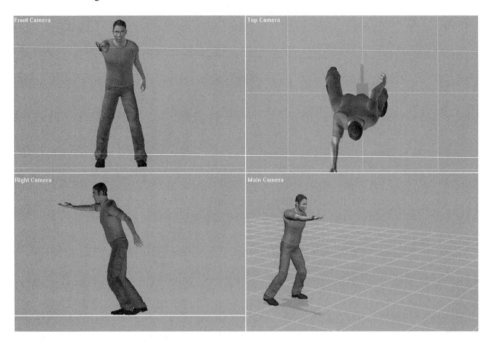

FIGURE 6.39
Simon posed on frame 80 of the underhand throw.

You should evaluate how well you are demonstrating that the character is managing its weight (using the weight principle of character animation), not by observing a keyframe in isolation but by looking at how the weight distribution appears in relation to keys before and after any specific evaluation point. The weight should seem to be thrown or supported in a way that demonstrates motion, not just so the character is standing, and therefore the weight is distributed a certain way. If you fail to do this, it will appear as if your character has unexplainable strength in certain places—or unexplainable weakness.

NOTE

ON THE DVD

39. Now you'll animate the end of the throw by working on frame 100. If you are working with the exercise files, you can load Throw-Underhand-Step-05 Follow Through.pz3, which is the starting point for this step in the animation. At frame 100, you want to end this animation with him coming back to rest. The easiest way to do this is to go to the Keyframes Editor, go to frame 1, and drag top to bottom to select all keyframes on frame 1.

Then, with the Alt key held down, drag these keyframes over to frame 100. You are basically making a copy of frame 1 and pasting it onto frame 100 so that Simon is automatically back at rest. Simon should now be posed on frame 100 to look like Figure 6.40. Now preview this.

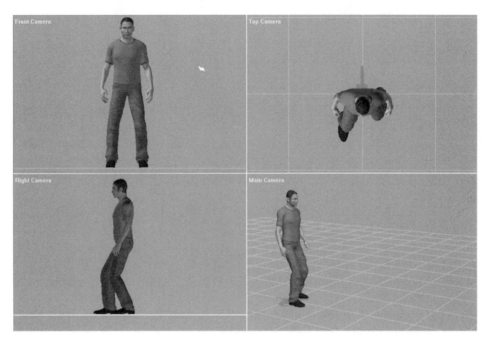

FIGURE 6.40
Simon at rest on frame 100.

40. Now as you know, when you're throwing a ball, you don't generally just go smoothly from standing at rest, recoiling, and throwing without some kind of a delay. So, we've introduced this delay by making some edits in the Animation Editor. At this point in the animation, we'll go over just what these timing changes are.

ON THE DVD

41. Open the Throw-Underhand-Step-07 Timing.pz3 from the Chapter 6 exercise files, and let's look at the keyframes. Everything before frame 40 is unadjusted to achieve the hold as shown in Figure 6.41.

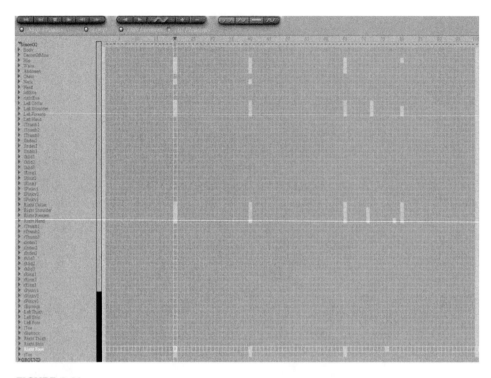

FIGURE 6.41
The keyframes are adjusted to create a hold to affect the timing of the throw, thereby
following the principle of animation timing.

42. The right foot is linear at frame 65 to keep the foot from going through the
    floor, as you saw earlier. Linear keys are set on the left arm and the right
    arm. Notice that the torso (the hip, waist, and abdomen) doesn't have lin-
    ear keys. You don't apply linear keys to the torso, even though you make
    linear keys here, because you can give the illusion, or the animation, of a
    hold by keeping certain body parts in place while others still show signs of
    life; in other words, the character is still but not dead. If you keep every-
    thing in place and perfectly still, it simply looks unnatural, as if there's no
    life. So, you leave a few other elements to be free to move through this
    spline interpolation.

43. Remember that this is not to say that there is no motion, it's that you're in-
    terpolating linearly (in a straight line). The combination of the two enables
    you to create the illusion that you are holding a live character in place.

44. Looking at the Object Properties parameter dials, if you select the Right
    Shoulder Front-Back, you have keyframes with the exact same value, but
    the first keyframe is set to a linear key.

45. Because this area is linear between them, you can get the motion to hold on this actor.

Remember, in Poser talk, the term actor refers to body part.

46. Between frame 40 and frame 65, not only do you have interpolation but also the same value. The result is that this appears not to move; however, because in the hierarchy of the structure of the character, this is a child to the hip, this is still in motion with relation to the hip. But the right collar, right shoulder, forearm, and hand appear to be static as a unit, so that there is no bending of the arm at this time, even though the arm may be rotating with respect to the torso. This gives the sense that he's thinking. He's choosing when he'll throw the ball. He is not forced to throw because his hand went back. He held it in position.

47. One of the added results of this kind of animation is that because the duration hasn't changed from 100 frames and the ball is being held back there, you'll have fewer frames to throw the ball. This means that the ball will be thrown faster. The end result is that it's less like a helium balloon effect and more like he's actually throwing a ball.

ADDING THE BALL TO THE UNDERHAND THROW

Now let's animate the ball:

1. Go to the Library Props/Primitives, and get a ball. Scale the ball to 30%, and raise it up to place it in the right hand. Also make adjustments at this point to ensure that the hand is grasping appropriately.

2. First you need to animate the ball traveling with the hand even though the hand isn't yet really grasping the ball on all keyframes. Work in the Left Camera View, and zoom in. Moving forward in 5 frame increments, place the ball in the right hand. When setting the character animation keyframes before, you animated it in 20-frame increments, but here 5-frame increments are required because the hand is moving very quickly and the ball will not stay in sync.

3. You may find that at times it's easier to just grab the ball and move it. Sometimes it will be much safer to just use the parameters. So just work in the Y-Z plane, without dealing with the X plane. You don't need to be concerned at the moment that the right arm moves left and right. You're only trying to keep the ball with the hand.

4. Because you set the keyframes for the ball every 5 frames, as you go from frame 50 through frame 70, you start to see how the ball is separating from the hand. Even by placing keyframes with 5-frame increments, this is happening. Remember as you slowed the character down to hold that pose and then released the fast pitch, you have a greater chance of being out of sync with the ball. For example, there is a keyframe at 70, and another keyframe at 75. They both seem to be relatively okay. Although you can fine-tune them, they are not really problem spots. However, when you go in between the 5-frame increments and look at frame 73, you can see that's clearly a problem. So you need to bring that back in and transition between them.

Bear in mind that it's not simply that the ball is not in the hand. It's that there's a curve of trajectory that the hand is following based not only on its movement but also on the rotation along the skeleton of the arm. This creates a unique curve. The ball being keyframed at frame 70 and 75 won't automatically create the same curve. So you need to go in between to frame 73 or some other in-between frame and create a correction keyframe to mimic the motion curve of the hand (as shown in Figure 6.42).

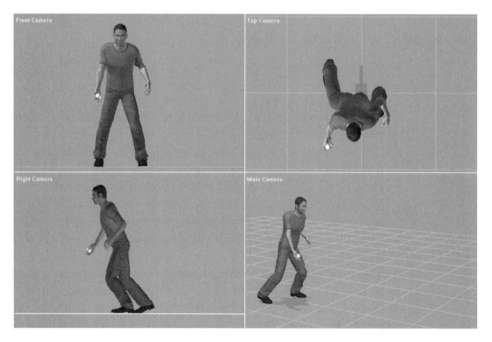

FIGURE 6.42
A correction keyframe at frame 73.

5. Look at frame 50, and come forward slowly to see a similar issue here, although not as bad. In frame 60, it's fine; in frame 63, it's not so fine. This is the type of issue that you must know to check when combining animations that must appear to be parented at one point and unparented at another.

6. At frame 75, the ball is in the hand. This is the point when it starts to leave the hand. The ball is traveling in the z-axis, so to send the ball out, go to the next keyframe, which is frame 80. Place the ball around 4.8 in the zTran. Make sure it is elevating in the yTran so that it's going up (because this is an underhand throw). Now that's starting to look good (shown in Figure 6.43).

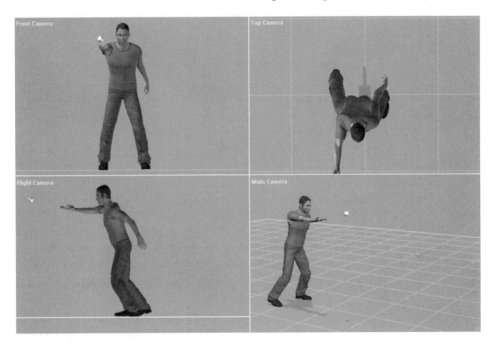

FIGURE 6.43
The ball is leaving now.

7. Go to the next frame, which is frame 85. Now, you just continue that trajectory, so bring it out and up a little bit more. The ball should now be positioned on frame 85 as shown in Figure 6.44.

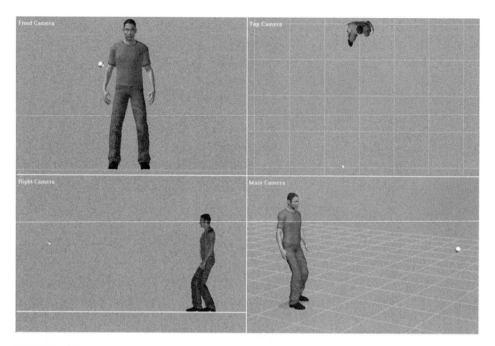

FIGURE 6.44
The ball is gone.

8. As you go to frame 90, you can start to make creative decisions, such as is the ball very heavy? If so, then the ball will start to come down. Of course, if the ball is very light, a few things could be happening. It would not only not start to come down quickly, but it may also not go very far because it may be reacting to resistance from the air. So, this becomes a matter of story-telling more than a matter of a mechanical animation process. In other words, it depends on what you are trying to communicate as the storyteller.

9. For this exercise, you'll simply have the ball come to its end point as shown earlier in Figure 6.44.

10. Now let's look at this from the front because earlier you positioned the ball well from a side view. Let's look at it from the Front Camera View because you know that there will be some issues. Work again in 5-frame increments to correct the position of the ball to match the right hand.

11. To adjust the curve of the trajectory of the ball, with the Ball and the xTran selected, go to the Graph Editor, and see how the ball is moving. You can see any strange movement in the ball's animation by looking at the xTran, yTran, and zTran here in the Graph Editor. Adjust the xTran curve in the

Graph Editor to look like Figure 6.45. Adjust the yTran curve in the Graph Editor to look like Figure 6.46. Adjust the zTran curve in the Graph Editor to look like Figure 6.47.

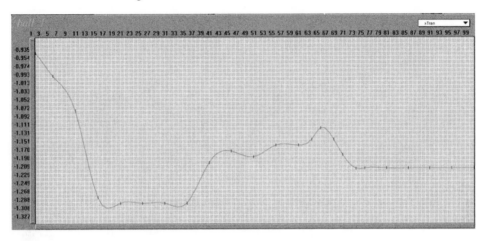

FIGURE 6.45
The correct xTran curve for the ball in the Graph Editor.

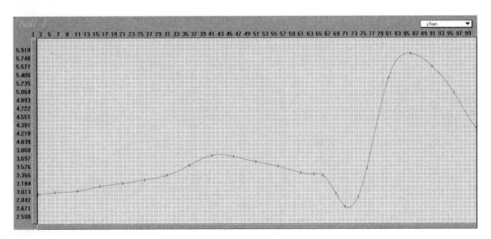

FIGURE 6.46
The correct yTran curve for the ball in the Graph Editor.

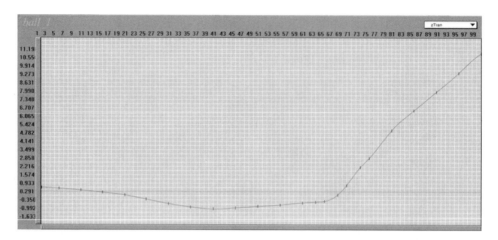

FIGURE 6.47
The correct zTran curve for the ball in the Graph Editor.

12. The final thing you have to do here is work on that hand grasp. Select the Right Hand. Working with the Right Hand Camera, zoom out a little bit, enough to clearly see the hand and ball (as shown in Figure 6.48). Orbit a bit to make sure that you can always have a sense of how the hand is grasping. You're just setting keyframes for the grasp, so be sure that the Grasp dial is selected for the right hand. Work in 10-frame increments. Be prepared to edit individual fingers of the hand at certain keys.

FIGURE 6.48
The ball grasped on frame 1 as seen from the Right Hand Camera.

13. The extent to which you have to do very accurate and detailed work here depends on how close you'll be seeing this aspect of the animation. In reality, when you are working in a production, maybe for a TV commercial, you have to make some judgment calls as to whether or not it's worth spending the time to make sure every finger is making contact with the ball. The important thing is to simply know how, in case you must.

14. To see the final animation, play the Throw-Underhand-Ball.mov movie in the Chapter 6 exercise file .

This completes the Throwing the Ball Underhand exercise, which combines several principles of animation to create 3D character animation in Poser.

Summary

You've just worked through the workflow for straight-ahead animation with overlapping motion to cause a 3D animated character to lift an object and place it on a shelf, and to throw a ball both overhand and underhand. As you've now learned, straight-ahead animation requires a bit more effort and practiced skill as compared to pose-to-pose animation. However, the most expressive character animation that you'll ever produce without the aid of reference video or motion capture will most likely be straight-ahead animation.

To truly learn how to apply the knowledge gained from this chapter, you really need to get out there into the real analog world and watch people move. Study them and observe the nuances, learn the patterns, and check out how social and age grouping combine to affect how people really move. Research topics such as biomechanics, physiology, and anything that delves into the reasons we move. Oh yeah, and have fun doing it too.

7 Animating to Reference Video

In This Chapter

INTRODUCTION

After you get the desire to produce realistic 3D character animation, you very quickly discover what a daunting task it can really be. Because we all know so well how people really walk, sit, stand, run, and move in general, animating a walk cycle or other bodily movement to truly simulate a realistic human motion can take what seems like eons to perfect.

Although there is no rule that says animation must be faithful in every way to reality, trying to achieve realistic motion and falling visibly short can really distract the viewer from the true value of your storytelling. So you've got to really give some serious thought as to whether your story really needs realistic motion or whether the expressive nature of the characters' interaction will captivate the viewer's mind in a compelling way that clearly communicates your ideas.

WHAT IS REFERENCE VIDEO?

Reference video is any video footage that can serve as a guide for animation. This is intentionally a very broad and vague definition of reference video because based on the workflow used to animate Poser figures to the reference video, you can use video of practically any type.

Reference video can be live action of a car chase or car crash, a rodeo event, or even a crazed mob in full-on attack mode. Each of these interesting scenario applications of video as a reference for 3D animation has strengths and weaknesses (assuming that the video is of sufficient quality for the task, of course). Cases in which an object or person (which will be mimicked in Poser character animation) is partially or fully obscured in the footage or the camera moves about in the footage both represent some additional challenges. In some cases, however, you may have to work with such video, such as when animating a live-action case for legal presentation or for forensic analysis, because you may not always have directorial control over the original capture of the reference video footage.

CAMERA

For purposes of this chapter, we'll be discussing reference video as video footage of real people in motion used as the basis for animating Poser characters. Although we'll be using footage captured with a consumer HD camera (JVC GZ-HD7), you can create great reference video using just about any low-end or high-end camcorder on the market. So, there are no real technical specs or hard-and-fast requirements of resolution, color space, frames per second, aspect ratio, or numbers of CCD (Charge Coupled Device) elements except to say that a higher quality camera with superior resolution improves your opportunity to create a great and predictable result.

The JVC GZ-HD7 was chosen to produce the reference videos in this chapter in part due to its 16:9 aspect ratio as well as its onboard 60-GB hard drive.

Non-HD cameras/camcorders have a 720 × 480 pixel resolution with a 4:3 aspect ratio similar to the shape of a traditional, older square-shaped TV screen.

NOTE

The benefit of the onboard hard drive is that every time you record a video clip, it is stored in the onboard hard drive as a video clip. After you're finished recording all the reference video, you can just copy the video clips to your computer and start processing them for import into Poser.

That being said, the higher the quality of the camera (camcorder) you use as well as your lighting and set preparations, the more useful your reference video will be. If you use a camcorder that requires a lot of light to capture a dancer's motion in a poorly lit room, you'll likely find the resulting video marginally useful at best.

LIGHTING

As with any video camera process, it is very important to have adequate and properly set up lighting to ensure an optimal result. The light kit used to record the included reference videos is the DayFlo-FX three-piece fluorescent 4200-watt kit. Although it's called "4200 watts," it doesn't actually use that much power at all. Each of the three light soft boxes has four fluorescent lamps that are 80 watts each. So as far as your wall socket is concerned, it's really (80 watts $\times$ 4 lamps) $\times$ 3 soft boxes = 960 watts. It's just that they produce the equivalent light of 4,200 watts of incandescent light. Besides the benefit of saving energy and the Earth by using this type of light, this light kit doesn't emit perceivable heat and doesn't make your actors sweat. You can even look directly at these lights without causing eye strain. They're like magic lights, or at the very least, really neat.

The real purpose of lighting when capturing reference video is not to capture beautiful footage but rather to capture beautiful motion. Lighting should be tuned and adjusted to help the camera capture high contrast between the motion actor and a static and (preferably) plain background as well as clearly defined motion markers on the motion actor.

REFERENCE VIDEO VERSUS MOTION CAPTURE

Technically speaking, animating to reference video is a primitive form of motion capture in that the process mimics the live-action motion in 3D. When you say "motion capture" (mocap) in the general context of 3D animation, everyone knows that you're referring to the combination of multiple cameras and markers or some such apparatus equivalent. So how does video reference stack up to motion capture? Well it's a mixed bag, where they both have their strengths and weaknesses.

MOTION CAPTURE

Mocap has incredible motion fidelity, meaning that the results are very realistic, resulting in an uncanny sense when the quality of the motion is even more realistic than the quality of the 3D modeling, textures, or character expressions. Mocap can also take a comparably shorter time to create great results than using reference video. Additionally, mocap is excellent at handling cases where the character may be partially obscured due to unique body poses or interaction with other objects and is great at handling multiple simultaneous live actors.

However, a good mocap setup could easily cost from $25,000 up to $1 million. So if you want to create 3D character animation at home or in a small company, mocap is usually not a realistic option. Depending on the system you use, there could be motion data editing after the capture process. There's also a bit to learn with respect to getting the mocap data into your 3D application via some file format conversion process. This means that there may be intermediary steps between capture and animation, which, in some cases, may involve integrating other applications such as Autodesk's MotionBuilder into your workflow.

Mocap generally records a keyframe on every frame of the animation for every motion sensor in your live actor mocap suit setup, which produces very lifelike motion. However, this also means that editing the motion after the fact can be a chore. For example, imagine that you're working for a customer who wants a realistic dance animation, so you hire a good dancer and use mocap to collect the motion for the animation. After a little work and two days later, everything looks great. Then the customer says that at the 8-second point, he wants the dancer to jump into the air. This is a problem because motion capture animation is like getting canned animation with an overabundance of information. Another example of this limitation shows up when you capture a realistic walk cycle and then try to create attitude and personality in the walk. In both of these challenging scenarios, you might consider doing some sort of keyframe reduction to either reduce the frames by a factor (1/2 as many or 1/4 as many keyframes per second) or use an adaptive keyframe reduction that reduces keyframes where the transformation or rotation channels for each body part changes rotation or position below a set threshold (in other words, where there's a significant change). These solutions yield limited success rates and are favored only in certain circumstances.

For all of its pros and cons, however, mocap is used more than any other animation mimic method in Hollywood because with proper planning, a skilled team, and great tools, mocap is nothing short of digital art in motion.

REFERENCE VIDEO

Reference video for use in Poser can be produced with just about any video camera or camcorder, so it's very affordable and accessible to most animators at the widest range of economic means. Reference video can also be sourced from preexisting footage such as movies, television, or any other video already recorded. So apart from the cost of gear to bring the video into the computer (which is already built-in to most modern computers), reference video (in comparison to mocap) can in some cases be free. The workflow for using reference video to animate in Poser is based on first identifying key poses in the reference video and then posing the Poser figure to match the live action figure in the reference video. As a result, significantly fewer keyframes are generated in the process, allowing for the resulting character animation. Editing such animation to customer demands is much easier than editing mocap animation.

On the other hand, the quality and usability of reference video for animation captured by a video camera is totally dependent on the skill of the videographer/animator to properly prepare and use a light kit, the live-action actor's motion, and a good understanding of both the video camera and the video capture process. Failure to understand or operate the lighting setup, camera operation, or video capture into the computer can result in marginally useful or downright useless results. Unless several video cameras are used together to capture the action from all sides, body parts will often be obscured or even go off camera. Because cameras capture the real world and store/present it in a 2D screen space, the video reference generally doesn't line up perfectly with the 3D characters being animated.

Reference video is more frequently used by smaller operations due to cost because most cannot afford a mocap system. You'll see this used in Hollywood only when the reference video is a source that must also be composited with the resulting 3D animation.

ENCODING THE VIDEO (PC)

If you're working with Poser on a PC, you'll need to encode the reference video as an .AVI video file. This is a native video format of the PC and is the only video that you can import into Poser on a PC. When encoding as an AVI file, it's important to understand when to use which AVI codec (variation of the .AVI video file format). The most versatile code is the *uncompressed* format. The beauty of the uncompressed format is that it doesn't introduce any lossy artifacts (degrading distortion) into the video image, and it handles any pixel resolution. The downside is that this format makes massive video files that eat up a lot of hard drive space and can even be difficult to preview on your computer due to the massive memory it requires for playback.

Indeo 5.1 is a popular codec that makes relatively clean smaller video files. For purposes of encoding reference video for Poser, the main drawback to this format is that it doesn't handle large or irregular aspect ratios (non 4:3) very well. So it works well with 320 × 240, 360 × 240, 640 × 480, 720 × 480, and 800 × 600 video. If you're wondering where you would ever get video with odd aspect ratios, such video really comes from preprocessing and cropping video to produce reference video that focuses on the area of action. For example, the reference videos in the Exercise files in the Chapter 7 folder of the DVD-ROM included with this book named Exercise-1.avi and Exercise-1.mov were originally produced by rotating an HD camera 90 degrees (just like when you're photographing a standing person with a still camera) to capture Chiaki's exercise motion. This was done because she stood in one spot and stretched her hands all the way up, making her height extend beyond the

ON THE DVD

limits of the default camera framing. Rotating the camera 90 degrees kept her within the video frame. After bringing the video in to Adobe AfterEffects, it had to be rotated -90 degrees to bring her back to the proper orientation. This resulted in an unnaturally tall video with a resolution of 1080 (h–width) by 1920 (v–height). After cropping and scaling down the video, the final video rendered at 800 × 600.

ENCODING THE VIDEO (MAC)

If you're working with Poser on a Mac, you'll need to encode the video as a .MOV (QuickTime) video. This is the native video format for the Mac and is the only video that you can import into Poser on a Mac. QuickTime is generally easy to encode with when working with odd aspect ratios.

Whether rendering reference video files on a Mac or PC, you should be prepared to handle very large video files. Rendered file sizes can span the extremes just by making simple adjustments in the application used to render the video. For example, the reference videos in the Exercise files in the Chapter 7 folder of the DVD-ROM included with this book named Exercise-1.avi and Exercise-1.mov can be rendered with a file size of 1.5 GB or 15 MB without changing the pixel resolution. Simply adjusting the bit rate (the amount of data used to display the video per second) and the codec can make a world of difference.

ON THE DVD

CHARACTER ANIMATION APPLICATIONS

Now we'll look at two character animation applications where you might use reference video:

2D Live Action: The live-action subject maintains a head-on or side view to the camera while performing the reference motion. The camera remains in a fixed location and orientation. This is useful for capturing body movement such as exercise and other simple movements that do not require the live action actor to turn in the y-axis.

3D Live Action: The live-action subject varies position and is free to rotate while performing the reference motion. The camera remains in a fixed location and orientation.

Note that in each of the preceding reference video applications for character animation, the camera remains in a fixed position with no change to the orientation and zoom. The video camera is simply a static recording device without assisting or compensating for any of the action being captured. Depending on the features of the camera's focusing system, after proper focus is established, it may be necessary to switch from automatic to manual focus so that the camera doesn't lose focus during the recording process.

PREPARING THE LIVE-ACTION MOTION ACTOR

With the ever-increasing use of motion capture in CG today, a new breed of actor has emerged, the *motion actor*. A motion actor is someone who acts by gestures and body movements as a motion source to later drive animated CG characters.

Although it is possible to simply point a camera at a moving person (the motion actor) and record the person as reference video footage, preparing the actor speeds up the process in Poser and increases the fidelity of the final animation with reference to the live-action footage.

The reference video we will use in this chapter shows Chiaki and Teri as the motion actors. As you look at Figure 7.1, notice that Chiaki has tan and blue markers on her elbows, wrists, knees, and ankles.

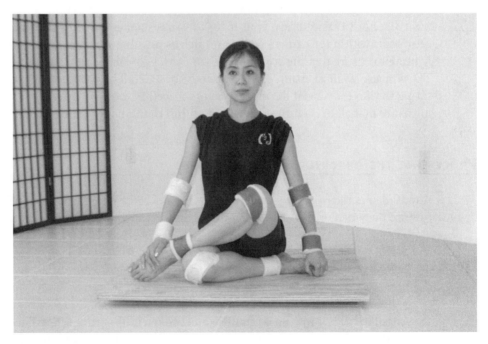

FIGURE 7.1
Live-action actor with blue and tan motion markers on legs and arms.

These are truly low-tech markers in that they are just made from colored tape wrapped around foam pads and positioned to highlight the position, orientation, and posing of the legs and arms.

When using tape and foam, be sure they are tight so that they do not move out of position while the motion actor is performing.

Two different tape colors are used to help identify left arms and legs from the right side. Using other colored tape as well as adding colored markers to other body parts (such as shoulders and toes) can also be helpful.

DIRECTING THE LIVE-ACTION MOTION ACTOR

The motions performed by the motion actor must be directed and observed carefully to help ensure that they will truly aid in the 3D animation storytelling process. Depending on your skill in directing, you may want to enlist the help of a skilled videographer or video director who can effectively direct actors to emote and really perform. In such a crew configuration, you would then need to function as a technical director (TD) and turn your focus to issues such as ensuring that the motion actors stay within the camera frame as much as possible and keeping an eye on the lighting to ensure that the critical details are always available to be recorded. As the TD, you also want to ensure that you get the best detail by balancing between capturing the largest view of the motion actors as well as zooming out only far enough to ensure that all of their motion will be within the camera's frame.

PROCESSING THE IMPORTED REFERENCE VIDEO

After video is recorded, depending on your camera/camcorder type, you'll either capture the video or copy the video clips from the camcorder to your computer.

If editing the video is beyond your current skill set, seek tutorials on the editing options of any video editing software compatible with the file format you will import into Poser.

After the video is in your computer (and broken into separate clips if necessary), you need to decide whether you must process the video to enhance lighting, crop out unneeded areas, or rotate the video. When these issues are resolved, you'll render the video in either .AVI for PC or .MOV for Mac, and you're off to Poser-land.

ANIMATING TO 2D LIVE-ACTION REFERENCE VIDEO

Now we'll actually begin working with some reference video in Poser; you'll be working with the Exercise-Step-01.pz3 project file from the Chapter 7 folder on the DVD-ROM. This exercise covers practical issues you'll run into when applying this workflow in production. There are some important things to be aware of here. You have a bit of freedom and a chance to be creative and play with the touch and feel of the motion mimicking in this workflow (as compared to working with mocap). There are some issues you need to be aware of (such as having to filter the incoming motion capture data, having to do keyframe reduction, and having to review the relationships of the autogenerated keyframes to best determine how to edit the data) that are unique to this workflow that you don't have to deal with if you are animating manually by the principles of character animation.

You'll start by working with the preloaded scene so that the video is already in place with the character.

You can use any character in this exercise. You don't have to use the one included in the exercise file, just in case you don't have all the components required for this character installed in your Runtime Poser directory.

TROUBLESHOOTING VIDEO IMPORTING

When troubleshooting issues while importing video into Poser for reference in a workflow involving more than one computer, be sure that the codec used to render the video in your editing software is also installed on the computer on which Poser is installed and on which the video will be imported.

Also, be sure that you are using the appropriate file type for your computer. If it's a PC, you should be using the .AVI video format. If it's a Mac, you should be using the QuickTime format. You should also make sure that you have the latest driver updates for your video card and that the video card has ample memory and is capable of OpenGL display.

The video reference is not intended to be a frame-accurate, pixel-accurate, temporal-accurate type of workflow. Instead, it's intend to be more like a student (the Poser figure) mimicking a teacher (the reference video motion actor).

For example, in this exercise, you'll have a ballet dancer doing some basic exercises, and the Poser character will mimic those exercises following the body shape of the video reference motion actor. So, be loose and have fun with the process as opposed to being very technical and fastidiously making sure every angle matches perfectly. This process is more art than science. Taking this loose approach opens up more possibilities for using reference video.

If, for example, you require that the actor in your reference video has the same proportions and body type as your Poser character, you'll find yourself very limited in which reference video actors you can use. So, instead, keep it loose, have the motion actor's body approximately match the Poser figure's body, and you'll be very pleased with the end result. Your work will be completed in a reasonable period of time, and you'll have more creative thoughts of how you can apply this workflow in your projects. You'll see how you can use more easily accessible actors for your projects. And by actors, I don't mean Hollywood actors. Your actors can literally be brothers and sisters and friends and family to produce reference motion for your Poser character animations.

ON THE DVD

After you have the Exercise-Step-01.pz3 file loaded, make sure that you set your end frame to be 687 frames because we are only working with a segment of this reference video. The reference video is actually quite a bit longer and goes all the way to frame 1125, but you'll get the idea of the workflow by frame 687.

When doing this type of work, I generally work with a dual or triple monitor system because I work with the QuickTime version of this reference video file on another monitor to get a clear view of the video without any Poser content getting in the way. QuickTime works well for this is because it scrubs very smoothly back and forth when you drag the play head, and it's very easy to work with.

When using the reference video externally in the QuickTime player, you want to have the same point of reference in time. In the QuickTime player, you'll change the position display from Standard to Frame Number (shown in Figure 7.2). This way, you can be on the same frame in Poser and in QuickTime—well almost.

Poser animation starts from frame 1. QuickTime video starts from frame 0. So there will be one frame of difference between Poser and QuickTime.

NOTE

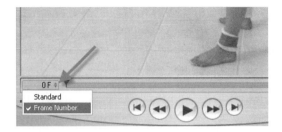

FIGURE 7.2
Changing the QuickTime position display to
Frame Number.

So, if you want to sync frame 10 in Poser with the QuickTime reference video, you go to frame 9 in QuickTime. Simply add one to the reference video when looking at it in QuickTime to sync up what you are seeing in Poser.

Now we'll look at a deconstruction of the workflow for using reference video in Poser to create character animation.

ON THE DVD From the Chapter 7 Exercises folder on the DVD-ROM, play the Exercise-Together.mov movie to see the Poser figure mimicking the motion reference video's motion actor. If you look very closely, you'll see some slight differences in the body because the body's proportions are slightly different between the Poser figure and the motion actor, which is just fine.

CHOOSING KEYFRAMES BASED ON REFERENCE VIDEO ACTION

One of the keys to getting this fun process to work is evaluating reference video to determine which points in the video are key to posing the 3D figure. It's important to use the QuickTime player to evaluate the reference video. This is where Quick-Time's capability to smoothly drag the play head back-and-forth along the timeline becomes very important. Based on key points in the reference video where body parts start or stop motion or where a body part has reached an extreme point or made contact with something, you'll want to make a list, a literal document listing of such key points identifying the frame number and some description that allows you to better correlate what the Poser figure is trying to achieve.

NOTE *Remember that unlike the Poser figure, the video cannot be rotated to show you what's behind. So with this limitation in mind, to reduce your confusion, creating descriptions for the list of keyframes extracted from the reference video is helpful when posing the Poser figure.*

With the QuickTime video Excercise-1b.mov at frame 0, you'll make a document list to indicate key points in the video that represent keyframes in Poser.

For example, as you look at the relevant keyframes in this video, you can make a note that on frame 10 in the QuickTime player, there is almost have a 90-degree elbow bend. So how do you come up with the keyframe descriptions? This is really a matter of whether you're working with a team or alone. In a team setting, there should be some agreement that the descriptions make sense to all who must use them. It's a bit more relaxed if you work by yourself. So, for example, on frame 10, my description is "Almost 90 degree elbow." It's visually accurate and, if I come back to work on this project six months from now, the description will still make sense.

As stated earlier, this reference video has different colors of markers (shown in Figure 7.3), which starts to become an issue as the motion actor really gets moving.

FIGURE 7.3
Color markers on the reference video motion actor.

In this project, our focus is on animating based on the left side of the motion actor's body posing in the reference video. You'll use the Symmetry menu item in Poser to easily reflect the left side to the right side.

As an example of how you extract the list of keys from a reference video for posing a Poser figure to create character animation mimicking the live action motion actor, the following is a listing of the keyframes on which the Poser figure should be posed to match the reference video for this project:

Keyframes	Description
1	Starting point
10	Almost 90-degree elbows
23	Upper torso eases back slightly
34	90-degree elbows up
68	Reaching for the sky
109	Hold
222	Bending over midway
334	Touch the floor
376	Palms on the floor
404	Palms stopped moving forward
419	Head preparing to face camera
434	Head facing camera
454	Head still facing camera
483	Head turns away and hands pulling back to raise up
494	Fingers about to leave floor
535	Back and arms straighten out
545	On her way to reach for the sky, again
590	Midway going to the sky
633	Reaching for the sky
664	Hold
687	Holding the "reaching for the sky" pose a bit more

When you're actually posing the character to match the reference video, it's often helpful to work in two camera views (viewports). So, switch to the two ports, and work in the Right Camera and the Main Camera (shown in Figure 7.4 and Figure 7.5).

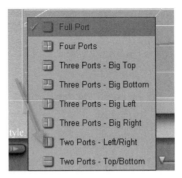

FIGURE 7.4
Selecting the two viewport mode.

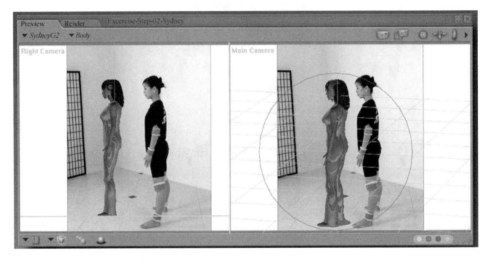

FIGURE 7.5
Right and Main camera viewports.

When working in the right camera, the reference video is not particularly important (because the right camera is an orthogonal view, and the reference video is shot in perspective). The purpose of the Right View is to check for floor contact with the feet (and later on with the hands when they touch the floor) and verify body symmetry. In the Right View, by simply moving the mouse over the floor, you can see the relationship of the floor to the character. The reference video is really important in the Main Camera view because this is where you can more closely match the figure posing to the reference video.

In the Main Camera, you'll want to scale and position the figure as close to the reference video as you can to get a good relationship between the figure and the reference video.

Go to frame 1 (shown in Figure 7.6), and take a look at the elements of the figure that will receive the most attention in the animation with this reference video. You'll be starting with the Left Collar, so be very careful when selecting it that you are not selecting one of the props or clothing (such as Tank, Casual_Pants, Hair2, and so on) while actually trying to select an element of the Poser figure.

Pay particularly close attention to this issue because getting this wrong can be very frustrating.

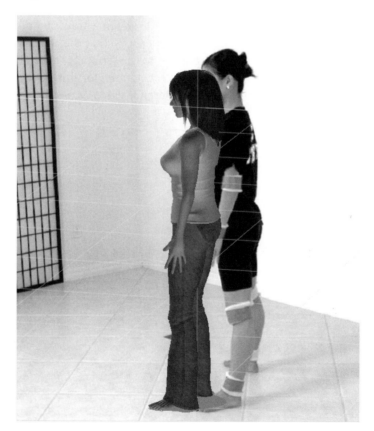

FIGURE 7.6
Frame 1 is the starting point in the reference video.

You'll use the parameter dials for all of the figure posing for this animation. You won't be using the editing tools at all.

1. So with the Left Collar selected, Twist, Front-Back, and Up-Down are all defaulted to zero. Select the Left Shoulder, and take note that Twist = 0, Front-Back = -4, and Up-Down = -76. The forearm is set to Twist = -22, Side-Side = -12, and Bend = -13. Use the Symmetry tool for the figure to select Left to Right to pose the right side of the figure. This is very easy because this reference video is simple. The exercise routine maintains a parallel relationship between the right and left sides of the body. Also, on frame 1, the hands are in their original default posing with nothing special happening to them yet.

2. From the keyframe list, the next reference frame you'll work with is frame 10 (shown in Figure 7.7). You can see that the arms are coming up in the reference video. It's important to use symmetry to reflect the left side of the body to the right side on each keyframe for this tutorial. Pose the left arm of the figure to match the reference video or use the following parameters:

	Twist	FrBack	Up-Down
Left Collar	0	0	0
Left Shoulder	0	-4	-76
Left Forearm	-22	-12	-75
	Twist	Sd-Sd	Bend
Left Hand	0	0	0

FIGURE 7.7
Almost 90-degree elbow.

3. On frame 23 (shown in Figure 7.8), there's a slight movement on the upper torso. If this isn't very obvious to you yet, open the reference video in the QuickTime Player, and drag the play head slowly back and forth between frames 10 and 23. You'll see that the torso is moving slightly. You'll animate that on frame 23. To assist in this subtle animation, with the Waist selected, set the Bend to -4. On frame 10, this value was set to 0, so this subtle change in the waist bend provides the small movement you're looking for.

FIGURE 7.8
Upper torso eases back slightly.

4. Go to frame 34 (shown in Figure 7.9). Here, in the reference video, you'll have the 90 degrees elbow up (from the keyframe list). This keyframe shows another reason why you want to use Right View because the 90-degree elbow is more easily observed from an orthogonal view. Pose the left arm of the figure to match the reference video, or use the following parameters:

	Twist	FrBack	Up-Down
Left Collar	12	5	0
Left Shoulder	-94	-96	0
Left Forearm	-22	-12	-93

	Twist	Sd-Sd	Bend
Left Hand	0	0	0

FIGURE 7.9
90-degree elbow up.

5. Go to frame 68 (shown in Figure 7.10), and note that on the reference video, the motion actor is reaching for the sky. Be careful not to deform the collar and shoulder when posing the left arm here. Examine the collar and arm pits in the Pose camera when setting this keyframe. Failure to pay close attention can lead to an artifacted and deformed image. Pose the left arm of the figure to match the reference video or use the following parameters:

	Twist	FrBack	Up-Down
Left Collar	-74	3	33
Left Shoulder	-94	-33	-6
Left Forearm	-22	-6	-21

	Twist	Sd-Sd	Bend
Left Hand	0	0	0

FIGURE 7.10
Reaching for the sky.

6. On frame 109 (shown in Figure 7.11), you'll be holding the pose from the previous keyframe with a slight adjustment to the Hip. Pose the left arm of the figure to match the reference video, or use the following parameters:

	Twist	FrBack	Up-Down
Left Collar	-74	12	33
Left Shoulder	-94	-33	-6
Left Forearm	-22	-6	-21

	Twist	Sd-Sd	Bend
Left Hand	0	0	0

	xRotate	xTran	yTran	zTran
Hip	13	0	-.026	-.041

FIGURE 7.11
Hold the pose.

7. Go to frame 222 (shown in Figure 7.12), where the motion actor is bending over midway. This pose requires some major hip rotation in the xRotate and a little movement in the xTran and yTran. There is also some animation of the arms, but it's not really significant at this point. Pose the figure to match the reference video, or use the following parameters:

	Twist	FrBack	Up-Down
Left Collar	-43	22	22
Left Shoulder	-93	-69	14
Left Forearm	-4	-8	-40

	Twist	Sd-Sd	Bend
Left Hand	3	0	14

	xRotate	xTran	yTran	zTran
Hip	64	0	-.232	-.292

FIGURE 7.12
Bending over midway.

8. In frame 334 "Touch the floor" (shown in Figure 7.13), you can see that the motion actor in the reference video is not quite touching the floor yet. So the Poser figure also should get close to the floor with her hands but not quite touch it yet. This is where working in the Right View really becomes advantageous.

9. You'll notice some differences between the body type of the live-action motion actor and the Poser figure and how the animation differs from the reference video. Because this is a 3D model and 3D character rigging is not perfect (compared to real human biomechanics), you'll run into some odd limitations at points in the animation like this, where you'll see some un-natural compression. You can fix this, for example, by pulling the torso forward so that the figure is not so compressed around the hips. Pose the figure to match the reference video or use the following parameters:

	Twist	FrBack	Up-Down	
Left Collar	-74	12	33	
Left Shoulder	-58	-33	-6	
Left Forearm	19	-6	-21	

	Twist	Sd-Sd	Bend	
Left Hand	0	0	0	

	xRotate	xTran	yTran	zTran
Hip	129	0	-.619	-.292

FIGURE 7.13
Touch the floor.

10. Go to frame 376 "Palms on the floor" (shown in Figure 7.14), where the palms of the hands are actually touching the floor.
11. Now you're going to switch to working with the hand cameras because ensuring that the hand contact with the floor doesn't result in the hands going through the floor visibly is critical to maintaining the illusion of the animation.
12. So select the Left Hand Camera to work on posing the Left Hand. A key visual cue in getting the hand placement right is the real-time OpenGL shadow provided by Poser. This quick real-time shadow tells you whether the hand is penetrating the floor. After you get the left hand set, pose the right hand manually.

The Symmetry menu will not help reflect the left hand to the right. You must pose the right hand manually here.

13. Pose the figure to match the reference video, or use the following parameters:

	Twist	FrBack	Up-Down
Left Collar	-80	10	35
Left Shoulder	-52	-26	-20
Left Forearm	22	-6	-17

	Twist	Sd-Sd	Bend
Left Hand	-4	-1	32

	xRotate	xTran	yTran	zTran	Grasp
Hip	131	0	-.585	-.241	-15.81

FIGURE 7.14
Palms on the floor.

14. Go to frame 404 "Palms stopped moving forward"(shown in Figure 7.15).
15. Here, you can see that the hands must bend. Select the Left Hand, and set the Bend to 30. If you temporarily go back to frame 376 with the Left Hand still selected, you can see the slight bend occurring. If you go back one more keyframe to 222, you can see it's quite different (-7). So as you're moving forward in the timeline, the animation of the hand becomes an issue to keep track of.
16. You don't want to break the illusion that this is the floor, so you want the hand to respond as though it's limited by the floor while also appearing to hold up (support) the weight of the body. To effectively pose the hands, you'll also have to get into the hand controls at this point because the way

the fingers splay to support the body is a part of the illusion that this is really happening and that she (the Poser figure) really has mass and body weight. At some point, you'll even want to get granular and deal with things such as spreading the fingers and even working with individual digits (especially the thumbs). The thumbs have a strange habit of bending so that they go through the floor, so you'll have to actually select the thumbs and edit them by manipulating each of the three segments (lThumb1, lThumb2, and lThumb3).

17. Pose the figure to match the reference video, or use the following parameters:

	Twist	FrBack	Up-Down	
Left Collar	-81	10	35	
Left Shoulder	-51	-25	-29	
Left Forearm	23	-6	-17	

	Twist	Sd-Sd	Bend	
Left Hand	-5	-3	37	

	xRotate	xTran	yTran	zTran
Hip	128	0	-.722	1.032

	Twist	Sd-Sd	Bend	
Neck	0	0	-4	

FIGURE 7.15
Palms stopped moving forward.

18. Go to frame 419 "Head prepping to face camera" (shown in Figure 7.16). Because the figure is now preparing to face the camera, set the Twist parameter of the Neck to match the reference video.

19. In preparation for the next key at frame 434, set a key for the Twist parameter on the Neck to 0 so that you establish the start of the neck's rotation to have the head face the camera. Later, you'll set another keyframe on the Neck Twist at frame 434, but to properly control the head turn, a key must be set now.

NOTE

Even though the value of the Neck Twist is already defaulted to 0, if you don't manually set the value to 0, the head will slowly begin turning from the previous Neck Twist keyframe to the next keyframe (frame 434 where the head will actually be facing the camera). Adjusting the Twist parameter dial and setting it back to 0 sets the required keyframe data.

20. Pose the figure to match the reference video, or use the following parameters:

	Twist	Sd-Sd	Bend
Neck	0	0	-4

FIGURE 7.16
Head preparing to face camera.

21. Go to frame 434 "Head facing camera" (shown in Figure 7.17). Twist the neck to now face the camera.
22. Pose the figure to match the reference video, or use the following parameters:

	Twist	Sd-Sd	Bend
Neck	43	0	-4

FIGURE 7.17
Head facing camera.

23. On frame 454, set keyframes on the figure so that the head is still facing the camera.
24. On frame 483 "Head turns away and hands pulling back to raise up" (shown in Figure 7.18), the Neck twists back to its default Twist value of 0. Now as you are going through these frames with the hands contacting the floor, you really should pay attention to ensure that the hands are not going through the floor.

FIGURE 7.18
Head turns away and hands pulled back to raise up.

25. With the neck now animated to have the head face the camera, an interesting problem creeps in. If you play back the animation to this point, you'll notice that the head turns at a point in the timeline where you have not instructed it to turn. This is due to the default spline interpolation applied by Poser between the keyframes. With the Neck and Twist selected, open the Graph Editor to view what is really happening here (shown in Figure 7.19). The default spline interpolation is causing the head to twist heavily before the figure faces the camera and slightly after the figure faces the camera.

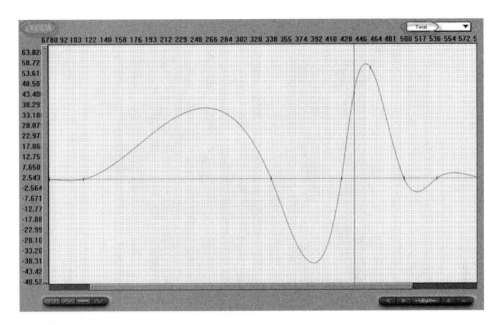

FIGURE 7.19
Excessive twisting of the neck displayed in the Graph Editor.

26. To solve this problem, select the keyframe at 419 and the two previous ones by dragging in the Graph Editor (as shown in Figure 7.20). Select the Linear interpolation button (also shown in the bottom left of Figure 7.20) to get rid of this twist problem. Repeat this selecting frames 494 to 535 as well. When you're finished, the graph should look like Figure 7.21.

Note that when you use Linear interpolation, Poser tries to help you by adding keys just before the start of your selection and just after the end. You'll need to manually select these and delete them.

NOTE

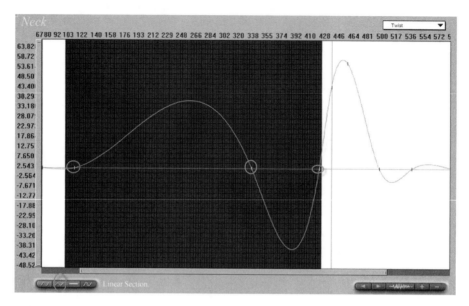

FIGURE 7.20
Neck Twist keyframe selected in the Graph Editor before being flattened with Linear interpolation.

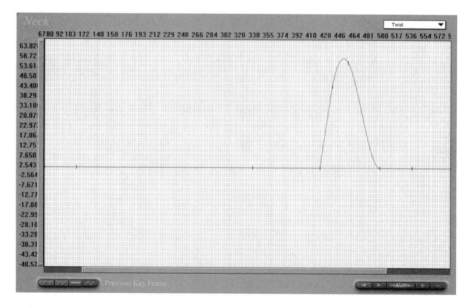

FIGURE 7.21
Neck Twist to have the figure's head face the camera in a way matching the reference is now corrected.

27. Go to frame 494 "Fingers about to leave the floor" (shown in Figure 7.22). The weight is coming back onto the legs.
28. Pose the figure to match the reference video, or use the following parameters:

	Twist	FrBack	Up-Down	
Left Collar	-76	11	34	
Left Shoulder	-56	-31	-54	
Left Forearm	20	-6	-20	

	Twist	Sd-Sd	Bend	Grasp
Left Hand	1	-18	73	-7.836

	xRotate	xTran	yTran	zTran
Hip	129	0	-.636	.893

FIGURE 7.22
Fingers about to leave the floor.

29. Go to frame 535 "Back and arms straighten out" (shown in Figure 7.23). The figure is starting to regain her balance. In the keyframe, pose the hip and straighten the arms and hands to match the reference video, or use the following parameters:

	Twist	FrBack	Up-Down	
Left Collar	-74	12	33	
Left Shoulder	-58	-33	-58	
Left Forearm	19	-6	-21	

	Twist	Sd-Sd	Bend	Grasp
Left Hand	37	0	9	-14

	xRotate	xTran	yTran	zTran
Hip	91	0	-.327	-.156

FIGURE 7.23
Back and arms straighten out.

30. Go to frame 545 (shown in figure 7.24) where we are at the midway point and going to reach for the sky again. As you can see, this process is just a matter of using simple Poser posing techniques to match a reference image that happens to be a part of a sequence of video.

31. Pose the figure to match the reference video, or use the following parameters:

	Twist	FrBack	Up-Down	
Left Collar	-74	12	33	
Left Shoulder	-58	-33	-58	
Left Forearm	19	-6	-21	
	Twist	**Sd-Sd**	**Bend**	**Grasp**
Left Hand	43	2	0	-14
	xRotate	**xTran**	**yTran**	**zTran**
Hip	76	0	-.249	-.267

FIGURE 7.24
On her way to reach for the sky, again.

32. Go to frame 590 "Midway going to the sky" (shown in Figure 7.25). In this
    step of the workflow, check that you have keyframes set for the figure to en-
    sure that midway between the keyframes the character is not wildly out of
    sync (visibly before or after) with the video. You can only see this by click-
    ing Play (because Poser won't update the reference video as you manually
    drag the play head).
33. Pose the figure to match the reference video, or use the following parameters:

	Twist	FrBack	Up-Down	
Left Collar	-74	12	33	
Left Shoulder	-58	-33	-48	
Left Forearm	19	-6	-21	
	Twist	**Sd-Sd**	**Bend**	**Grasp**
Left Hand	37	0	9	14
	xRotate	**xTran**	**yTran**	**zTran**
Hip	61	0	-.172	-.156

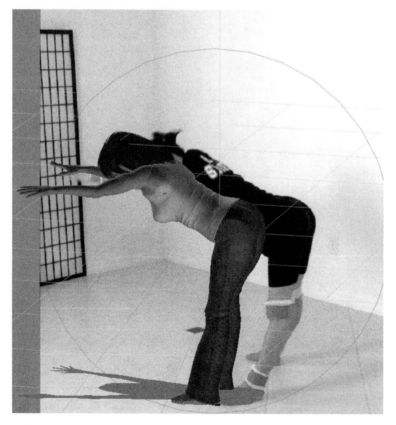

FIGURE 7.25
Midway going to the sky.

34. Now go to frame 633 "Reaching for the sky" (shown in Figure 7.26). You're basically using the same technique as before to cause the figure to reach for the sky. You don't copy and paste frame data from previous frames with this workflow because when working with a reference video, you want to benefit from the nuance in posing provided by the live-action motion actor.

35. Pose the figure to match the reference video, or use the following parameters:

	Twist	FrBack	Up-Down	
Left Collar	-74	30	33	
Left Shoulder	-58	-33	-27	
Left Forearm	19	-6	-21	

	Twist	Sd-Sd	Bend	Grasp
Left Hand	37	0	9	-14

	xRotate	xTran	yTran	zTran
Hip	12	0	-.017	-.156

FIGURE 7.26
Reaching for the sky, again.

36. Go to frame 664 (shown in Figure 7.27), which provides a keyframe where you make a slight adjustment to xRotate (change the value to 6) to rotate the hips up. You are just holding the "reaching for the sky" pose here.

FIGURE 7.27
Holding the "reaching for the sky" pose.

37. You end on frame 687 by holding the pose some more as shown in Figure
   7.28.

FIGURE 7.28
Holding the "reaching for the sky" pose a bit more.

38. Play this all back to see how much the 3D character now matches the video reference. You'll see that it's not a temporally perfect match but rather like the visual relationship between a teacher and student.

USING 3D MOTION REFERENCE VIDEO

Because reference video often has motion that occurs in 3D space (shown in Figure 7.29) and doesn't have actors performing action parallel to the camera, additional issues must be addressed to successfully use such video as an animation reference within Poser.

FIGURE 7.29
A live-action motion actor moving in 3D natural space.

Markers placed on the actor's left and right sides (as shown in Figure 7.30) prove even more useful in such reference video because as the actor moves faster, and their arms and legs blur with motion (as shown in Figure 7.31), it becomes a bit difficult to clearly identify whether you are looking at the right or left arm or leg on certain keyframes.

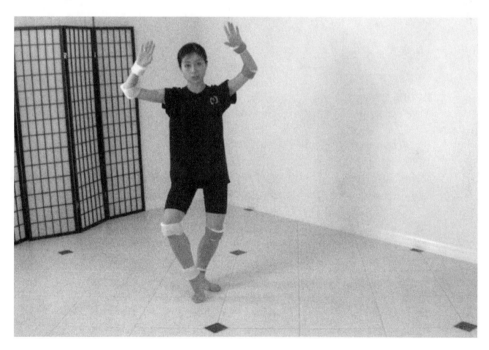

FIGURE 7.30
A live-action motion actor with colored motion markers.

FIGURE 7.31
A live-action motion actor with blurred fast-moving legs.

When working with fast-moving actors with 3D motion reference video, adequate lighting is even more critical as shown in Figure 7.32. Poorly lit fast-moving actors also have poorly lit markers, which will hinder your efforts when using the reference video as a background in Poser.

FIGURE 7.32
Good lighting on the left; poor lighting on the right.

When capturing 3D motion reference video footage, spend a lot of time considering the size of the actor with the video frame as a percentage of the overall resolution at the camera's video format. So if you're capturing the video with an NTSC DV camera, you'll need to keep the actor closer to the camera (even in adequate lighting) than you would when capturing the video with either an HD or HDV camera. Failure to do so can result in significant loss of pixel resolution, which makes it difficult to match the Poser figure's posing and motion to that of the reference video actor. This is because the NTSC camera's video resolution is relatively lower than HD and HDV (see Figure 7.33 and Table 7.1).

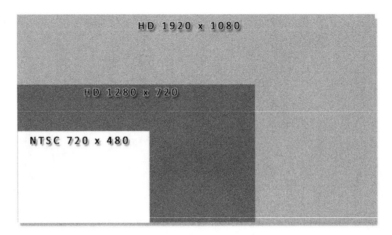

FIGURE 7.33
Various video formats overlaid.

TABLE 7.1 VIDEO FORMAT RESOLUTIONS

NTSC	=	720 h × 480 v
HDV	=	1440 h × 1080 v
HD	=	1280 h × 720 v
HD	=	1920 h × 1080 v

So if an actor is 10 feet away from an NTSC camera, the level of detail available within Poser will be equivalent to the same adequately lit character 22.5 feet away in HDV or HD video.

Level of detail here, for example, refers to the amount of pixels used to show the actor's face or any body part. Level of detail is most critical when distinguishing between the position and movement of body parts on the left and right of the reference video actor.

NOTE

As with the "Exercise" video tutorial we did previously in this chapter, you should scroll through the 3D motion reference video in a video player with frame number display (not the default time display) and note the keyframes that indicate key points in the live-action actor's motion. These will indicate the frames in Poser where you'll need to pose your 3D figure. For example, in the Exercise files in the Chapter 7 folder provided on the DVD-ROM, there is a 3D motion reference video file named Dance-1a.mov. Play this QuickTime movie to see how the actor moves

ON THE DVD

in 3D, and then set the QuickTime player to display frames and not time. If you were going to use this as the motion reference for a Poser 3D character animation, you would use the following list of keyframes:

Keyframes	Description
1	Starting point
29	Balancing end
53	Rotate right foot lightly
69	Flat footed
84	Left leg halfway up
113	Left leg all the way up
129	Right foot down
142	Half twist
166	Full twist
189	Wings out
205	Dip
230	Wings out
251	Right foot plant
273	Left leg 90 degrees
292	Left leg all the way up
330	Final stance

After the 3D motion reference video is in Poser, you need to approximate the position and orientation of the Poser Main Camera so that the video reference floor and the Poser Floor align approximately.

Then you can add the Poser figure you want to animate, and position and orient it on frame 0 to match the reference video actor.

To keyframe the Poser figure with 3D motion reference video, you have two choices:

■ Select the Poser figure Body, and position and orient the figure to match the reference video actor's body on each keyframe from your previously identified list of keyframes. Then pose the figure's arms and legs to match the actor on the keyframes.

The reason that you choose the Body and not the Hips is because the body acts as a container for the whole character. When you position and orient the Body, the Poser figure moves and rotates like a wooden doll. When you position and orient the Hips, the Poser figure uses IK and tries to solve the figure posing. Such IK assistance creates difficulty when following this workflow.

■ Position, orient, and pose the figure on each previously identified keyframe to match the reference video actor. In this method, you can either leave the IK on for the legs and arms and drag the appendages to pose the figure, or turn off IK and use the dials to orient each segment of each arm and leg.

I tend to use the first method because it provides a better preview of which sections of the animation will require foot-to-floor contact correction.

SUMMARY

This chapter showed you a new way to view Poser's application in the character animation process that expands your horizons and possibilities. The workflow presented here requires some practice. When you get the steps and issues clear in your head, both your production planning and volume of character animation production will benefit greatly.

8 Poser and Cinema 4D— Integrated Character Animation

In This Chapter

- Why Integrate Poser with a 3D Host?
- PoserFusion Versus interPoser
- Cloned Simon: Using PoserFusion to Add Poser Character Animation to Cinema 4D
- Karate Simon: Using PoserFusion to Add Motion Captured Poser Figures
- Using interPoser to Bring Poser Figures into Cinema 4D and Add Hair

WHY INTEGRATE POSER WITH A 3D HOST?

So you've travelled the journey and mastered the art of bringing your Poser figures to life. What's next? The next step in your evolution as a character animator is to integrate your animated Poser content into a host 3D application where the capabilities of the CG world are virtually boundless. Poser is focused on helping you design and animate 3D characters. Taking these characters into a 3D host lets you expand on what you began in Poser. Another reason for integrating Poser with a 3D host is that certain features found within Poser, such as adding hair and cloth, are tedious and cumbersome in comparison to adding these same features to your Poser characters within a 3D host. So let's look at how we make it all come together.

ADVANCED LIGHTING

Besides rendering your Poser figures with the basic light models found in Poser, rendering your Poser figures in a 3D host application such as Cinema 4D, Maya, or 3D Studio MAX gives you more advanced and sophisticated light models such as smoky volumetric light, inverted volumetric lights, inclusive/exclusive light assignment, and even programmable lights controlled by the transformation or behavior of other 3D animation scene elements.

ADVANCED RENDERING

The level of photo realism offered in leading 3D host applications is not only beyond the rendering capabilities offered in Poser but also the intimate level of control over aspects of rendering in 3D hosts is far greater. Functions such as multiple types of motion blur using various algorithms and processes, radiosity (rendering light bounced off of objects to create photo-realism), multi-pass rendering (various aspects of a scene such as shadow, color, reflection, transparency, and many more features are rendered into separate layers of a sequence of Photoshop files providing incredible post-render control), cartoon rendering (shown in Figure 8.1), and post-rendering effects are just a sampling of the great benefits to rendering your Poser figures in a host application. The effect of many of these rendering capabilities can help you produce imagery so powerful that the figures may only slightly resemble what you can deliver when working exclusively within Poser.

FIGURE 8.1
Cartoon rendering of Simon in Cinema 4D.

PARTICLE SYSTEMS

Particle systems allow you to control large groups of objects (particles) to behave in ways that mimic nature and physics. This is very helpful when trying to create schools of fish and flocks of birds (shown in Figure 8.2), billowing rising smoke, rain, snow, leaves blowing down the road, or even dirt being emitted from the ground as a car peels out at high speed. A special class of particles is used to create fluid simulations, which allow you to create dynamically interactive bodies of water such as pouring water into a glass and simulating a fish tank or even a lake or the raging ocean. Particles can add a sense of complexity to your animation scenes, which helps sell the illusion of your story.

FIGURE 8.2
Particle system in Cinema 4D used to create a flock of birds in a 3D animation scene with Poser's Simon imported with PoserFusion.

SOPHISTICATED CLOTH

Not only can clothing be modeled in the 3D host application (which cannot be done in Poser) but it also can be made to fit the Poser figure with various levels of form hugging, as well as be made to dynamically move and bend with the figure's animated movement. The clothing can even sash and take on the characteristics of various fabric behavior (shown in Figure 8.3) such as denim, silk, cotton, wool, and any other fabric that you can imagine. The use of cloth also extends beyond the application of making curtains, clothing, and table cloths. It even includes uses such as creating balls that really squash and stretch when they bounce, tires that visually show the weight of a car, conveyer belts that actually work, wine glasses that shatter when hit by a bullet, and even (drum roll) tank treads that really work.

FIGURE 8.3
Hat added to Poser figure imported with PoserFusion in Cinema 4D.

SOPHISTICATED HAIR

For those who have ventured into Poser's Hair room, you know that you can grow hair for your Poser figures, although it's not the easiest of processes. 3D host applications provide more sophisticated and complete hair solutions for your Poser figures. Cinema 4D has a fluid hair solution that generates realistic hair very, very fast. You can even comb, brush, cut, curl, and style the hair with frizzing, kinking, and coloring. One caveat you'll need to consider when adding hair to Poser figures in Cinema 4D is that the figures need to be seen by Cinema 4D as polygon objects. For this, you will need to use the interPoser plugin (covered in this chapter). The bottom line is that 3D host applications can dramatically enhance the effective and interactive use of hair on your characters to change their appearance and personality.

EXTENSIBILITY

Poser's claim to fame and significant contribution to the 3D film-making process is the design and posing of 3D characters. Bringing the characters into the host 3D application affords a wealth of extensibility by means of the host application's own strength and commitment to expanding its feature set and integration with other applications. As an example of this, Maya (Autodesk®), Cinema 4D (MAXON®), and 3D Studio MAX (Autodesk) have various integration capabilities with Poser; Vue (e-on software) is used to create landscapes with realistic vegetation and ecosystems; and RealFlow (Next Limit) is used to create fluid simulations. Bringing your Poser characters into such extensible development environments allows you to tell your story the way you intended to.

POSERFUSION VERSUS INTERPOSER

Several years ago, if you wanted to bring your Poser figures into a host 3D application, you were limited to partial solutions such as exporting the figure as an OBJ file and magically getting the proper textures reapplied, or (if compatibility allowed between the version issues of the day) you could use the Poser Pro Pack to bring your figure into a host application.

Now we have options—really good options—as described next.

POSERFUSION

PoserFusion (Smith Micro Software) ships with Poser Pro and is a Poser plugin installed into your host 3D application. This is most certainly one real reason to upgrade from Poser to Poser Pro.

With PoserFusion, you design, pose, and animate your character in Poser and save your project as in any standard Poser work session. You then switch to your host application and use the Poser plugin menu item to add a Poser object to your scene. You then browse for the Poser project file (.pz3) previously saved. This immediately presents your fully animated Poser figure in your host 3D application. Clicking the Create materials button (shown in Figure 8.4) magically locates all needed Poser textures and builds the appropriate materials in your host application, and finally, assigns them where needed to complete the integration of your Poser character into your favorite 3D host workspace.

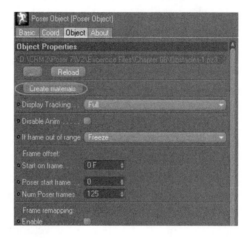

FIGURE 8.4
PoserFusion's Create materials button in
Cinema 4D.

As you move through your timeline, you see the Poser character animate, and all other animation built in the 3D host application happens in the same 3D space. Rendering now uses the 3D host application's toolset and no longer relies on Poser.

Following are the pros and cons for using PoserFusion:

Pro: Very fast and easy to use.

Con: No direct posing control of the Poser figures from within Cinema 4D. You can't easily add Cinema 4D hair or clothing to the imported Poser figures. Sluggish response when dragging the timeline playback control.

INTERPOSER

interPoser (Kuroyume's DevelopmentZone) is a plugin add-on for Cinema 4D *only*. With interPoser, there are two workflows to integrate Poser and Cinema 4D:

Workflow 1: Save your Poser project, and import it into Cinema 4D via inter-Poser. Character animation is inherited from the saved Poser .pz3 project file.

Workflow 2: Add Poser figures into Cinema 4D via the interPoser. In this workflow, you can animate the Poser figures in Cinema 4D by adding Poser poses via interPoser. You can also directly pose the figures using an interPoser implementation of the Poser figure dials accessible within Cinema 4D's Attributes Manager (shown in Figure 8.5).

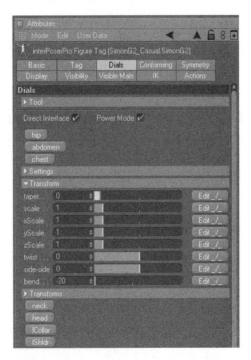

FIGURE 8.5
interPoser's Poser figure parameter dials in
Cinema 4D.

One of the great benefits of interPoser is that the Poser figures import into Cinema 4D as polygon objects. So, you can select polygons in the crown of the figure's head and grow luscious, highly interactive and easy-to-style Cinema 4D hair. You can also use Cinema 4D's Dress-O-Matic cloth workflow to design and fit clothing right onto the imported figures and watch the clothing sash and blow in the wind as the character moves. Having the figure as a polygon object also allows you to directly deform the shape of the figure using Cinema 4D's world class modeling tools.

Following are the pros and cons for using interPoser:

Pro: Direct animation control of the Poser figure within Cinema 4D. Ability to access the figure as a polygon object and add Cinema 4D hair and clothing.

Con: Only available for Cinema 4D. More complex to use than PoserFusion. Additional cost to Poser Pro purchase.

Although each of these solutions can appeal to different animator's needs, for some, both solutions are equally needed. I use both of these in my project workflows.

CLONED SIMON: USING POSERFUSION TO ADD POSER CHARACTER ANIMATION TO CINEMA 4D

NOTE

This project requires that you have Poser Pro and Cinema 4D 10.5 installed. Maya or other PoserFusion-compatible 3D hosts have similar workflows.

On this project, we'll use PoserFusion to integrate the Poser figure animation of Simon walking past the obstacles, which we produced in a previous chapter. Follow these steps to integrate the animation with Cinema 4D:

ON THE DVD

1. In Poser, load Obstacles-1.pz3 from the Chapter 8 folder in the Exercise files on the DVD-ROM. You need to be able to separate elements of your Poser scene and have them brought into Cinema 4D as discrete Poser objects. This turns out to be particularly useful as you'll see when working in Cinema 4D. So again, you have these two very simplistic obstacles (shown in Figure 8.6) of two cylinders. Nothing else is in the scene.

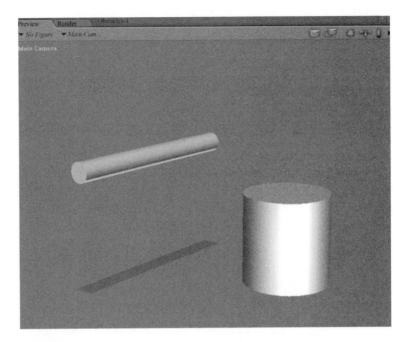

FIGURE 8.6
Obstacles project in Poser.

2. Load Avoiding Simon.pz3 from the Chapter 8 folder Exercise files. Here you have Simon from the object avoidance animation previously animated. If you play this animation, you'll see him avoiding the obstacles even though they aren't part of this scene. So you just have him now, separate from the obstacles themselves (see Figure 8.7). You'll import both of these two Poser projects into Cinema 4D using the PoserFusion plugin.

FIGURE 8.7
Just Simon from the object avoidance animation.

3. Now in Cinema 4D, you can look at how the PoserFusion module of Poser-Pro allows you to integrate the Poser figures in your host 3D application. In this case, Cinema 4D is the 3D host application, but this is the same workflow for working with Maya or other 3D hosts that are supported by Poser-Fusion. This won't be a tutorial on Cinema 4D because we are really focusing on the integration of PoserPro (via PoserFusion) with Cinema 4D.

4. In Cinema 4D, open the Cloned Simon-Start.c4d project from the Chapter 8 folder on the DVD-ROM. If you rend this very basic scene, you'll see it's just two poles on the floor (shown in Figure 8.8) with some lights in the sky. You can see that there is a camera through which the upper-left viewport is looking. The camera is looking at a camera target (invisible null object). You can also see that the camera has a motion path. Over time, the camera's motion is seen in the perspective view. So as the camera moves, the upper-left perspective viewport window is moving as well. Also in the scene are lights, sky, and environment; some instance copies of lights; and the infinite floor (all shown in Figure 8.8).

ON THE DVD

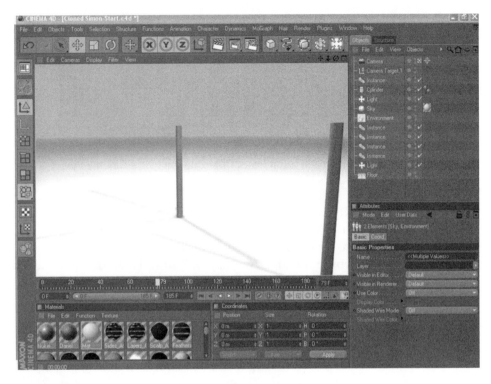

FIGURE 8.8
A rendered image of the Cloned Simon-Start.c4d project.

5. To import the Poser content, go to the Plug-ins menu, and choose Poser Object (shown in Figure 8.9). This adds a blank Poser object to the Cinema 4D Object Manager, which will act as a sort of container and controller for the actual Poser content after it's imported. To import the Obstacles-1.pz3 Poser object, in the Attributes Manager, go to the Object tab and browse for the Poser content in the Chapter 8 folder in your Exercise files on the DVD-ROM. This imports the tank and the bar.

ON THE DVD

FIGURE 8.9
The PoserFusion Poser Object option in the Cinema 4D
Plugins menu.

6. For now, rename this Poser object as "Obstacles" to differentiate it from the other Poser objects that will be added. Add another Poser object, and browse to the Chapter 8 folder in the Exercise files on the DVD-ROM to set its content to Avoiding Simon.pz3. This will load the actual animation of Simon avoiding the obstacles.

ON THE DVD

Due to the amount of work that the PoserFusion plugin does, it's not the most fluid application in Cinema 4D, so you won't be able to scrub the animation playback head on the timeline.

NOTE

7. Click on different points of the timeline to see how the character advances. You can see it's really going through the animation now. If you click off of the Poser object (into an empty space in the Objects Manager), you'll see that no materials have been applied to this Poser figure yet (shown in Figure 8.10). It's just gray.

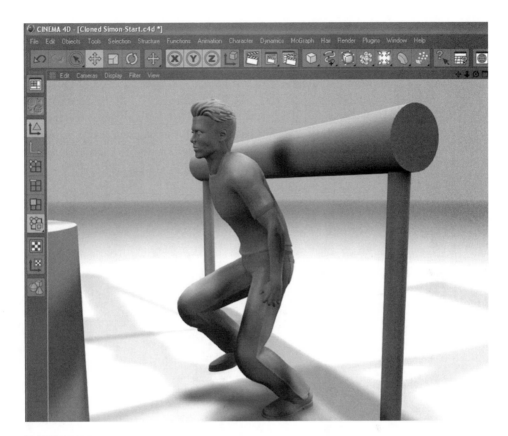

FIGURE 8.10
The PoserFusion imported Simon has no materials applied.

8. To create and apply the materials for imported Poser content in the selected PoserFusion object, in the Objects Manager, select the Poser object
again. In the Attributes Manager, select the Object tab, and then click the
Create materials button. This goes through the Poser runtime directory
and finds all the materials needed to build the Cinema 4D materials for the
selected Poser content and applies them to the Poser object.

*For a stable work experience, it's very important to wait until all of the materials
are built before you continue working in Cinema 4D. Failure to wait may result in
an unstable application or a crash.*

9. If you click off of the figure (into an empty space in the Objects Manager),
you can see that textures are applied to the Poser character. In the Objects
Manager, rename that Poser object to "Simon 1". Copy and paste this
Simon 1 object twice, and rename the copies as "Simon 2" and "Simon 3".

10. One of the features of PoserFusion is that you can offset the timing of when the imported Poser character animation occurs, independently of where the Cinema 4D animation play head may be.

11. Now go to frame 60. Here, it appears as if you have only one instance of Simon, even though you have three copies of him because three copies of Simon's animation start at the same time. To offset the Simon copies in time, select Simon 2, and in the Attributes Manager, set the start to frame 30. This causes Simon 2's animation to start 30 frames later. Set Simon 3's to start on frame 60. Now we have Simon at three different states in the animation (shown in Figure 8.11).

FIGURE 8.11
The three copies of Simon are now spaced 30 frames apart offsetting their respective animation sequences.

12. Now let's look at how you can manipulate Poser objects imported with Poser-Fusion by making them into editable Cinema 4D polygon objects. Choose the Obstacles Poser object in the Objects Manager, and press the B key to convert the selected Poser object into a null object containing two polygon objects,

with one being the tank and the other being the bar. Rename the objects as "Tank" and "Bar" in the Objects Manager to prevent further confusion.

NOTE

Converting from a Poser object to a polygon object is a one-way process that converts a Poser object into a Cinema 4D object. This removes any PoserFusion control from the imported Poser content and will treat it as a regular Cinema 4D object from this point forward.

13. The benefit of this conversion to polygon objects is that you can now apply Cinema 4D materials to these imported objects. Go to the Materials Manager's File menu, select Shaders, and then choose the Danel and Nukie shaders. To apply the Danel shader to the materials, drag the Danel material onto the Bar object and drag the Nukie material onto the Tank object. The rendered result of these materials is shown in Figure 8.11.

14. To see the final result of this project, play the Cloned-Simon.mov in the Chapter 8 folder in the Exercise files on the DVD-ROM. You'll see how the three Simons can stagger in time, separated by one second apiece.

ON THE DVD

15. The final task performed in this project is to set a light to exclusively light the three Simon characters without adding any more light to the other scene elements. Select the Light object in the Objects Manager. In the Attributes Manager, select the Scene tab, and set it to Include (so that its contents will be the only things it lights). Drag each of the Simon Poser objects (one at a time) into the large Objects field (as shown in Figure 8.12).

FIGURE 8.12
The three Poser objects of Simon are dragged into the light Scene Objects Include field.

16. The result of this action is that the light from this one light source only lights the Simons. This is a very effective method of solving lighting problems within a scene integrating Poser content and other Cinema 4D content, including any number of additional lights. This is helpful when the Poser figure appears dark, but the rest of the scene appears bright. This method is used to bring the lighting into harmony. Figure 8.13 shows the final result.

FIGURE 8.13
Lighting corrected with an inclusive light being used to add light only to the imported Simon Poser figures.

KARATE SIMON: USING POSERFUSION TO ADD MOTION CAPTURED POSER FIGURES

In this project, we'll look at how motion captured data applied to oppose a figure can then be imported into a 3D host application (Cinema 4D) with PoserFusion.

1. From the Chapter 8 Exercise files on the DVD-ROM, open Karate-Simon-1.pz3 in Poser to see the motion capture (mocap) animation applied to Simon (shown in Figure 8.14). This mocap was downloaded free from *http://www.mocapdata.com*. The mocap data is a bit rough and choppy at a few points, but it's a great free resource for you to use for Poser animation. The free downloaded mocap has already been edited and cleaned up a little before being applied to Simon.

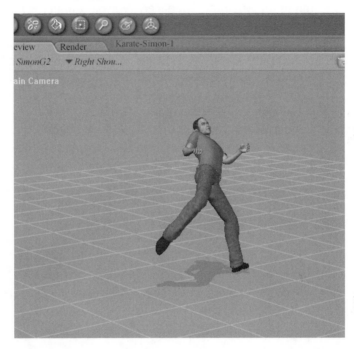

FIGURE 8.14
Karate mocap from *mocapdata.com* applied to Simon in Poser.

2. To work with PoserFusion, now switch to Cinema 4D. Open the Exercise Files/Chapter 08/Karate-Simon-1/Karate-Simon-Start.c4d Cinema 4D project to load the Cinema 4D animation scene elements into which the Karate-Simon-1.pz3 Poser object will be imported. This is a very simple animation, which includes the camera moving and some birds flying by.

3. The camera is targeting a null object (Camera Target) because the Poser content object imported via the PoserFusion plugin is not a standard Cinema 4D object. The Poser object acts as a container and controller for the imported Poser object. If you try to make the camera target Simon, you would notice that Simon would often move out of the camera's view because although

Simon moves, the Poser object does not. So animating the camera target by keyframing it to be visually centered on Simon at key points in time keeps him in view of the camera.

4. To import Simon, from the Plugins menu, add a Poser Object. In the Poser object Objects tab of the Attributes Manager, browse the Exercise Files Chapter 08 folder on the DVD-ROM, and load Karate-Simon-1.pz3. Simon (by default) loads with no materials. Click the Create materials button in the Attributes Manager, and wait for all the materials to be built in Cinema 4D's Material Manager before doing anything else.

5. Select the light. Simon needs more light to better match the scene. The light is currently set to the Include mode on the Scene tab in the Attributes Manager. Drag the Poser object into the Objects field so that the light only lights Simon. Don't worry about lighting the rest of the scene because some extra lights are already taking care of this.

6. Render a frame of this animation to see the rendered image of the Poser figure perfectly lit and in balance with the rest of the scene (shown in Figure 8.15).

FIGURE 8.15
Mocap-animated Karate Simon ready for animation rendering in Cinema 4D.

NOTE

If you're very familiar with the Poser Firefly rendering features, it's important to note that Firefly won't be available to you here. You'll need to depend on the rendering features of the host 3D application instead.

7. Look at the movie Karate-Simon.mov in the Chapter 8 folder on the DVD-ROM to get a much stronger sense of the integration of the Poser figure via PoserFusion in Cinema 4D by looking at the finished rendered video.

USING INTERPOSER TO BRING POSER FIGURES INTO CINEMA 4D AND ADD HAIR

Another way to import Poser figures into a host application (specifically into Cinema 4D) is to use the interPoser Pro plugin (from *Kuroyumes-DevelopmentZone.com*). This plugin (unlike PoserFusion) doesn't only work with the saved Poser scenes but also with all of the figures, poses, and props in the Poser runtime folder. All of your content is accessible from within Cinema 4D via interPoser Pro, which, in effect, turns Poser into a character library for Cinema 4D. That's huge! To use this within Cinema 4D, follow these steps:

1. From the Plug-ins menu, choose interPoser Pro. Then in the Runtime Explorer (as shown in Figure 8.16) choose Poser Runtimes, and then Poser 7 (or Poser Pro if that's how your runtime folder has been set up).

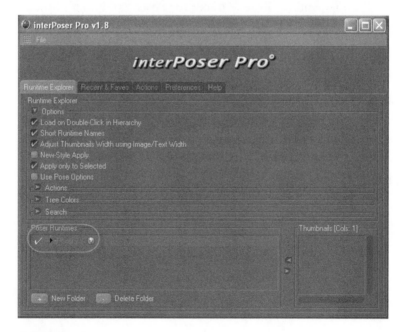

FIGURE 8.16
interPoser Runtime Explorer in Cinema 4D.

You may want to adjust the Tree Colors in the Runtime Explorer since the default color of drab green makes it difficult to see the Runtime content names.

2. Expand the Characters folder as shown in Figure 8.17.

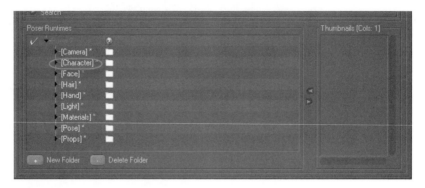

FIGURE 8.17
Expand the Characters folder.

3. Expand the Poser 7 folder (or Poser Pro if that's how your Runtime content is setup) as shown in Figure 8.18.

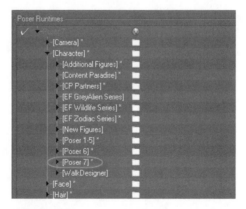

FIGURE 8.18
Expand the Poser 7/Poser Pro folder.

4. Expand the Simon G2 folder as shown in Figure 8.19.

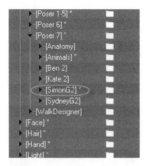

FIGURE 8.19
Expand the Simon G2 folder.

5. Choose SimonG2_Casual as shown in Figure 8.20.

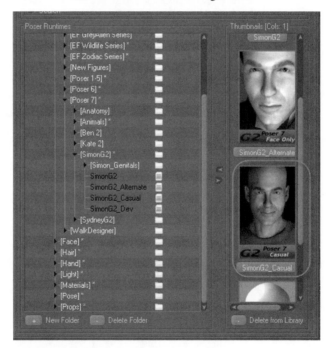

FIGURE 8.20
Choose SimonG2_Casual.

6. After you do this, you'll see the hourglass icon as interPoser Pro is importing the geometry and textures for Simon and is building the required Cinema 4D materials. When completed, you can close the interPoser file
requester.

7. In Cinema 4D, you now see Simon's materials in the Materials Manager (shown in Figure 8.21). The Poser figure is now available in the Cinema 4D viewport. With Simon selected in the Objects Manager, press the O key on the keyboard to frame Simon into view. If you deselect the figure, you can see it's fully textured and ready.

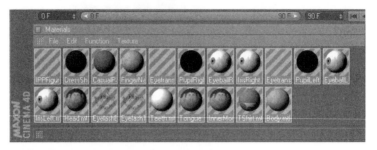

FIGURE 8.21
Simon's materials in the Materials Manager.

8. When your Poser figure is in Cinema 4D, you can pose the figure in one of two ways. First we'll look at how you pose the figure using Poser poses from the runtime library. In the Plug-ins menu, choose interPoser Pro and go to the Runtime Explorer. Drill down through the hierarchy by choosing Pose, Universal Poses, Action, Fighting (as shown in Figure 8.22).

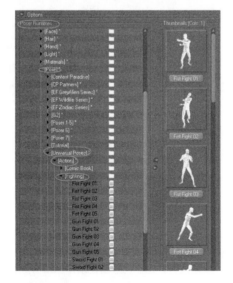

FIGURE 8.22
Navigating the Runtime Explorer to get fighting poses for Simon.

9. Here you see icons of various fight poses (shown in Figure 8.22). Making sure that you first have Simon selected in the Objects Manager, in the Runtime Explorer, choose the first one, Fist Fight 01, to pose Simon at the current animation frame (much like working within Poser). Go to frame 20, and apply Fist Fight 02 to see Simon once again accept a new pose.

NOTE

You must have the Poser figure selected before clicking the poses in the Runtime Manager because interPoser allows you to work with multiple figures in an animation. Selecting a Poser figure in the Objects Manager before applying poses allows interPoser to apply the pose to the selected figure. This way, interPoser Pro knows which figure you're referring to.

10. Unlike working with PoserFusion, you can drag the timeline and see your animation happening with interPoser. Go to frame 40, and apply Fist Fight 03.

Clearly, it's easy to animate your imported Poser figure with interPoser by adding runtime poses at various frames on the timeline (shown in Figure 8.23).

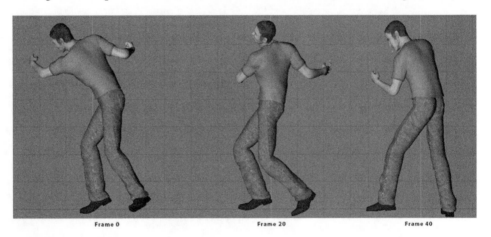

Frame 0   Frame 20   Frame 40

FIGURE 8.23
Poses applied to Simon on frames 0, 20, and 40.

Now let's look at how you animate Poser figures in Cinema 4D via interPoser without using runtime poses. In this workflow, you animate the Poser figure in Cinema 4D directly, using the Poser parameter dials mimicked in the interPoser interface in the Cinema 4D Attributes Manager. The parameter dials that you're already so familiar with in Poser are directly accessible to you in interPoser Pro. This brings Poser's amazing character rig control to you in a 3D host application.

1. To access the parameter dials, select the Simon interPoser tag in the Objects Manager (shown in Figure 8.24). This displays the interPoser controls in the Attribute Manager tabs. Select the Dials tab to access Simon's body parts (or *actors* as Poser calls them) dials. In Dials/Tool, click on Direct Interface (shown in Figure 8.24) to list the body parts. Although you can drill down to this level of intimate character control (listing all body parts) as you also see in Poser, in general, when animating a figure's gross motions, this is actually a bit too much information. So switch to interPoser Pro's Power Mode (shown in Figure 8.24) to display only the most common elements of the character to be animated. This really increases the speed and fluidity of the animation workflow.

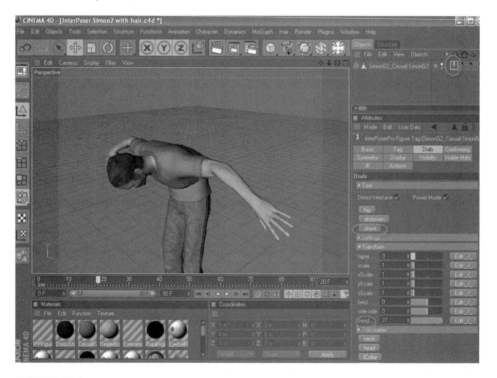

FIGURE 8.24
Simon bending. The interPoser Dials tab is also selected.

2. To see how you control the body parts, click on the Abdomen, and then go to Transform to see the familiar controls such as Twist, Side-Side, and Bend (among others). These controls operate interactively when dragged just like when working in Poser. So just as in Poser, you use these parameter dials to pose the figure.

3. Animating in interPoser is quite easy. It uses its own independent auto key system. You just pose the figure on various frames and play back the animation in Cinema 4D. On frame 0, Simon is standing up straight with his arms stretched out in the T-Pose. Go to frame 20, and adjust the bend of his abdomen to 48.

You can enter number values into dials to drive them beyond their slider limits.

NOTE

4. Select the Chest, and set the Bend to 27. Go to frame 40, and bend his torso the other way now. Select the Abdomen and set the Bend to -20. Select the Chest and set the Bend to -20 as well. Go to frame 60, and set the Bend for both the Abdomen and the Chest to 0 bringing Simon back to his original T-Pose. Now you have this very simplistic animation of a crazy Simon bending forward and then backward.

Applying all that you've learned about animating Poser characters in previous chapters in this book, you can easily bring your imported Poser figures to life in Cinema 4D via interPoser.

Now we'll demonstrate the value of having the imported Poser figure accessible at the polygon level in Cinema 4D. You'll do this by adding the Cinema 4D Hair to Simon. At this point, you're actually finished working with the interPoser plugin itself. Now you'll work with the geometry of this figure directly, which should be fun!

1. Select the Polygon tool (shown in Figure 8.25). Working in Cinema 4D's right viewport, choose the Live Selection tool (shown in Figure 8.26).

FIGURE 8.25
Cinema 4D's Polygon tool.

FIGURE 8.26
Cinema 4D's Live Selection tool.

2. To select polygons on the left and right sides of Simon's head, be sure to uncheck Only Select Visible Elements (shown in Figure 8.27). In preparation for adding Cinema 4D Hair to Simon, with the Live Selection Tool already active, draw to select polygons at the top of Simon's head as shown in Figure 8.28.

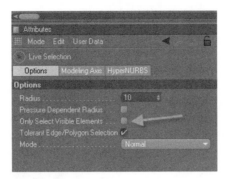

FIGURE 8.27
Only Select Visible Elements must be unchecked.

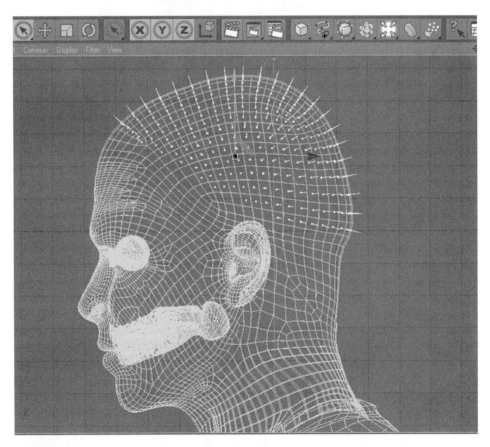

FIGURE 8.28
Polygons at the top of Simon's head are selected to receive hair.

3. Now to add the hair to Simon's head, in the main menu, select Hair. Instantly, Simon sports the most aggressive afro ever seen by mortal man. This hair is a bit much. It's wild on just about every level. Go to frame 0, and get out of the Hair tool by choosing the Move tool (just to the right of the Live Selection tool). Play the animation to see the dynamic hair simulate freely now (as shown in Figure 8.29).

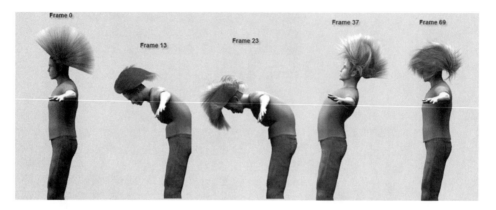

FIGURE 8.29
The Cinema 4D hair is dynamically responding to the animated Poser character movement.

4. You can clearly see that even though Poser does give you the ability to add hair to your figures within the application itself, you'll find that working with Cinema 4D hair on your imported Poser figures is a far more empowering workflow because the hair simulation is comparatively very fast. The other great benefit of adding hair to your Poser figures via this workflow is that the toolset for editing this hair is extensive and intuitive.

SUMMARY

When it comes to creating great looking 3D characters, Poser is a highly valued tool for any animator. Staying entirely within Poser for your full animation production, however, will invariably impose limits on your workflow and limit your digital storytelling to a single great application: Poser. In this chapter, you've seen how you can build on all of your hard work in Poser to deliver truly impressive 3D character animation by integrating the Poser content with a 3D host application using either PoserFusion or interPoser.

Now create some great 3D character animation, and leave the spinning 3D logos to the newbies.

Appendix: Animation Principles Quick Reference

This appendix provides some key information to aid you in bringing Poser's characters to life. Although some of this information is scattered throughout the book, this appendix is a consolidated quick reference that you can visit frequently.

ANIMATION PRINCIPLES

The rules governing how to best bring characters to life are called the principles of animation and are shared by animators around the world and through the years. They are meant to replace hopelessness and trial and error with proven methodology and will help you on your journey to becoming a character animator.

SQUASH AND STRETCH

Using the principle of *squash and stretch*, you create the illusion of weight and volume for a character or object as it moves (shown in Figure A.1). This is achieved by scaling the object independently in the x-, y-, and z-axis in such a way that although the object changes shape, it maintains its volume. The amount of squash and stretch that you use really depends on what your storytelling is calling for. For example, in a more cartoon-styled animation, squash and stretch may be very exaggerated. But in a very realistic animation, squash and stretch will be minimal and only applied to prevent the motion from looking like everything is made from hard plastic.

Because character animation is often supported by inanimate objects (such as a ball, as shown in Figure A.2) also being animated, squash and stretch is often applied to them as well. You should definitely expect to use this principle of animation often.

FIGURE A.1
A jumping penguin with the animation principle of squash and stretch applied.

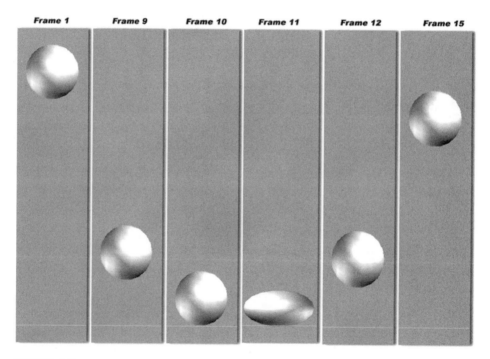

FIGURE A.2
A bouncing ball with the animation principle of squash and stretch applied.

ANTICIPATION

The animation principle of *anticipation* builds the expectation of a coming major action in the animated character such as when the character is about to blow out a candle, throw a ball, yell, or do some action that is best exaggerated by taking the kind of deep breath that engages the whole body.

Anticipation can best be described as a backward motion preceding the main forward motion. So if a character is about to blow out a candle and takes a deep breath that pulls the character back, the viewer knows to expect the character to then move forward to blow. Coupling the use of timing with anticipation can really accentuate the animation. As an example of this, if the character pulls back to blow out the candle and then holds in the breath for a moment, the anticipation of what comes next really builds.

The extent to which you use the exaggeration of anticipation is greatly determined by the needs of your story and the level of realism of your animation. The more realistic the animation style you produce, the less exaggerated your anticipation needs to be.

STAGING

Because you have a very limited time onscreen to tell the bits and pieces that make up your story, as a filmmaker, you must be very creative and effective in how you communicate the key aspects of your story to the viewer. The animation principle of *staging* is where you address this issue. Here are some of the things that factor into staging your animation:

- **Camera shots:** The use of close-up, wide angle, reverse, and long shots.
- **Framing:** The selective framing of content in the shot.
- **Sequence:** The use of gags and preparatory actions that build to a main event.

When looking at the staging of your animation, take clear responsibility for everything onscreen as it relates to effectively communicating your story to the viewer. This includes lighting, positioning, and supporting characters with props and appropriate backgrounds. Be sure to keep the focus on the key aspects of your story. A basic error to avoid in this regard is to make sure that very busy and detailed backgrounds are not seen directly behind your character, that is, unless that's the whole point of the shot.

Remember, when it comes to staging, you're in charge and responsible for the viewer's experience of your story.

STRAIGHT-AHEAD AND POSE-TO-POSE ANIMATION

Straight-ahead animation is when you pose the character as you go through the timeline. This allows for very spontaneous animation and maximum creativity, however, it also requires greater skill and care to produce cyclical motion such as walking because the rhythm and patterns of motion inherent to walking may not be very obvious to novice animators. This type of animation is great for noncycling motion such as standing, sitting, lifting, and throwing (as shown in Figure A.3).

When animating straight ahead in Poser, it's essential to return to earlier keyframes and check that earlier motion is behaving as you had intended. This is because the motion curves that control each body part in the character are affected by keyframes that occur immediately before and after the active keyframe. Use the Graph Editor to edit the motion curves and the Keyframes Editor to edit the spacing and spline interpolation of the keyframes.

FIGURE A.3
Straight-ahead animation used to create the motion of Simon throwing a ball.

Unlike straight ahead, *pose-to-pose animation* is very staged and preplanned. In this type of character animation, key poses are established as the prime basis of the whole animation. All other work is a matter of tweaking and transitioning between these key poses. Walk cycles are excellent candidates for the use of this animation principle (shown in Figure A.4).

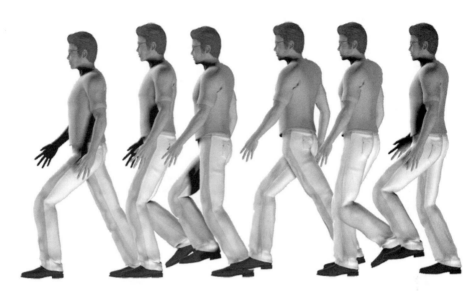

FIGURE A.4
Walk cycle created with pose-to-pose.

FOLLOW THROUGH AND OVERLAPPING ACTION

Follow through is used to complete character animation by allowing body parts and props to catch up. As a walking character comes to a stop, the arms would come to rest, a leg might complete the final step, and loose clothing might settle down, all to conclude the motion to a believable point. Failure to use follow through results in abrupt mechanical and highly unnatural looking animation that distracts your viewers from your story by making them think "something's wrong."

Overlapping motion is observed as the relationship among primary, secondary, and tertiary movement. For example, in the case of creating walking character animation, the primary movement is caused by the legs. If the character's legs are animated perfectly, and the character walks across the room but keeps his hands firmly at his sides, unless your story calls for a really goofy looking guy, this will look very odd. Secondary movement is the arms being animated to support the walk. As a result of selling the illusion that this walking animation is realistic, the character's loose clothing may move, trail, and sash in response to the primary and secondary movement, thereby creating tertiary movement. This all adds up to create overlapping motion.

EASE-IN AND EASE-OUT

A car starting to move from a resting state doesn't simply go from 0 mph on frame 1 to 100 mph on frame 2 (at least, not if you want humans to relate to it very well). To convey that an object is realistically going from being in motion to a rest state, you use *ease-in*. To get an object realistically from a rest state to a state of motion, you use *ease-out*. In Poser, this is most elegantly handled in the Graph Editor (as shown in Figure A.5).

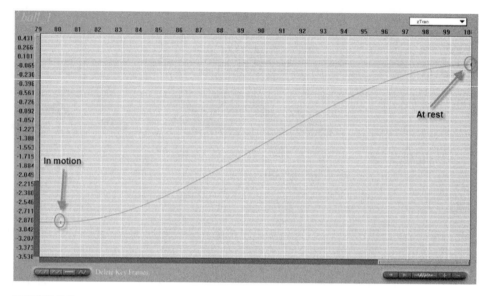

FIGURE A.5
Graph Editor showing ease-in and ease-out motion curves.

ARCS

Arms swing, head turns, and generally all body part movements should either form *arcs* or be the products of compounded hierarchical arcs. This works to help ensure that body motion is both natural and flowing in a way pleasing to the eye.

TIMING

In 3D character animation, there are two key aspects to the principle of *timing*:

- When each object, body part, or character is moved (transformed)
- When (in time) other principles of animation (i.e., exaggeration, anticipation) are used

Additionally, by moving the keyframes in the Keyframes Editor, you gain direct control over the character animation timing. Timing of character animation requires performing some iterative trial and error, looking at the motion playback, and even at times getting a second opinion to really get it right.

EXAGGERATION

Exaggeration is turning up the volume on key characteristics of a character's movement or facial gestures to more effectively convey their intent or personality. So if an old man is tired and walking, a good use of exaggeration might be to have him slumped over, and walking slowly with trembling and hesitation to show effort for each step. In reality, even an old man may find that to be a bit much, but your viewing audience will truly get the meaning that this 3D character is really old.

Exaggeration works even better when the exaggerated movement or character can be onscreen with a less exaggerated counterpart. So if the old man walks next to some young kids, the exaggeration can really give your story a very visible payoff.

WEIGHT

It's not enough to have well-designed, great-looking characters who move fluidly. They must appear to require effort to move. A key factor in conveying that they require effort to move is the use of the animation principle of *weight*. As a real-world example of this, when you bend down to lift an object (as shown in Figure A.6), you must shift your weight around a few times to complete the motion. Capturing this activity in your character's movement gives the subtle visual support to sell that this really is a believable character moving and not some mechanical automaton.

Additionally, when a 3D character must lift, push, carry, or throw an object, the object's weight should be conveyed in how much effort is required by the character to interact with the object. So a character throwing a bowling ball should definitely struggle, walk differently, and distribute his weight differently from a character throwing a golf ball.

FIGURE A.6
Character lifting a heavy object, demonstrating the weight animation principle.

APPEAL

The animation principle of *appeal* is where the real storytelling comes through. This is a combination of the design of the character, how the character moves, the facial expressions and gestures, and your ability to sequence and string them all together to not only tell a story but also to tell it in a way that intrigues the mind of your viewer. Appeal is not limited to the story lead good guy or leading lady. A villain (shown in Figure A.7) or supporting character should also have great appeal (as is needed to ensure they can effectively contribute to your story). When the animation principle of *appeal* is well done, you'll reach past the eye of your viewers and engage their minds.

FIGURE A.7
An example of an appealing villainous character.

KEYFRAMES EDITOR

Poser character poses are stored in keyframes along the timeline. While working in the Pose room posing your figure along the timeline, you can go between keyframes and continue to make adjustments, but you can't move the keyframes or see their positions relative to each other. Additionally, a keyframe for a figure on a given frame may be for all actors within the figure or for select actors only.

Although working in the Pose room does allow for visually fluid activity, to gain full control over the keyframe positions relative to each other, you need to work in the *Keyframes Editor* (shown in Figure A.8).

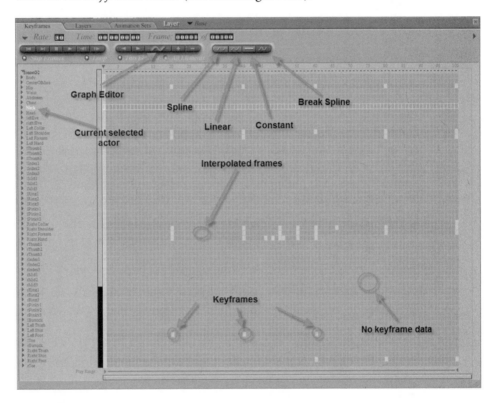

FIGURE A.8
The Keyframes Editor interface.

In the Keyframes Editor, keyframes are indicated in bright green. Keyframes can be moved by simply dragging them. To copy a keyframe to a new location, hold the Alt key down, and then drag the keyframe. Starting from outside a group of keyframes, drag a selection box around keyframes to temporarily group them. Selected keyframes can be moved or copied together.

If animation frames have no keyframe or interpolated frame data, they are shown as light brown. Interpolated frames are indicated in dark green and cannot be directly manipulated here. Interpolated keyframes are the motion between the keyframes. The behavior of the interpolated keyframes is determined by the interpolation mode of the preceding keyframe.

Spline: This is the default interpolation and is indicated in bright green. This interpolation begins at a keyframe, accelerates to full speed, and then slows down when approaching the next keyframe to create very smooth and fluid animation.

Linear: This is indicated in brown and maintains a constant speed between keyframes with no acceleration. This is suitable for mechanical motion and is also used in character animation to limit motion such as feet not going through the floor and feet staying planted on the floor.

Constant: This is indicated in gray. This interpolation type can be considered a noninterpolation because rather than smoothly transitioning an object between the transformation settings of the keyframes, constant is used to produce step-function animation. If a ball is keyframed to be on the floor on frame 1 and to be in the air on frame 30, with frame 1 set to an interpolation of Constant, the ball will remain on the floor from frame 1 to frame 29 and then suddenly be in the air on frame 30.

Break Spline: This is indicated in olive green and is used to end the last used interpolation type. This is very useful when you want to blend interpolation styles on one animated object.

The arrowhead to the left of the currently selected actor (as shown in Figure AP.8) is used to access all of the animation channels (i.e., twist, bend, up-down, etc.). Each animation channel can have its own independent keyframes and interpolation methods.

The currently selected actor (and to be even more specific, the currently selected actor's animation channel) is the basis for the animation curves displayed when you select the Graph Editor.

Graph Editor

The *Graph Editor* (shown in Figure A.9) shows the animation curve for the currently selected actor's currently selected animation channel. So if you have the Up-Down of the Right Shoulder selected, and you are in the Graph Editor, the animation curve you see will be for the right shoulder up-down. As you select different actors and animation channels, the Graph Editor updates to give you that animation curve data.

In Figure AP.9, you see spline interpolation of eight keyframes. These keyframes can be dragged up and down with no keys pressed on the keyboard. To drag them left to right, hold the Ctrl key or first make a selection of the area containing the keyframe(s) you want to move, and then drag left to right. With an area selected containing keyframes, hold the Ctrl key down to move them all up and down. With an area selected containing a keyframe, hold the Alt key down, and drag to make copies of that keyframe.

The same interpolation methods are available in the Graph Editor as the Keyframes Editor.

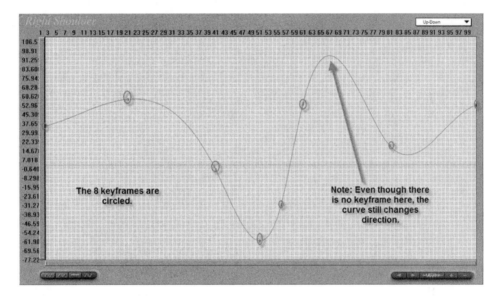

FIGURE A.9
The Poser Pro Graph Editor.

Index

License Agreement/Notice of Limited Warranty

By opening the sealed disc container in this book, you agree to the following terms and conditions. If, upon reading the following license agreement and notice of limited warranty, you cannot agree to the terms and conditions set forth, return the unused book with unopened disc to the place where you purchased it for a refund.

License:

The enclosed software is copyrighted by the copyright holder(s) indicated on the software disc. You are licensed to copy the software onto a single computer for use by a single user and to a backup disc. You may not reproduce, make copies, or distribute copies or rent or lease the software in whole or in part, except with written permission of the copyright holder(s). You may transfer the enclosed disc only together with this license, and only if you destroy all other copies of the software and the transferee agrees to the terms of the license. You may not decompile, reverse assemble, or reverse engineer the software.

Notice of Limited Warranty:

The enclosed disc is warranted by Course Technology to be free of physical defects in materials and workmanship for a period of sixty (60) days from end user's purchase of the book/disc combination. During the sixty-day term of the limited warranty, Course Technology will provide a replacement disc upon the return of a defective disc.

Limited Liability:

THE SOLE REMEDY FOR BREACH OF THIS LIMITED WARRANTY SHALL CONSIST ENTIRELY OF REPLACEMENT OF THE DEFECTIVE DISC. IN NO EVENT SHALL COURSE TECHNOLOGY OR THE AUTHOR BE LIABLE FOR ANY OTHER DAMAGES, INCLUDING LOSS OR CORRUPTION OF DATA, CHANGES IN THE FUNCTIONAL CHARACTERISTICS OF THE HARDWARE OR OPERATING SYSTEM, DELETERIOUS INTERACTION WITH OTHER SOFTWARE, OR ANY OTHER SPECIAL, INCIDENTAL, OR CONSEQUENTIAL DAMAGES THAT MAY ARISE, EVEN IF COURSE TECHNOLOGY AND/OR THE AUTHOR HAS PREVIOUSLY BEEN NOTIFIED THAT THE POSSIBILITY OF SUCH DAMAGES EXISTS.

Disclaimer of Warranties:

COURSE TECHNOLOGY AND THE AUTHOR SPECIFICALLY DISCLAIM ANY AND ALL OTHER WARRANTIES, EITHER EXPRESS OR IMPLIED, INCLUDING WARRANTIES OF MERCHANTABILITY, SUITABILITY TO A PARTICULAR TASK OR PURPOSE, OR FREEDOM FROM ERRORS. SOME STATES DO NOT ALLOW FOR EXCLUSION OF IMPLIED WARRANTIES OR LIMITATION OF INCIDENTAL OR CONSEQUENTIAL DAMAGES, SO THESE LIMITATIONS MIGHT NOT APPLY TO YOU.

Other:

This Agreement is governed by the laws of the State of Massachusetts without regard to choice of law principles. The United Convention of Contracts for the International Sale of Goods is specifically disclaimed. This Agreement constitutes the entire agreement between you and Course Technology regarding use of the software.